AN INTRODUCTION TO

Husserl's Phenomenology

AN INTRODUCTION TO

Husserl's Phenomenology

JAN PATOČKA

Translated by Erazim Kohák

Edited with an Introduction by
James Dodd

OPEN COURT
Chicago and La Salle, Illinois

Open Court Publishing Company is a division of Carus Publishing Company.

Copyright © 1996 by Carus Publishing Company

First printing 1996

Printed and bound in the United States of America.

Translated from the original Czech texts on file at the Institut für die Wissenschaften vom Menschen, Vienna. (Though the institute in Vienna handled the rights to Patočka's works during the era of Soviet dominance, the rights are now administered by the Jan Patočka Archive at the Center for Theoretical Study in Prague, the main depository for Patočka's original manuscripts.)

Library of Congress Cataloging-in-Publication Data

Patočka, Jan, 1907–1977.
    [Úvod do Husserlovy fenomenologie. English]
An introduction to Husserl's phenomenology/Jan Patočka; translated by Erazim Kohák; edited with an introduction by James Dodd.
    p. cm.
    Includes bibliographical references and index.
    ISBN 0-8126-9338-8 (cloth : alk. paper)
    1. Husserl, Edmund, 1859–1938. 2. Phenomenology. I. Dodd,
James, 1968– . II Title.
B3279.H94P336 1996
193—dc20   96-39052
                                               CIP

Contents

Editor's Preface

In the near twenty years since his death, the Czech philosopher Jan Patočka (1907–1977) has been little known outside of central Europe. He is, however, without a doubt one of the most important figures in modern central and east European intellectual history. Patočka was a philosopher of great erudition who wrote extensively, and not only about phenomenology: in his long and productive career he also authored an impressive variety of essays on the history of philosophy, aesthetics, and politics and made significant scholarly contributions to the study of Jan Amos Komensky (better known to English readers by the Latin form of his name, Comenius).

In recent years it has become easier for readers in the West to gain access Patočka's writings, and thus be in a position to appreciate his work. A number of his books and essays have become available in French, mostly due to the translation efforts of Erika Abrams, and recently the Institute for Human Sciences in Vienna has completed a five-volume collection in German of selected writings, edited by Klaus Nellen. The translator of the present work, Erazim Kohák, now Professor of Philosophy at Charles University in Prague, has also published a collection of English translations of a number of Patočka's essays under the title *Jan Patočka: Philosophy and Selected Writings* (Chicago: University of Chicago Press, 1989), a volume that also includes an extensive interpretive essay by Professor Kohák. *An Introduction to Husserl's Phenomenology* is one of Professor Kohák's translations of three major works by Patočka being published by Open Court Publishing Company, the other two of which are *Heretical Essays in the Philosophy of History* and the forthcoming *Body, Community, Language, World*.

An Introduction to Husserl's Phenomenology itself is of twofold interest. For Husserl scholars it offers a fascinating—and often brilliant—interpretation of Husserl's work, of his conceptions of logic and consciousness, time and corporeity. For Patočka scholars, or those interested in the reception of the phenomenology of

Husserl and Heidegger in eastern Europe, this book counts as Patočka's definitive statement on Husserl, and is essential to understanding the role played in Patočka's own philosophy by his understanding of Husserl.

I first encountered the work of Patočka—and Husserl—as an undergraduate student in a seminar on phenomenology conducted in the late 1980s by Professor Kohák, who at the time was a member of the Department of Philosophy at Boston University. For whatever I understand of Husserl, and of philosophy in general, I owe a great deal both to Professor Kohák's seminars and to early drafts of his translations of Patočka's writings.

Part of the editing of this book was carried out in Vienna at the Institute for Human Sciences, which houses the Jan Patočka Archive. I would like to thank the director of the Institute, Professor Krzystof Michalski of Boston University, who himself is a scholar of Husserl and Heidegger as well as a teacher and friend. I would also like to thank the director of the Patočka Archive, Klaus Nellen, for his support during my stay in the Institute, where in 1995 I enjoyed a generous fellowship as a Jan Patočka Junior Visiting Fellow. Thanks must also go to the staff and other fellows of the Institute for providing both excellent working conditions and a stimulating intellectual environment ideal for undertaking such a project.

Yet, above all, anyone who undertakes Patočka scholarship owes a debt of gratitude—and admiration—to the *samizdat* publishers who preserved Patočka's writings at a time when he was branded a nonperson by the once implacable Czechoslovak authorities. One hopes that, in the face of so uncertain a future in the former Soviet-dominated areas, we can say today that such risk, as well as Patočka's own personal sacrifice, was not in vain.

James Dodd
Vienna, 1995

Editor's Introduction

The founder of modern phenomenology, Edmund Husserl, is one of the most intriguing figures in twentieth-century philosophy. One reason for this is that Husserl, perhaps more so than any other philosopher of the early decades of this century, represents a transition from one philosophical culture to another. For his thought bears the stamp of two very different intellectual worlds: on the one hand, one can discern in his writings the philosophical posture of the mid- to late-nineteenth century, characterized by a deep commitment to the idea of science as the prism within which everything both social and natural is fused; further, that this science is not only explanatory, but rational, systematic, and above all *complete*. It is not fortuitous that Jan Patočka, in the final pages of this book, likens Husserl's philosophy to that of Fichte and Hegel. Here, too, Patočka tells us, is an example of the profound conviction that the essence of "science" in general is the realization, both in thought and cultural edifice, of the very truth of the world, and that its history is the history of this self-actualization. Patočka sees such a self-actualization not merely as the "idea," the "end" of science, what it "ought" to do and be, but as something that exists as the concrete essence of science, and therefore of European culture in general.

On the other hand, Husserl's thought prepared the ground for the development of a very different philosophical attitude, one that had already made itself felt in Europe by the end of the nineteenth century. This attitude is characterized by a profound distrust of all system, of any claim to hold the ultimate key to reality in its myriad of manifestations. This attitude can be described, in a provisional manner to be sure, as a modern version of skepticism, one that acknowledges, if not embraces, a higher degree of destabilization and ambiguity than the skepticism that arose out of the empiricism of the eighteenth century. It is a strong, though mostly indefinite, disillusionment with a particular development of certain tendencies of the Enlightenment, and seeks to articulate this disillusionment on various levels, whether philosophical, social, or political. Above all, it is marked by an unease with the nineteenth century's insistence on the total character of knowledge and the rationality that justifies it; it seeks to criticize the apparently naive conviction that the systematic possibilities of science and philosophy imply that our knowledge of the world can exhaust the meaning of the whole, of the forms in which life can have significance.

Husserl is an intellectual creature of both these worlds and their respective attitudes; and therein lies what is fascinating about his thought. His work enables us to ask a very important question, one which is basic to a thoughtful reflection on any form of skepticism, in any age: namely, if it is so that skepticism arises out of a rejection, or at least unease, with certain claims to knowledge and truth, does that mean that the significance of these claims, their importance and place in our lives, is *ipso facto* decided, and negatively at that? Or is it rather the case that the very possibility of skepticism is an opportunity better to understand the nature of the role that ideas of science, culture, and reason play in life? Should not such a skepticism be conceived as a "countermovement" within the Enlightenment itself, one that opens a clear perspective on something with which we were too enthralled, or perhaps which was simply taken too much for granted, for us to be able to see it? Husserl's philosophy enables us to ask such a question about the skepticism of our times in a way that escapes the trappings of a turgid polemics, for it is both a manifestation of the movement and the countermovement of the Enlightenment: it accepts that reason is basic, yet develops a critical apparatus wherein what this "reason" means, or could mean, is problematic.

If I preface this "introduction" to phenomenology with broad comments about Husserl's place in the history of philosophy, it is because the technical nature of his writings has a tendency to eclipse an appreciation of their general significance. This is not to say that technical matters are unimportant or unnecessary; Husserl expects a great deal that is philosophically decisive to come out of methodological considerations, and the detail and complexity of these reflections arise out of an enormous effort to be clear and precise. What is important to note here is that any introduction to Husserl's phenomenology poses a double task: it must be both an introduction to "phenomenology" per se, to the nuts and bolts of phenomenological method, as well as an introduction to "phenomenological philosophy," to phenomenology as a philosophical genre with its own self-understanding and goals. The two, to be sure, are inseparable: phenomenological method is no mere tool, an instrument which, in order to be understood, only requires that one know how to use it; this "method" is comprehensible only from the perspective opened by the understanding of the task of philosophy as Husserl understands it.

Specifically, for Husserl, to practice phenomenology as a science means not only to think rationally, but also to recognize the world as intrinsically rational; such recognition, even if it presupposes a training in logic and argumentation, is nevertheless an "understanding" that goes far beyond "methodology." It is incumbent upon the reader to grasp the attitude and intellectual motivation that lies behind such an assertion, and to see the tools that Husserl crafted, tools of descriptive analysis and transcendental argumentation, in light of such convictions—not only to be able to ascertain Husserl's historical significance, but also to see the possibilities inherent in the organon of phenomenology as such.

In *An Introduction to Husserl's Phenomenology,* Patočka pursues this double task. He recognizes that an introduction to phenomenology and to phenomenological philosophy requires an interpretive effort, one which can articulate the nascent significance of otherwise relatively abstruse texts. Patočka is, however, an important philosopher in his own right, one who writes not only to present Husserl's thought to a general audience, but who approaches it with his own concerns and interpretation of what is at stake in philosophy in general and Husserl's work in particular. Accordingly, this book is a thoughtful engagement, sometimes critical, with the guiding idea of phenomenology as Husserl understood and practiced it, with the intent of uncovering latent possibilities to serve as the basis for further development of phenomenology beyond Husserl.

These concerns are most evident in the first chapter wherein Patočka outlines the conceptual framework within which the introduction is to proceed. Like Husserl in *Crisis of the European Sciences,* he presents this framework by way of an interpretation of the idea of Western science as well as its history. Although both Husserl and Patočka present phenomenology as a chapter of this history, Patočka's interpretation is, in many ways, quite different from what one finds in Husserl's Vienna Lecture of the *Crisis*. For like any interpretation, Patočka's is at once an explication and a criticism; in this case, it is an interpretation of Husserl's self-understanding, which is in turn an extension of this understanding of the history of philosophy.

The criticism stems from a very different assessment, on Patočka's part, of the history of the idea of science. To be sure, both philosophers see the idea of science as constitutive of European civilization. Yet even if Patočka traces roughly the same course of development and focuses on the same basic principles as Husserl does, he nevertheless recognizes as decisive a different aspect of the idea of science—thus, inevitably, he comes to a different understanding of the constitutive nature of reason, a different sense of the totalizing character of the rational.

For Husserl, the history of science is the history of the development of consciousness, which he thematizes as a type of self-discovery: consciousness, as the actualization of a particular mode of relation to and among things, discovers in itself the possibility of universality. Since the starting point is consciousness, universality is grasped as a type of *knowledge;* for it is as a knowing consciousness that the relation between consciousness and the world is realized. Yet universality is not simply a character of a knowledge of things but, rather, a special relation of consciousness to its own innermost possibility of living: thus Husserl speaks of a universal life, of a self-conscious life in the horizon of the pursuit of knowledge. Such a life strives for totality, for it recognizes the horizon of its pursuit as part of its inmost essence; it sees that the horizon itself is its own condition of being, that out of this striving arises knowledge as a project, an *institution*. In grasping its own origin, the conditions of its possibility, it is complete.

Something else goes with this: not only self-consciousness, but self-responsibility is basic to the logic of a really existing, concrete rationality ("science"). For to be aware of life as the horizon of knowledge means to recognize as one's own precisely the general movement of revealing the order of the world. Universality is possible only if, as a subject, the consciousness of this order is the goal of my own life, if I am self-conscious by virtue of this activity. "Reason," then, is not only a tool, a manner of ordering discourse, but also a mode of life, and one that is necessarily universal; for the correlate of such a responsibility, that of which I am conscious in such responsibility, is nothing other than the world as a whole—that is, the world not as an aggregate of things, but as a region of the general possibilities of conscious life, of "knowledge" and "science."

Patočka, likewise, sees as decisive both this relation to the whole of what is, and the conviction that to be in relation to the whole is to be oriented towards a certain order. Like Husserl, his description of the rise of philosophy is also the history of the development of the relation to the world as a whole in a horizon of universalization. Yet Patočka does not identify this whole as the horizon of possible *knowledge;* at its most basic level, it is not the relation between the subject that knows and the world that is known. In these pages Patočka is critical time and time again of the idea of the access to the whole as an accomplishment of a sense-bestowing subjectivity which, within itself and in accordance with its own inner activity, "creates" the relation between itself and its object; the horizon of universality, then, is not for Patočka *eo ipso* a subjective achievement, however much "universality" and "knowledge" are historically intertwined. This criticism is not a minor one, but goes to the heart of Husserl's assertion that phenomenology is a transcendental idealism. That the meaningfulness of experience can be reduced to a pure, transcendental subjectivity; that the meaning of all that is, even of the horizon in which anything that is manifests itself, can be grasped solely from the standpoint of subjectivity—this is the very basis and justification for the idea of phenomenology not only as a transcendental science but as a rigorous science.

Patočka argues, here and elsewhere, that the subjectivism which underlies this rigor is a prejudice. It is, however, no mere prejudice of Husserl's, but a defining tendency in the history of modern philosophy. Its origin can be traced to Cartesian rationalism and a scientism that seeks to reduce the world to that which can be manipulated or controlled, to a language of elements and rules where any identity, any significance is mapped out and defined in advance. Here, to be "rational" means not only to follow, as it were, nature itself throughout all its manifestations, thus letting it appear as it is, but rather to force it to reveal itself in its generalities, to transform it into an image, a schema the structure of which can be mathematically manipulated. What Husserl called "physicalistic objectivism," the reduction of the world to abstract models of causal efficacies, is a direct descendant of this view of the nature of the rational; it identifies the rationality (thus meaning) of the world with the strict, calculable regularity of its models. It understands the essence of the relation between subject and world from the perspective of the ability of the subject to manipulate and control the other term of the relation, thereby making human beings in Descartes' words, *les maîtres et possesseurs de la nature.*

Husserl himself, to be sure, is critical of physicalistic objectivism, precisely in the way it conceives of the mode in which we are in relation to the rationality of the world. For it is intrinsically self-defeating: in seeking to thematize the general access to a meaningful, rational order, it cuts away the sense of its own meaningfulness by claiming that, in order for the world to mean something at all, it has to be emptied of all meaning save its accessibility to manipulation; the order of the world is translated into an abstract schema wherein whatever appears or manifests itself, does so only in the most empty and meaningless of orders.

Greek science—here, Husserl and Patočka are in agreement—is characterized by a different conception of the access to meaning: the relation to the world is not one of mastery, but of letting be what is, letting what is show itself as itself. As Patočka notes, this is the motivation behind Husserl's adoption of the concept of "phenomenon": the task of a "phenomenology" is to thematize the question of how access to the order of the world is possible; it does this not by asking what means are requisite in order to "reach" the "external" world, but by recognizing that the question of this access is more a question of how the world *presents itself to us* than how we "picture" it or "construct" it.

One could say, then, that despite its subjectivism—which has its ultimate source in Cartesianism—phenomenology is in part a rebirth of a much older conception of "science." In part only: for in Husserl the subject is not left quasi-thematized in the shadows, as it is in Greek philosophy; phenomenology, as a reappropriation of Cartesianism, points out not only that the world shows itself and presents itself in its being, but also that we, as subjects, are open to the world, and that the key to the secret of manifestation in general thus lies in the subject. The conditions for the possibility of knowledge are found not in the object, but in the openness of the subject to the object, an openness that is always prior to the manifestation of the world.

Even so, it is important to be attentive to what is common to Greek philosophy and phenomenology—for, in the end, it is what is common to Greek thought and the science of any epoch that forms the very basis of the tradition. In Patočka's account, the Greeks are the ones who discovered the very sense of the world as a whole—i.e., that the whole has a sense different from that of any given individual. Yet what does "discovery" mean here? It does not mean that cultures before Greece were not aware of the whole, of the world; in fact, the argument is that such an awareness is necessary in order to experience, to be in the presence of any given thing. However, to thematize awareness, to make it into an "object" of reflection or inquiry—this is something that goes beyond mere being in the presence of things, developing something that is only hinted at in our awareness of things. It is a thematization of the sense, always at work in our understanding of individual things, that every entity that we encounter in the world is always encountered within a context, whether of our activity or of relations to other things. Things are never meaningful in themselves, only with others; they point to a context that is always more a horizon than an object. As such, this context is nothing over and above the thing, but intrinsic to it; to have something to do with something, to handle it or to understand it, is to always be at the same time moving in the horizon of its signification. That means, in a sense, to always be oriented beyond the immediate dimensions of its givenness, even when we are most involved with the particularities of the object at hand.

This thematization of the horizon of the world in Greek thought accounts for its mathematical character, in two basic senses. The first has to do with a fascination with the idealizing possibilities inherent to mathematical techniques. The act of counting, of bringing together individuals into a collectivity while at the same time retaining the quality of each as a singular instance, then idealizing this collation into a general expression of "counting in general," is an example of a direct thematization of the worldly horizon of things. For formalization is an expression not only of the possibility of a general access to entities (i.e., that anything at all can be described by way of mathematical forms and construction), but that this horizon of the whole is itself an order, one that cannot be discovered by gathering together descriptions of particular things. It is an order that can only be grasped within the consciousness that, for anything at all "to be," it must be placed within this horizon; it must be ordered in accordance with these general, universal forms.

A second sense is the Greek sensitivity to the *mystery* of things. Certain mathematical phenomena, those which have to do precisely with the consequences of orienting thought more closely to the general horizon of things as such, inspire wonder. The infinite divisibility of the line, the incommensurability of the sides to the hypotenuse—all this at once highlights the presence of horizon of the whole in entities and, in one fell swoop, opens up an access to the mystery of all things, the mystery that all this *is*. It is as if, as Patočka puts it, an infinity were suddenly discovered at the very core of the familiar objects of our everyday surroundings; as if we suddenly became acutely aware of the strangeness of our world, a strangeness that had nevertheless always been there, had always played a part, however subtle, in our experience.

Both of these dimensions are present in Husserl's thought. It is not an accident that Husserl's philosophical reflections began with the questions having to do with the origin of mathematics, in particular with the problem of number. *The Philosophy of Arithmetic* represents the first step in Husserl's attempt to express the sense of the world as both horizon and order; yet here, unlike in Greek philosophy, Husserl articulates this order from the perspective of the subjective openness to this horizon. He does this by stressing the origin of number in the *synthetic* character of collation. Not only does he stress synthesis but also, again in contrast to Greek philosophy, he preserves it, and precisely because of the subjective starting point of these analyses. The Greeks hypostatized mathematical objects as special realities, "super"-natural in their immutability and perfection; thus, they in turn understood the order of the world, which is at the same time the horizon within which all things are grasped, as a super-thing, something immutable and static. Even if a constructing activity is necessary to be able to access such objects, that does not mean that the objects themselves have this character of being-constructed. By contrast, Husserl focuses precisely on the synthesizing process presupposed by the consciousness of ideal objects. This is something he always maintained, even after his critique of psychologism in *Logical*

Investigations, and which formed the very basis of his philosophy right up until the *Crisis.*

Here one can also see why the critique of psychologism is so important. For the world as a whole can be thematized only within the activity of idealization; otherwise we are merely dealing with individual things and our vague notion of the specific contexts into which they are set. Without idealization we would never have access to the dimension of experience to which any thing or context as such necessarily points; we would never be fully aware that facts are never complete as fact, but are always nestled into and borne along by some movement towards universality. Thus psychologism, which seeks to reduce all of our thinking as such to factual processes in real space-time, not only fails to recognize that what is intended in "ideal" objects is intrinsically beyond fact, but in turn threatens to misunderstand the nature of the "factual" as well—namely, that facts can be experienced only by a consciousness that is oriented towards their meaningfulness, and that means by an idealizing consciousness.

At the same time, however, psychologism highlights a key aspect of this consciousness of the ideal by approaching it as a *process.* It recognizes, indirectly, the synthetic character of the relation to ideality, thus to the order of the world. For all idealization is an activity, a movement, even if it is false to understand this movement as an empirical process, as something that is always bound to a given time and place—as if what a number "really is" is a certain "picture" that I have constructed of it in my mind. The task, then, is to thematize this generative synthesis, again not as an empirical process, but as a "pure" process, neither a "fact" nor something that ultimately has its origin in a "super" objectivity.

In the chapters that deal with "pure logic" and Husserl's "subjectivism" (chapters 3–6), Patočka traces the development of this attempt to elaborate a philosophy that recognizes, at the very origin of meaning in general, a pure generative synthesis. Though critical of Husserl's subjectivistic turn, Patočka nevertheless recognizes that the focus on the structures of consciousness opened the way for various important insights into the nature of meaning and reason. The high point of this line of inquiry, on Patočka's view, is *The Idea of Phenomenology.* Here, the phenomenon, understood as the result of generative synthesis, is both that within which the world shows itself as itself, as well as something that is achieved by the openness ("intentionality") of consciousness. The difference between this being open and that which shows itself is interpreted by Husserl in terms of the difference between the "immanence" of pure consciousness and the "transcendence" of the world. Yet the dynamic here is such that neither immanence nor transcendence is privileged: even if a "reduction to immanence" is the task of phenomenology, that does not by itself imply that the immanence of consciousness is the *origin* of the intentional relation. It is not as if immanence somehow envelops the world within the absolute being of consciousness; it is not as if the world could only be what it is because I am conscious of it. Rather, in this text we see Husserl stressing the open character of intentionality, thereby mitigating the effects of his subjectivism in formulating the problem at hand; for the argument is that even if we limit our description to the pure immanence of consciousness, we still find in it an intrinsic relation to transcendence. The idea of "transcendence in immanence" is a recognition that the immanence of consciousness is the *opportunity* for transcendence to show itself, that it is precisely as a meaning that the world is "transcendent" in the first place, that its horizonal character is manifest.

Yet that means, on the other hand, that for all the "respect" and "openness" that consciousness has for the autonomy of the transcendent, it is nonetheless an openness that imposes, and must impose, a certain structure. Consciousness is open only to the meaningful, to that which appertains to a certain thesis in accordance with which consciousness approaches the world. Thus the synthetic character of all meaning is identified as the synthesis of a thesis, a structure of subjective comportment that corresponds to the order of the world that can be manifest only within such a comportment, in the "immanence" of its movement. Therein lies the temptation to overemphasize the thetic character of consciousness—which is precisely what Husserl does.

Husserl's subjectivism, on Patočka's view, distorts the two-sided character of the synthetic origin of meaning: it asserts that the clear and distinct articulation of the structure of pure immanence, of the thesis of the world, is the goal of a philosophy that seeks to understand the origin of meaning in general. The very "impurity" or relativity of transcendence is castigated as an obstacle to such an articulation—as if the mere structure of being open to the world, the thesis that orders conscious comportment, exhausts the order of the world that appears "in" consciousness as a phenomenon.

To be sure, it is far from being the case that this subjectivism is the last word in Husserlian phenomenology. In the final chapters of this book, Patočka deals with two aspects of Husserl's thought that point to paths of reflection that could lead phenomenology beyond the limits imposed by such a prejudice: the analyses of time consciousness and of the phenomenon of the body.

The problem of time consciousness is particularly interesting, for it raises the question of the very nature of being oriented to a horizon on its most basic level—for "horizon" is not only a powerful spatial metaphor, but a temporal one as well. These analyses demonstrate that to be open to a horizon, to the world, is not to be a being who stands before a horizon, peering off into the distance at silhouettes of whatever is standing "against" it. On the contrary, we do not just sit and wait for objects to unfold before us; we are, in the progression of our lives, "in" things, not just next to them. For the world is not a backdrop for the picture show of things; it is the horizon of ourselves as well, of our life as beings who are open to the order of the world. The synthesis, then, which lies at the very origin of the meaningfulness of all that is, is not something we do, but a movement that we are; this means that the synthesis of an originary temporality, a primordial movement, lies at the very core of subjective comportment.

Being open to the world, however, is not only a temporal-historical mode of being, but a corporeal one as well. This final chapter (chapter 8, "Incarnate Being") is perhaps the most original and important part of the book. Here Patočka takes up in detail Husserl's phenomenology of the body, a theme in his corpus that is more often than not passed over in Husserl scholarship. Of course, it is not the case that the problem itself is unknown, for the importance of the body in phenomenology in general has often been stressed, especially in the work of Sartre and Merleau-Ponty. But it has not often been recognized that the phenomenological analyses of corporeity in the second volume of the *Ideas* has something important to tell us about Husserl's phenomenology.

In particular, the phenomenon of the body is important for understanding the thesis that the openness to the world is possible only by way of idealization. All meaning, all synthesis for Husserl is an objectification; consciousness is in tune with the order of the

world only insofar as it is the movement of an idealizing objectification. If that is so, then the subject-body as a thing means that,
on some level, this movement of *thought* discovers itself within the
world as a *thing*, an object. Though, undoubtedly, it is an unusual
object: because it is precisely the movement of the synthesis of
meaning, it can never be merely objectified, but must always har-
bor within it an element of the openness to things, thus exhibiting
the trait of pure subjectivity. And an originary one as well: for the
body, precisely as the locus of the pure subject, is the center from
which the synthesis of the world takes place, the center of an orientation to something that can never be an object but which
makes any relation to any object possible.

That the body is the center, located in the world, of the very
movement of consciousness itself, means that consciousness cannot be likened to an infinite streaming of a light which, emerging
out of everywhere and nowhere, "reveals" the presence of entities
in the world. Consciousness is something located, bound to a
place and a reality that it cannot escape—it is something essentially
corporeal.

If that is so—and, we should note, Patočka follows the philosophical implications of these analyses much farther than Husserl
ever did—then the idea of subjectivity or consciousness as a pure
region in the sense of a self-closure cannot be upheld. The very
subjectivity of consciousness means an openness that is less a
"lying in wait" for the world to come along than it is a passing
over into the becoming of things, thus an "experiencing" in a very
strong sense of the term—what I experience, that I become. The
synthesis that is this openness, even if it can still be spoken of as an
"achievement" (insofar as it is active, a movement), is inimical to
the idea of a fixed, closed order, an invariant structure.

This is, then, in broad outlines, the interpretative approach that
Patočka takes in his introduction to Husserl's phenomenology.
This book can also serve, as one might expect, as an introduction
to Patočka's own philosophy as well. In the course of *An Introduction to Husserl's Phenomenology*, the reader will be introduced
to all of the philosophical questions Patočka spent a lifetime pur-
suing: for example, the possibility of an "a-subjective" phenomenology which, while thematizing the synthetic character basic to
the relation between subject and object, nevertheless rejects the
Cartesian insistence on finding in pure consciousness an invariant

structure which would serve as the basis of rigor. There is also evident in these pages Patočka's deep interest in the nature of historical being; the meaning of corporeal existence; the historical character of openness to meaning—all of these are concerns, ideas, and insights to which Patočka dedicated various writings, including *Body, Community, Language, World,* "The Natural World and Phenomenology," and *Heretical Essays in the Philosophy of History.*

In closing, let us return to the thesis with which we opened, concerning the nature of Husserl's philosophy. Husserl's thought bears the stamp of two very different periods of European philosophy, one confident in the inevitable systematization of knowledge in a global totalization of consciousness and culture in general, the other far more skeptical of any sense of finality in matters of truth. Husserl's thought does not simply reflect these two attitudes, but also gives us the means to formulate, in a profound manner, the question of the nature of reason, of its significance for life. As skeptics—and I mean this not as a philosophical position per se, but rather as a general *ethos* of contemporary philosophy which, in contrast to the era of systems, finds figures such as Wittgenstein, Derrida, and Rorty to be far more sympathetic—how does the idea of the "order of the world" stand with us?

I believe that Patočka has shown, in this work and others, that Husserl's phenomenological philosophy enables us to think of "order" and "structure" in such a way that, though not relativistic, nevertheless passes beyond the invariant, fixed, static structures which were the ultimate goals of a host of Cartesian, Kantian, and idealist philosophical programs. Even more important, perhaps, is that the historical reflections of the later Husserl enable us to understand that the attempt to find a fixed order of things, which culminated in the nineteenth century and which still lives in ever-changing forms in technical civilization, is not merely the result of a prejudice, "the history of an error" that we can vaguely sum up as a quest for domination. Rather, this "error" is founded on the original openness to the world as an openness to an order; thus, in a deeper sense, on the truth of human life. It is itself a possible comportment that arises out of the recognition that the world can be "present" or "given" only as an order, and ultimately only to a ratiocination; further, that it is within our activity alone—the activity of community, of culture, of "life" understood as a movement that actualizes itself in projects, concerns, interests—that we are in relation to the whole of what is. That things are possible only within a horizon means that they are possible only within an order; or, better, the movement of an ordering. The horizon of the world is not an empty abyss out of which things emerge as if *ex nihilo,* but a rhythm that cannot be separated from the very movement of our life.

To think through the consequences of this, to take the first steps towards the ontology suggested by such an approach to the problem of the world as a whole, is only possible if we recognize that the attempts of the past to push science and philosophy to its extremes were actually a manifestation of this aspect of human life, that it is a life in possibility, a movement that is as its deepest level "worldly." For the lesson is important, in that these past attempts—to which Husserl's phenomenology ultimately belongs, however much it anticipates other possible ways of understanding order—reveal something basic to the essence of order and structure, thus of "reason," even if they ultimately misunderstood rationality as something fixed and eternal, a world of forms, natural laws, or Absolute Spirit.

Chapter 1

Phenomenology as a Philosophy and Its Relation to Traditional Metaphysical Approaches

Edmund Husserl's phenomenology represents a concurrent reflection about the meaning of things and about the meaning of human life. What makes Husserl's approach distinctive is that (1) it seeks to be a rigorous science and (2) it singles out such rigor not only as one instance but as the central, most important, and profound access to meaning; as such, science can claim a fundamental, crucial significance for human existence. Science ought to and can provide human lives with a "spiritual meaning," the content and aim of life we need in order to be truly at home, at one with ourselves, with our life, and with our world. Nor will it provide that meaning by serving as a *means* to something other, something further, but as itself in what it does, by scientific activity as such.

What, though, is science? We recognize numerous sciences of various types, from mathematics to entomology, from comparative anatomy to selenography. We even have a special science of science itself, the philosophy of science, epistemology, whose problems include the question of what is and what is not science. Yet when we cite all such sciences, which must necessarily be scientific so that even the seemingly least among them must be representative of science as such, it sounds paradoxical to claim that we should consider the doing of science, independently of its utility, as something sovereign which bestows meaning and a goal upon all else in life. The practice of entomology appears to us as a game comparable to stamp collecting. From this perspective, the formulation in terms of which we sought to characterize Husserl's phenomenology—as a concurrent reflection on the meaning both of things and of human life, in the mode of rigorous science—appears at first as an exaggerated affectation. If we are to realize that such an affectation is not what it is all about, we need to review the origins of the idea of science and of the quality of being scientific, as they are accessible to us within the historical horizon containing both their birth and evolution.

It was the ancient Greeks who first discovered science in the sense of a consistent sequence of reasoning, in the form of mathematical theory. What was common to all such teachings, to arithmetics, geometry, optics, astronomy, statics, was that by grasping several fundamental concepts and propositions whose content seemed commonplace or even banal—at first sight at least—it became possible to go on to startling, important, and often fruitful conclusions which were not merely asserted but proven, valid concurrently with their premises. The full content of those initial propositions would be unfolded only by all the propositions that could be deduced from them.

The Greeks, though, were not only the first to discover the format of systematic deductive inquiry. They were also the first who did not take the world for granted.

Still the mythical humans, despite their liberation from the automatism of instinct and from the integration in the global mass of natural processes, remained within the world in a sense like the stone, the crystal, the plant, or the animal: like such existents, the mythical humans in their birth and in their perishing, their functioning and their transformations, continue to relate explicitly only to *parts* of all there is, never to the world *as a whole*. For the mythical humans know already before they ask: their knowledge, passively suggested to them as something imparted, something told— a legend, a myth—fills the preconscious emptiness within them already beforehand. Now the Greeks are the first who ask explicitly about the whole which embraces all, ourselves included, and therewith confront the simple wonder of all wonders: that all of this *is* and that the being of that totality is not something obvious like the particulars of life. While anything partial is based on particulars, sequences, and finally on the whole to which all belongs, the whole itself, circumscribed by the abyss of nonbeing from which all emerges and into which all disappears in its turn, is not based on anything. Our relating to this wonder can be compared only to those relations in which we pass from an accustomed stance into a different mode of life, to the transition from a dream, to the discovery that all had been otherwise, to suspicions suddenly aroused by something we had long passed unconcerned: it is a strangeness, a wonder, an awe, it is *thauma, thaumazein,* from which, according to Plato, wisdom is born. It is worth noting that Aristotle cites as an instance of such an awe-evoking situation the mathematical example that the hypotenuse is incommensurate with the side of a square; what evokes wonder here is that a certain ordinary experience—that if one thing will not fit lengthwise within another, we need only find a third small enough to fit within each—does not apply here, that there is no magnitude small enough to fit both the side and within the hypotenuse, defined with mathematical precision.[1] Ordinary imprecise experiences have their limit, and mathematics, the rigorous theory of precise magnitudes, lets us reach that limit very quickly. The simple task of dividing a segment confronts us at a stroke with the need to choose between the inevitability of the irrational necessity of coming to a halt or of continuing to infinity. Infinity, wholly alien to human experience in ordinary life, suddenly confronts us as the inner matter mysteriously present at the very core of things, showing them forth as paradoxical rather than obvious. In such instances, the noble game of mathematics suddenly becomes all too real, more real because more truthful than ordinary life. The Greeks discovered many such paradoxical situations at the interface of everydayness with the ideal abstractions of mathematics: the infinite empty space without which everything would be immobile, the movement whose first and last moments cannot be determined, the arrow in flight which stands still at any given moment—each such paradox pointing again to the mysteriousness of the ordinary and the familiar so that we could almost say that the more commonplace something is, the more mysterious it is,

---

1. See Plato, *Theaetetus* 155d; Aristotle, *Metaphysics* A 2, 982b12; 983a15. [Ed.]

the more ever before us, constantly manifesting itself, the more dark and impenetrable. The most persistent situation of all, however, is one which is the framework for all the others, the ever present whole and its being, the whole within which and through which everything is and outside of which there is nothing. Just as the division of a straight line forced us to cross the threshold of the mystery of infinity, so the idea of the whole forces us to cross the threshold of the mystery of being, forcing us to see that outside the whole there is nothing—to confront this nothing in thought face to face as the background without which we cannot see the whole and so neither anything particular—at least in its being. The infinite in the segment, the infinite emptiness, defying grasp, extending beneath all that can be grasped, the movement which has limits but neither a start nor an end—all that is but an introduction to the mystery of all mysteries: things flow forth from things, ones presuppose others, but the fact contained in all their duration and alteration, that they are, presupposes nothing that we could call a "thing" in the ordinary sense of an entity which we encounter.

What is the significance of this remarkable concurrence of mathematics and of the question of the whole of being, a concurrence which is both chronological and objective? It would be hard to suppose both arose in approximately the same epoch and in the same nation at approximately the same time by mere coincidence. Mathematical entities are of very different kinds but all have that much in common that we do not encounter them ready made in the world like a table, a house, a forest and an animal, a star and a cloud. To be sure, a house or a table are the works of humans; they are also understood as such, though only when we are concerned with actually making them, while far the more common approach to them is through *using* them and for that they are always ready to hand. We are in no sense aware of participating actively in experiencing them; our experience of them is passive, even and especially when it is a practical experience. Even what I change, rework, add to, or adjust about a thing is just a response to something a thing asks for, what it itself somehow "wants," what it lacks, what needs to be added or deleted and so forth. In ordinary use it is as if things themselves asked for what we do with them, as if they were asking to be cared for, an achievement that has its own melody, its own characteristic course and results which lead on to further tasks. Likewise language, the words which call our attention to things and through which we orient to them, are experienced as something external, something that is not the product of explicit activity; that is why words are so closely associated with things.

Every use, being an activity, aims at some goal of which, however, we are for the most part also not consciously aware as being the product and the work of a decision. Goals, too, seem to be somehow given, the day's program bears us along, prescribing for us, and even on those rare occasions when a decision intervenes, it is determined by traditions, customs, generally speaking by possibilities which are already present and which force on us what we do. In that sense, *doing* is a progression along a pregiven track.

In ordinary use, mathematical entities like numbers, segments, straight lines, or triangles might perhaps make the same impression as things ready at hand. They differ from them insofar that they *are not* without our active participation. They are not like the things we use: those we construct and thereafter they live their own autonomous lives without us. Numbers, straight lines, and circles are only in active counting and construing, never of themselves and for themselves alone.

What autonomous activity leads to mathematical entities? Surely in arithmetics we have to deal with the generation of sets that are not geared to our immediate needs or interests, in which a member retains the validity of a member under all circumstances and through all possible substitutions and variations, so that it does not matter who carries out those operations, or when or in what situation they do so: that then makes it possible for us to agree on anything whatsoever that can be subordinated to the conception of such a quantitative set as long as questions about it can be answered from the conception of that set. In geometry, too, we are dealing with such an objectification: the indefinite, imprecise world of our impressions and of subjective, ungraspable perspectives is to be made equally accessible to everyone; for that purpose we make use of certain privileged configurations taken from ordinary observation (straight lines) which we strip of all that would stand in the way of a perfect objectification, so we carry out an *idealization*, their transformation into an object which as such does not occur and cannot occur in the world presented to us. Only on the basis of such operations can we now pose meaningful, profound questions about things whose answers do not refer ever again to the givenness of things themselves—thus we know a priori, for instance, that we can find a number corresponding to any set of entities, regardless of its magnitude. Still more remarkable—and historically requiring still longer period to be brought fully to mind—is the objectification of shape. Still Leibniz did not believe that it could be possible to express any concrete, sense-given shape whatever mathematically.

Now perhaps we can dare attempt to determine the relation between mathematics and the question of the world as a whole, touching on what is common and what is distinctive between them. Just as particular things in the world become truly objective—intersubjectively identical—only by means of an explicitly objectifying act and its meaning correlate, mathematical objectivities, so also the *world as a whole* is originally nothing objective. It is pre-present, as obvious, in the "functioning" experiential sequences, in the reference of their "and so on" which leads us from one given to the next, from one present to another present. It must, however, be first *explicitly torn out* of this everyday obvious functioning before we can note that this process of approximation, perennially incomplete, presupposes the being, the existence of a *whole* which requires an act of transcendence, at once free and necessary—free insofar as it can be done only once we *break free* of what is momentarily given and so forced on us, and necessary, because to deny it would mean to deny experience itself in its functioning. As with mathematical entities, there is here something independent of the given, something which its objectification presupposes and which for that very reason is not passively accepted, strictly speaking, but rather something accessible to us not from *external givenness* but from *internal freedom.*

The world thus is not an evident entity like its parts which we encounter as soon as we open our eyes or reach out with our hand. It is originally concealed and must first be uncovered, opened up. Wherein and how does it conceal itself? In nothing other than in things themselves, those things that are accessible to us. Every one of them by being here, by "speaking" to us so that we understand it, points beyond itself. The table and the chair point to the room they furnish, that room to a home, that in turn to successive circles of strangeness all the way to the wilderness of a practically effectively infinite nature we cannot master; the peace of the home at the table points to activity, to the day's doings, to work, to the community with its innumerable cells and interrelations; the wood of the chair points to lumber, to a growing tree, to the coherence of extrahuman life. Each of these relations evokes, as indices and references, the divisions of time paced by the great lights of the sun and the movements of the starry heavens. All that and a thousand other things are already here the moment we sit down in the morning room at the table for refreshment and work. Yet I do not *see* these things or, better, I do not become distracted by them and in them. Thanks to the coherence we noted, things are here as what they are—they themselves, in the original, not in some appearance or re-presentation, but what concerns me are my task and my accomplishment at a given moment and at a given place— my concern is breakfast and work, duty and rest, the way and the goal. The world (*svět*), the circle of light (*světlo*) in which I see every activity and thing facing me, all I determine to do, vanishes totally in the clarity of that determination. Just as nothing can be seen in pure light, so, too, the light of the world submerges within the things we see until it appears identical with them. Thus the world conceals itself in the things it brings to light and does so precisely by bringing them to light, by showing them forth and so making them accessible—freeing them for us and giving us access to them. We do not originally see and live the *world as a world* but rather as the things and projects within it.

If mathematical activity is the foundation of all explicit, deliberate, active objectification by which things cease to be *only* what appears *to me* and become equally accessible *to all,* then the task of mathematics is to *continue* the primal objectification, in that opening up and rendering accessible which the world that conceals itself carries out by concealing itself. The mathematical activities of colligation, comparison, subordination, and measurement *constitute* the possibility of a constant presentation, a presentification identical for all, a definition and an overview of things. *Note it well:* that presentation is constituted here, not simply presented and given; we need to grasp it, transform it from mere possibility into act—just as humans need to grasp the world as a world and not merely as presented things and projects in an explicit act.

Undoubtedly, the original beginning of such explicit objectification is a practical one, based on the need to predict, to plan, to reach mutual agreement about realities, about the measurement of a field, about the amount of the harvest and its division, about the time it will last. However, the significance that mathematics acquired in Greece and subsequently in all Western history lies in its part in the discovery of the world.

How did the Greeks discover the world? That is, not under what circumstances, nor for what reasons or from what causes, but rather in what guise and mode did the world open itself and become manifest to them? Conventional wisdom, *communis opinio,* appealing already to the tradition of antiquity, would have it that the world was discovered as *physis* and that, consistently with that, physics was the first theory about the world. Modern thinkers have accordingly taken physics to be a kind of a preface of a theory of material nature and its forces, a primitive physics in the modern sense of the world. *Physis,* however, might have a different meaning in the original Greek.

Originally, the Greek *physis* did not mean an aggregate of things but an activity, a majestic drama to which we ourselves belong and not as spectators, but rather that both we and things are expended for it and consumed in it. The emergence from the night of nonbeing, the interconnection and fusion of generation and perishing of beings which mutually, in their binding interrelation, make room for each other and destroy each other in turn, this primordial happening, primordial movement, and primordial process are the way in which the world emerges in Anaximander's famous statement, in the reflections of his Ionian followers about generation and perishing, in Heraclitus's vision of the world as fire. It is a drama which, like a fire, engulfs and consumes all and in which nothing lasts except for that engulfing and consuming itself.[2]

Thus, from this point of view, what is concealed in the mundane overt presence of our projects is this all-consuming drama. Here it becomes manifest that things and beings stand on a shaky ground, that they sink into what is no thing. Nothingness belongs to the world, even though not among the things of the world. The depth of the abyss, inaccessible by reflection on mere things,

---

2. For the text and a discussion of Anaximander's *apeiron* fragment, see Kirk, Raven, Schofield, *The Presocratic Philosophers,* pp. 106–26. According to the account given by KRS, the doctrine of *ecpyrosis,* the periodic destruction of the world by fire, was actually a later Stoic doctrine that was attributed to Heraclitus; though, to be sure, the importance of fire in cosmic matters for Heraclitus should not be underestimated. See KRS, p. 185. [Ed.]

opens up beneath them. The all-embracing coherence which pre-cedes all particulars, magnificent and merciless, is explicitly here as soon as the mundane fixations of our projects cease affecting us. Now, however, humans can see in truth how and what they are, as *brotos,* mortals who share in the discovery of things by an explicit integration in the drama of the world. Only now are they revealed as worldly beings who by their entire nature are not self-enclosed but rather related to the world and to its vertiginous drama. In their *hic et nunc,* humans are related to the whole. This whole bestows meaning on all particulars. Does this whole which bestows meaning on things, does most of all that ground of all meaning which consists in their emergence and disappearance, in their belonging to the whole, in that they *are*—does this whole itself have a meaning? What is this whole? In what sense can we say of it that it is? What does it mean to be? Such are the questions which now emerge, questions which will not be silenced and which will continue to affect humans once we have grasped the possibility of uncovering the world itself, the world concealed in the clarity of our projects.

Philosophy sets out along the path of these questions and of answers which in turn give rise to new questions. It would know—not only mere things but the whole which manifests itself transiently in all things, letting them participate on its primordial movement and consuming them therein. It would know the whole that is undoubtedly present, since parts are presented to us, but which eludes us as a whole. It would know the whole of which humans are so integral a part that the meaning of this whole becomes their own meaning. It seeks to embrace the all-embrac-ing, to comprehend the comprehensive. In the process it turns to those special manifestations and contexts of human life which are the repository of our inexplicit familiarity with this whole apart from direct contact with revealed particulars: such is *logos,* lan-guage, meaningful discourse. With the art of discourse about things, *dia-logos,* the Greek thinkers transformed language into a tool for working out constant, unchanging meanings on which we can depend, to which we can return so that they are always avail-able, perennially present. Through them they then present for themselves permanently the *shape of things,* independent of their contingent manifestations here, then, and there. Then on the way to that which can *always* be overlooked but which at the same time has a global, fusing character, the Greek thinkers encounter mathematical operations and mathematical constructs. They, too, are independent of the transience of manifestation: they are firm, common for all. In addition, they have the immense advantage: what is true of them can be ordered as a system and exhausted by a rigorous method which, except for certain rules of admissible and inadmissible ordering of propositions, admits nothing external, disruptive, and uncontrolled in its progression.

Thus, gradually, on the basis of the discovery of the world as a process of manifestation and in the effort to comprehend, embrace, and surround this manifestation there emerges philosophy as a science and science as a part of philosophy, that is, of global comprehension. Science (as for instance mathematics) is a component of and a contribution to philosophy. Its intention is to penetrate beyond appearing particulars to the whole that bestows meaning, to penetrate this whole itself, comprehending it as an organic unity in all its interlocking, internally necessary, and reciprocally implied parts. Being and the world, understood as a *kosmos,* an organic whole, become the goal of Greek philosophy and science. Logic and mathematics are the organs, the tools, and at the same time the models of this philosophy: it is from them that it learns to understand the drama of the world as a mere "course of events" in a transtemporal sense, from them it learns the art of drawing the whole out of individual meanings. Precisely this fusion of the two brought about that systematization of science which has no parallel elsewhere: systematization presupposes care, care for the whole independently of individual utility and purpose. While even the greatest achievements of pre-Greek science are technical directions for reaching this or that result, here suddenly the mind focuses on something other than successful task and achievement—it is focused on the whole which is here for itself and as such holds an "interest" of its own. Hence also the sudden advancement of Greek science over all of its predecessors.

We cannot sketch here even the chief phases of the fortunes of this conception of philosophy as a science, as an *episteme* which seeks to arrive at the whole of appearance by discovering that within it that is firm, ever present, and in that sense eternal. This conception seeks to master the discovery of freedom for the world by a freedom to an ongoing, definitive objectification, so transforming the primordial whole into an all-embracing object, into a kind of superthing, into that cosmic organism, harmonious in all its members so that the process of manifestation is transformed into a mere appearance of a permanent substance. At the same time, that is linked with a special conception of the meaning of humanity: it consists in using imitation, realization of the cosmos in the individual and in the human community, to forge a firmly grounded, defined, and delineated unity—so that the cosmos becomes not only a measure of being but also the norm of human life.

Precisely this objectively oriented practice, in this understanding of humanity in terms of a completed organism of things in the cosmos, reveals the limits of the Greek understanding of being, of the world, and of humans—of oneself and of the other. To the Greek mind the discovery of the whole did not mean at the same time a discovery of human being with each other in its fullness, in its originality. Humans, to be sure, were discovered originally in terms of their relation to the *kosmos*—as worldly being—though not together with the originality of their relation to others which can be realized only in a turn no less profound than the turn from individual things to their global coherence. For in the obviousness of our daily dealings with things in which the world is concealed there is also contained the concealed overtness of our relation to other beings of our kind. The projects we undertake are focused on our personal, exclusive goals but they are meaningful only in reciprocity, in the mutuality of mirroring and mutual penetration with others. As long as the turn from things to the world is not carried through to this dimension, as long as there is no realization of the originality of the living relation in which others cease to be mere things (even if governed together with me by the same cosmic norms of harmony and justice), the discovery of the world cannot take place except along the lines of the impersonal and so of the "lifeless"; hence also the appeal for the Greek philosopher of what is comprehensive and transcendent, global and permanent, though lifeless and internally empty, of ideas, of mathematical entities, of logical relations. In a world so understood there cannot ultimately dwell the meaning of manifestation, such a world is stripped of it and vacuous—it has to be transcended if we are to overcome the fossilization brought about by the discovering and uncovering, but impersonal and so ineffective philosophizing in the matrix of transtemporal presence in its unity with rigorous science.

Modern philosophy and science intended to continue in the
work of antiquity ever since their beginnings in the sixteenth and
seventeenth centuries, but their understanding had already been
recast in terms of a more *personal* understanding of the global
drama. For that reason, humans no longer understood their life
from the perspective of integration (in the process of manifestation, in the harmony of the cosmic organism), but rather from a
standpoint which seeks to transcend integration, givenness, facticity—from the standpoint (figuratively speaking) of a *command*
that opposes the given and the fixed.

Knowledge, too, now lives from this perspective. It does continue to be borne by the idea of a mathematical uncovering of
what is permanent and substantial in worldly realities. On the
other hand, however, it is no longer simply a way of coming to
terms with the whole of the world, of integrating our mind within
its harmony, but rather is—or wants to be—a realization, as Bacon
puts it, of the *regnum hominis,* seeking to make us, in Descartes'
words, *maîtres et possesseurs de la nature.*

The *maître et possesseur de la nature* must then be understood
as superior to its objects—superior and autonomous, masters of
their own, in their self-confidence masters of their own home—
this is where we find Descartes' basic discovery of the role of self-
confidence: to be in the world means to be as a self-confident
being whom no one and no thing can drive out of the ultimate
bastion of self-certainty. Thus this bastion will inherit the role
played by *logos,* mathematical entities, ideas, and forms in ancient
philosophy: it will be a permanent, reliable foundation of the
world of appearance—such reliability will in turn be meaningful in
terms of our mastery, our progressive conquests within it. For self-
confidence is not only a mirror, it is also the self-consciousness of
a humanity which stands above things because its life is grounded
in a command and so is fundamentally a will.

Mathematics thereby acquires a new impetus and a new significance: it becomes the principal tool of this project, accompanied
by a progressive objectification. It does not merely introduce precision into the world but transforms it, rendering it susceptible to
mastery in a real, concrete manner. Mathematics itself becomes
self-consciously formal and abstract, focusing its main interest and
power on abstract formalization—that is, into the project of its
own mastery. Utilizing indirect mathematization and the lawlike

correlation of its entities with the given, mathematics incorporates physical reality within its scope and piece by piece other realities as well. Continuing the trend of abstraction inherited from Greek mathematical philosophy, it renders reality itself abstract: what it considers real is whatever corresponds to mathematical relations; overlooking their termini, their content, mathematics apprehends only the network of relations or perhaps only the structure of this web of relations.

Such a formally oriented science aims at effectiveness, that is, at releasing forces for action and domination, for ordering the world, for transformation of things for purposes foreign to them; they come to be understood purely as a means which humans have not only a right but a duty to exploit and expend. Humans are no longer integrated within the world as having a calling to it, rather, they become the ruthless rulers of an abstract object to which they have only an abstract relation. Science is no longer fruitless, it no longer lets things be what they are, but transforms them into mere means which are meaningless in themselves.

The abstract person and its relation to the world are will and domination. This will shatters the ancient *kosmos* and all its legacy, things no longer constitute an organic whole. The world is no longer an equal participant in a shared drama, rather, we are free with respect to it, it does not represent a fundamental limit for us but rather is for us a stage, a reservoir of raw materials, the basis for action in which it ultimately figures as a mere subordinate component. Because we, too, are objects in the world, we deal with humans similarly, generating not only a technology of things but in conjunction with it a technology of the organization of human resources. The abstractly personal relation to the world is thus a technology which becomes its own purpose. In a basic contradiction in the being of humans: to be the world-constituting being and at the same time a thing in the world—this abstractly personal relation leads to an actual subjugation of humans by the aspect of will and domination as such.

The contradiction of this abstractly personal understanding of the place of humans in the world manifests itself in the theoretical self-objectification and practical self-reification of humans. Theoretical self-objectification is the contradiction which extends mathematical physics into an empirically causal theory of mind and of its cognition. Empiricism can be understood as a protest of human

beings with their active integration in the world against mathematical metaphysics, though a powerless protest which does not
remove this metaphysics because it is itself based on it. In reflective *psychology* the empiricists attempted to grasp the manner in
which images are produced in our minds on the basis of a causal
relation to them. They were guided by the understanding that
experience has its lawlike structure on whose basis things can
appear and become manifest; thus they discover the *reflective
method* which seeks to set about tracing the order of our experience, basing itself on the self-certitude of consciousness and
marked by it. However, they cannot understand this order in its
distinctive nature, independent of causal conditioning, so that
they do not give up the physicalist model of being integrated in
nature; on the other hand they do arrive at a skepticism about its
validity because they know no experiential syntheses other than
the contingently empirical. These shortcomings of empiricism,
however, leave room for corrections and modifications of the
reflective method in the direction which Husserl's phenomenology will take.—Practical self-reification is that process of ruthless
rationalization of all social relations which makes humans a tool
for ever further and more general objectification.

It was Kant who uncovered the abstractly personal relation of
humans to the world as a problem that needs to be resolved by a
phenomenalization of the mathematical model of reality and by
superordinating practical life, that is, the harmonic interaction of
the will with all other wills, to phenomenal nature. Not psychological reflection, but rather a descent to the covert *logic of the
constitution of objectivity* becomes the context of the question of
the world.

Subsequent thinkers posed the question of the world in a new
way: as a matter of a revitalization of withered human relations,
restoring them to an inward form in which the other, without
ceasing to be other, loses its strangeness and externality and
becomes no less an internal content of our lives than we of its.
That gave rise to the problem of a concretely personal conception
of the world which transcends the abstractly personal conception
as no more than its starting point and as the ground that makes it
possible, though it finds the overall meaning, otherwise absent
from it, only in a community of mutual respect and mutually
interchanging individualities.

The concretely personal conception hopes to attain this global construction of the meaning of the world and of being by unfolding a new logic, capable not only of construing the relation of the subject to nature but also a system of spiritual relations in a historical evolution. It will succeed where ancient metaphysics was shipwrecked: it will be a logic of action and movement, not merely a logic of a changeless structure, of transtemporality. It will, however, be at the same time a logic of the whole, an exhaustive logic, the logic of the final uncovering, obscured by nothing.

It will become such an uncovering when the idea of such logic will contain the phenomenon itself with its positive and negative side, when it will absorb nonbeing, nothingness into itself and will relate being and nonbeing, this contradiction, to each other, thus conjoining what in the logic of finite differentiation of individual things must ever remain disjointed.

The idea of such a logic, in its various forms—radical or mitigated—of a logic applied universally or only anthropologically-partially, is the final bequest of Greek philosophy to the present time. In it lives the Greek idea of philosophy as a science, as an *episteme* rather than a mere *doxa,* that which simply seems and appears, as well as the idea of the unity of science and philosophy.

This logic, as Hegel conceived of it and as it has been subsequently modified, is one of the foci of present-day philosophical discussion. Today, though, few would dare defend it in that form, as a closed system and in the completeness that was to make it the logic of the concrete.

Face to face with this focus of contemporary discussion, methodologically continuous with empiricism and its reflective method, another conception of the question that led to the rise of Greek philosophy is emerging, of the question for the drama of the world, for being which bestows meaning on all that is and sets each particular a priori into a meaningful framework. It is a conception which also sees the meaning of philosophy in setting humans free for a prevenient continuity of the world and of being, but so analyzes the continuity that as a consequence of these analyses we might doubt whether that continuity can itself ever be surveyed as a whole, mastered, and exhausted.

For this mode of posing the philosophical question the central philosophical concern will still be the way in which each particular we experience acquires its meaning—how it appears to us, how it manifests itself, shows itself in what it is. Appearance, manifestation, *phainesthai* in Greek, will be its fundamental problem: hence the name, *phenomenology*.

Phenomenology will no longer revive the project of an all-embracing logic of being. Though it will not be blind to the problem of logic, it will take it for a purely objective doctrine of meaning, of meaning as expressed and formulated, while the activities in which meaning takes on its actual form in a lawlike manner remain outside its purview. It will turn, rather, to psychology, though profoundly transforming it into a doctrine concerning the constitution of a meaningful order of experience in things. Thus it will build on Descartes as well as on Kant, though in its own original manner which will gradually exclude all possibilities of slipping, in tracing the consequences of radical reflection, back into the all-exhaustive form and configurations of the absolute logos instead of that attention to the elements of streaming personal and living experience in which its reflection must move.

Consistently with that, phenomenology will not consider as its highest goal the transformation into principles, reasons, causes, its ideal will not be an explanation subordinated to the principle of sufficient reason, but rather a comprehension of the thing, that is, of all that has to do with meaning, in the structured richness of its nature and substance.

Furthermore, phenomenology will not be a philosophy of the older, argumentative type, focusing on the analysis of internal contradictions and the intricacies of systems and seeking to formulate abstract solutions, it will seek, rather, to resolve philosophical problems on experiential grounds, *seeing* the things themselves, moving from abstract schemata to the fullness and depth of the sphere of life.

Thus phenomenology does not intend to demonstrate, as positivism and all the offshoots of empiricism, that science is mere description, perhaps an explanatory, reductive description of realities, of entities in their sets, moments, and relations. It is about the meaning of existents and about being as the presupposition for the description carried out by empirical science.

The world appears to it as the foundation of that meaning—it seeks to detail the fusing, overarching, transcendental role of the world in its analyses. At the basis of the world, however, it discovers something that traditional philosophy had always passed over and ignored—time and temporality, so that the meaning-bestowing ground of being itself in its nature becomes a temporal drama, a movement above which understanding cannot carry us since every understanding presupposes it; a movement which opens up the world as a genuinely open-ended drama, repeated ever anew in different ways.

The founder of phenomenology, Edmund Husserl, nonetheless insisted that it is possible to comprehend this ultimate ground, to forge a comprehension that would tear it out of namelessness and make it accessible to all. How did he arrive at his questions and his conclusions? Will his proposal that phenomenology be the foundation on which all science and philosophy ought to build, prove tenable, and how should we understand his claim that phenomenology, though giving up any claim to an exhaustive and definitive validity, is a rigorous science? In what sense is he carrying on the enterprise first proposed by Greek science and philosophy?

Chapter 2

The Philosophy of Arithmetic

Husserl was a mathematician by professional training. His interest in philosophy developed out of the foundational problems of one of the mathematical disciplines, arithmetic. His first major work, *Philosophy of Arithmetic* (1891), is devoted to them.

Husserl understood the foundation of his discipline as a combination of logical and psychological methodology. A logical analysis of the discipline leads to basic axioms which include concepts undefinable in virtue of their simplicity. The concepts of quantity, intensity, location, time, etc. cannot be defined, just as primary relations and relational concepts like equality, similarity, gradation, whole-part, multiplicity-unity, are not susceptible to a formal logical definition. What can be done is *to single out* the concrete phenomena from which they are abstracted and to clarify the mode of such abstraction. The *psychological explanation* which that brings to the fore must be suitable for placing us in a position to note those abstract moments ourselves and to duplicate in ourselves the entire process of abstraction with all its components.[1]

The primacy which Husserl attributes to the psychological method in dealing with foundational questions is linked to his unquestioning acceptance of the classical theory of definition and makes no attempt to develop methods which could meet the

---

1. Edmund Husserl, *Philosophie der Arithmetik, Husserliana* (hereafter Hua) XII, pp. 118–20.

demand for a purely logical, that is, for a systematically self-sufficient closure without reference to other disciplines.

Husserl's clarification of the fundamental mathematical concepts
of multiplicity, unity, and number is an example of such a psychological determination of what is logically undefinable. Husserl seeks
to uncover the psychological origin of these concepts.

Thus Husserl was guided from the start by an effort to contribute to the clarification of the same questions which occupied
nineteenth-century mathematicians and philosophers like Bolzano,
Frege, and others who were concerned with a rigorous, logically
deductive construction of the mathematical disciplines.[2] His
method, however, is entirely different from the beginning. He
does not aim at a mere axiomatization of the discipline by objectively logical methods. He seeks to *grasp the origins* of fundamental concepts and perspectives in corresponding subjective activities.

The psychological method by which Husserl seeks to achieve this
is a reflection on and an analysis of the lived experience of elementary thought processes. Nothing suggests that Husserl in this phase
deviated in any way from his teacher in psychology, Franz Brentano,
who considered such a reflection an *empirical* method based on
facts. It is important, however, that Husserl applied this method precisely to the lived experiences by which we arrive at the fundamental
mathematical conceptions of multiplicity and quantity. On the one
hand, the arithmetical concepts of multiplicity, quantity, and number
would forcefully present their character as meaning units which are
general and ideal, yet at the same time objective and identical in
diverse thought processes dealing with identical meaning units. On
the other hand, however, the discipline of arithmetics clearly showed
that basic arithmetical relations are not possible without a specific
mental activity, that they are not a mere internal schematization of
relations imposed upon us by external objects, as they appear to us
in passive experience. Thus in his thought we encounter a new version of the Locke-Leibniz antithesis, *nihil in intellectu quod non
fuerit in sensu—nisi intellectus ipse:*[3] as the tension between the

---

2. As illustrative, see Gottlob Frege's analysis of number in *The Foundations of Arithmetic*. Bernard Bolzano's (1781–1848) *The Paradoxes of the Infinite* was an important influence on Georg Cantor's later development of set theory. [Ed.]

3. That is, Locke's claim that there are no innate ideas, in contrast to Leibniz's rejoin-
der that there are no pure ideas that are not innate. The contrast can be readily made by
comparing book 1 of Locke's *An Essay Concerning Human Understanding* to Leibniz's
New Essays on Human Understanding, essay 1, chapter 1, §§23–34. [Ed.]

experiential starting point (from individual givens, facta, even if they are the facta of inner experience, of reflection) and the autonomous activity of the mind which nevertheless reaches objective results. In time, this tension must lead to a modification of the empirical starting point: the subjective will have to be so conceived as to lead to grasping objective concepts and truths, objective in the sense that we can always return to them as identical and that they are also identical for various subjects. On the other hand, however, this objectivity must itself prove to be something that is not wholly independent of the subject's activity.

For now, though, in the phase of the *Philosophy of Arithmetic,* this contradiction is present in full force.

Husserl's account of the genesis of number (quantity) is the following.

Quantity (Husserl relies basically on the classic Euclidean definition: a multiplicity of units) is a kind, a specification of multiplicity.

Quantity and multiplicity are abstract concepts. The foundation from which they are abstracted are concrete groups of objects of thought (not of things merely but of any objects whatever). Relevant to this abstraction, to be sure, are not qualities or any aspects of things fused in an aggregate but rather the way in which these objects are brought together in a unity, the special relation into which they are introduced.

Husserl now distinguishes two kinds of relations, primary and psychical.[4] This distinction is an *application of Brentano's differentiation between physical and psychic phenomena* to the realm of relations. "Physical" phenomena are, for Brentano, for instance color, tone, landscape, odor, warmth which are localized entirely in the "external world," "psychic" phenomena are those which are characterized by an "intentional" relation to the object—that is, the presentation of a color, a judgment about something, and so forth.[5] Similarly, for Husserl, primary relations are those in which the relation contains its fundamentals or members nonintentionally, psychic relations the ones that contain them intentionally. Primary relations are such that the fundamentals (members) of the relations are linked in terms of content: equality, gradation,

---

4. Husserl, *Philosophie der Arithmetik,* Hua XII, pp. 66ff.
5. Franz Brentano, *Psychology from an Empirical Standpoint,* pp. 80, 85, 97. For Brentano, psychic phenomena are always either presentations (*Vorstellungen*) or are based on presentations; a presentation, then, is always a presentation of something, of an object—see also below, chapter 4.

continuity, the connection between extension and quality (for instance, color), logical entailment. The content of one member requires an other, and a specific other. Equality or similarity are relations which can be fulfilled only by a member having a certain characteristic content.

By contrast, psychical relations are such that the contents are linked *only* by the act of our mind. The object does not require the psychic relation, it is wholly indifferent to the content and is not subject to any content variation.

The colligation of objects of the mind in a unity is now a *psychic relation*. It consists in the unification of any objects whatever, considered not in terms of concrete content but simply as "something," unified by an act of the mind. This ingathering can continue ad infinitum, there being no reason why it should cease. Multiplicity consists in this type of mere gathering without specifying the kind of gathering (one + one + one + . . .). A multiplicity specified as a definite type of an aggregate (one of + one of, one of + one of + one of, . . .) constitutes a quantity.

Thus quantity grows out of the purely psychic relation of colligation or, in other words, from an ingathering unification. Reflection, that is, a viewing of this purely psychic intentional relation, constitutes the process of colligation as an object, generating the concept of quantity.

Throughout Husserl's theory we can see the original contradiction between his empirical psychological method and the universally rational, ideal result he seeks. An empirical method can do no more than accept the given individual data (here the observation of particular internal processes in reflection), derive empirical abstractions from them, and finally formulate hypotheses which serve to clarify given observations. However, what really needs to be clarified does not have the character of such data but rather of ideal generalities. Such generalities are the basis of the most rigorous truths of the exact sciences, independent of experience. How can we arrive at them from individual empirical data?

In addition, empirical processes like reflection on individual lived experience has a subjective reality as its object. How can an abstraction from such an empirical procedure arrive at anything other than empirical generalizations, from subjective processes at that, at objects such as quantity and number, which implicity contain necessary and universal cognitions?

Hence the ambiguity of Husserl's concepts of multiplicity, quantity, and unit (of something): on the one hand they designate objects, on the other hand something subjective, and about that something subjective it is not clear whether it is taken in its empirical contingency or whether it is simply assumed that it has some necessary structure, capable of being grasped directly, which these analyses elaborate.

Without being clearly aware of this distinction, Husserl strives in his analysis of the origin of the primordial arithmetic concepts for something other than the *empirical* laws of this origin: he is striving to grasp the *necessary* laws, *perceived in their necessity*, of the way we arrive at those concepts.

The paradox of this way of arriving at them is that even though we are analyzing a subjective process, it is one which can lead to an objective, objectival structure. What must be the nature of this subjective process so that its own free activity, independent of the characteristics of the given objects, could in turn give rise to something objective?

Thus though the use of the expression "psychic relation" is understandable, it is also an ambiguous one: on the one hand, this relation can be understood as a psychic reality, on the other hand as something ideal, a universal unity.

Those who stress the aspect of the ideal unity in this equivocation and who interpret the *Philosophy of Arithmetic* in light of Husserl's later development claim that Husserl is here *de facto* already engaging in a "constitutional" analysis of number, that he is considering the way in which an ideal unity is constituted by certain typical thought processes.[6] "That there are structures," Walter Biemel tells us, "which must be produced in thought in order to exist . . . is, *in nuce,* the *idea of constitution*."[7] To be sure, Husserl is here simply letting himself be borne along by the natural meaning of ideal formations as general unities, not yet posing the problem of how the universal can "appear" in the particular, the inactual in the actual, because he does not yet see it clearly.

Consequently, if we read into the text the distinction between the perception of the particular and the perception of the general

6. As representative let us cite Oskar Becker, "The Philosophy of Edmund Husserl"; Walter Biemel, "The Decisive Phases in the Development of Husserl's Philosophy"; and Robert Sokolowski, *The Formation of Husserl's Concept of Constitution*, p. 19.

7. Walter Biemel, "The Decisive Phases in the Development of Husserl's Philosophy," in *The Phenomenology of Husserl*, p. 153. [Ed.]

(be it an ideal entity, a lawlike regularity, or structure) and the distinction between consciousness in the contingent particularity of its processes and in its function of making possible the experience of the contingent and the particular, *then we can read these analyses as if* they were dealing with what later will become a purely phenomenological description and constitutional analysis.

That Husserl here really wavers is suggested also by the circumstance that the concept of multiplicity and of quantity (of basic number) is here generated, according to him, by a reflection about "collective interconnection," originally a subjective activity. This subjectivity becomes an object in the act of reflection; it had not been that hitherto.

At the time (1891; Ed.), Husserl also had not yet developed the conception of subjective experiencing as intentionality which makes objective reality always a unitary "pole" correlated to lawlike experiential multiplicities. He is still holding on to Brentano's conception of the intentional act in which the object and the act correspond to each other statically—the object corresponds to the concept, a thesis to a judgment, rejection or refusal to love-hate. Only in the case of the primordial arithmetic concepts has a dynamic moment entered in; the objective unity of number and of multiplicity here corresponds to the *procedure* of colligation.

Thus Frege's objection, formulated in 1894,[8] is not without justification: in the *Philosophy of Arithmetic* Husserl fluctuates between a subjective and an objective conception of the concepts of multiplicity and quantity, which appear now as objects, now as something subjective, and again as subjective processes of conceptualization.

For that matter, Husserl himself, in his "Prolegomena to Pure Logic,"[9] speaks critically of his standpoint at that time as subjectively empirically psychological. Likewise Roman Ingarden does not believe that the *Philosophy of Arithmetic* is already a constitutional analysis of multiplicity and quantity.[10]

Despite all this, Philosophy of Arithmetic *is at the root* of all of these future concerns. Once Husserl manages to clarify the

---

8. See Gottlob Frege, "Review of Dr. E. Husserl's *Philosophy of Arithmetic.*"
9. Husserl, *Prolegomena to a Pure Logic,* vol. 1 of *Logical Investigations,* p. 42. Also, as evidence of Husserl's change of heart between the *Philosophie der Arithmetik* and the *Logical Investigations,* with respect to Frege's position, see ibid., p. 179, n. 1 to §45. [Ed.]
10. Roman Ingarden, "Discussion de la conference Biemel," in *Husserl,* Cahiers de Royaumont, p. 67. Ingarden, to be sure, asserts (wrongly) that the objectivity of ideal entities and their "constitution" by mental activity are mutually exclusive.

problems sketched here—the substantival objectivity of ideal unities and the special character of the laws pertaining to them which
are independent of empirical generalization, also the nature of the
subjectivity capable of arriving at such objective laws—he will have
presented the most substantive part of his philosophy.

Philosophy of Arithmetic is significant in two other respects as
well. For one, Husserl here shows himself as a brilliant master of
analysis, especially of analysis of subjective mental processes. The
distinction between primary and psychic relations (despite the
ambiguity noted above) is an insight which will later lead to an
understanding of the characteristic trait of mathematical formations—that they are not given empirically but rather must be
freely *constituted by a spontaneous activity*. Another brilliant insight
of the *Philosophy of Arithmetic* is the differentiation between the
intrinsic and the symbolic (later, merely signitive) conceptions of
number[11]—which will later lead to analyses of purely significative
acts and their fulfillment; and among symbolic conceptions the
discovery (contemporaneous, to be sure, with Mach and
Ehrenfels[12]) of "figural" moments,[13] that is, of configurational
qualities which function as a substitute for the actual perception of
a definite quantity.

Finally, we encounter here one other characteristic trait of
Husserl's foundational analysis then and later, the idea that an
inspired solution of professional problems is not incompatible
with a lack of foundational clarity. This became evident to him in
the case of Helmholtz and Kronecker and of their nominalist theory of numbers as mere names for designating any object whatever: these great specialists neglect foundational considerations in
their eagerness to confront complex *technical* tasks, without
devoting an appropriately deep analysis to such considerations.
Such an approach does give rise to valid and important recogni-
tions, though their meaning remains obscure. These great mathematicians blindly adhered to a *symbolic process of numeration*, one

11. Husserl, *Philosophie der Arithmetik,* Hua XII, part 2, chapter 10: "Numerical
Operations and the Concept of Real Numbers" ("Die Zahloperationen und die
eigentlichen Zahlbegriffe"), pp. 181–92; chapter 11: "Symbolic Multiplicity-Presentation"
("Die symbolischen Vielheitsvorstellungen"), pp. 193–221.

12. Ibid., pp. 203ff, "Figurative Moments." [See also Christian Ehrenfels, "Über
Gestaltqualitäten"; and Ernst Mach, *The Analysis of Sensations*—Ed.]

13. Ibid., pp. 177–78. [Husserl in this context makes frequent reference to Hermann
Helmholtz's 1887 essay "An Epistemological Analysis of Counting and Measurement"; see
also Leopold Kronecker's "Über den Zahlbegriff."—Ed.]

which is of first-rate importance to mathematical technique, and consequently they projected its symbolics, the perspective of mere names and symbols, into the very foundation of the discipline of arithmetic and so entirely dismissed number as a special entity—as the true realm of actually perceivable multiplicity and quantity. From this insight there emerges one of the fundamental ideas of Husserl's future philosophy and philosophical critique: the need to trace the entire genesis of meaning, to turn from its merely symbolic derivation to where the matters themselves point, to its most primordial sources—otherwise the meaning of the discipline degenerates, bringing on a crisis of the corresponding science.

In order to disentangle arithmetics from the contradictions suggested here it was *first of all* necessary to stress the objectivity of ideal entities, of objects, units, classes, quantities, multiplicities as well as of the rigorous and immediate laws which hold for these entities independently of individual empirical givens; at the same time clarifying the objectivity of units of meaning, of concepts, axioms, etc., as they relate to objectivities (whether real or ideal).—A further *fundamental, correlative task* was to clarify the relation of this entire ideal region to subjective life, to those conscious processes which have access to essential laws, an access which in turn cannot be accidental (a contingent access could not bring about an awareness of essential relations as such): the idea of a psychological grounding of scientific principles must pass through a series of profound transformations to achieve a resolution of all contradictions and ambiguities.

Now the objectivity of the ideal realm could not be assured in all its extent and depth on arithmetic grounds alone, nor on the grounds of mathematics as such in its usual sense. To be sure, mathematics, specifically arithmetic, does center on ideal concepts such as multiplicity, quantity, something (object) as such; still, the problem of a rigorous justification exceeds every individual mathematical discipline already because any justification presupposes, in addition to *objects,* also *meanings* as ideal entities, and no mathematical theory is a theory of meaning in general. The relations of objects and meanings involve a different and a more fundamental theory and, in Husserl's conception, logic is precisely that theory. Thus the question must be posed first of all on the grounds of logic.

For that reason, Husserl seeks to resolve the entire initial task (that of assuring the objectivity of ideal constructs) in a series of logical investigations (*Logical Investigations*). Especially the first part, "Prolegomena to a Pure Logic,"[14] demonstrates the need for an autonomous science of logical objectivities—entities on the one hand, meanings on the other—independent of empirical psychology. The second volume then deals in part with partial questions that belong here (for instance the theory of meanings as ideal objects (*idealia*); the idea of a pure logical grammar, that is, a systematization of meaning from the simple to the complex with the help of syntaxes; furthermore in the area of ideal laws of objects a systematization based on a theory of the whole and its parts); then in part with a substantial part of the second task—the study of subjectivity in its substantive relations to the object.

However, it turns out that a systematically constructed logic in the required sense does not yet exist. The old formal logic may be a science of rigorous laws of meaning, but those do not yet constitute a complete theory of the form of all possible theory as such. The efforts of modern thinkers such as Descartes and Leibniz did move in the direction of such a universal *mathesis;* actually, though, they resulted only in the birth of new, special mathematical disciplines: analytic geometry in the case of Descartes, calculus and logistics in that of Leibniz. The development of the science of logic demonstrated the same trait that the *Philosophy of Arithmetic* noted in the case of the great modern mathematicians, that technical success overwhelmed the effort to clarify the foundations.

Hence the unsatisfactory state of contemporary logic: logic is traditionally understood as an organon, a tool, not as a science with a theoretical significance and domain of its own, and as a philosophy of science logic remains bound by this tradition.

This situation is reflected in the fundamental question much discussed by logicians at the time: is logic a theoretical discipline or a practical doctrine, or in other words, is it a *scientia* or an *ars,* a skill? The delimitation and characterization of the nature of the entire discipline reflected this question: for some it was a theoretical discipline whose subject matter is essentially independent of psychology, dealing with mere form of cognition without reference to content, thus being a demonstrative and so an a priori

---

14. Husserl, *Logical Investigations,* volume 1, "Prolegomena to Pure Logic."

discipline much like arithmetic; for others it was a practical
art, founded essentially on psychology, that is, on an empirical
discipline, consequently also dependent upon experiential content
and a posteriori in all substantive aspects.

The supporters of the first thesis were drawn for the most part
from the followers of Kant (and Herbart[15]), joined by isolated
individuals belonging to no school but carrying on the trends of
the seventeenth century, Bolzano the greatest among them. The
supporters of the opposite thesis, highly numerous and, in
Husserl's time, predominant, were empiricists or thinkers influ-
enced by empiricism.

For all their divergences, both trends recognized the function
of logic as a philosophy of science, but did not equally accept the
need for logic as a theoretical discipline. For that reason Husserl,
too, starts out by stressing the need for a firm, lucid foundation
and construction of science.[16] *Practical results do not yet guarantee
flawless theoretical construction*. A rigorous construction of a science requires a special theory of what makes a science scientific, a
logic of science. That logic teaches that rigorous cognition—science—combines evidence, that is, the evident givenness of cognitions, with the systematic coherence of individual sciences. This
coherence leads to the conception of the *form of justification*
which is independent of the particular contents of a given science
as well as neutral to this or that science. Philosophy of science
deals with scientific justification—on which all scientific progress
ultimately rests—with the coherence of justification, that is, with
scientific theory and with science as a complex of theories relevant
to a particular set of objects. Thus the task of philosophy of science will be to evaluate the validity or invalidity of theories. Logic,
as a philosophy of science, will therefore be a normative and
specifically a practical science: it does not merely note but rather
evaluates and prescribes, teaching how to carry out a genuine science. It belongs to the essence of a normative theory that it justifies general axioms which, with respect to a particular idea or ultimate goal, determine the characteristics an object must possess to
measure up to it as to a norm we apply to the subject matter.

The normative and practical nature of logic is thus a matter of
course. Why then the conflict whether logic is a science (that is, a

---

15. I.e., the German philosopher Johann Friedrich Herbart (1776–1841). [Ed.]
16. Husserl, *Logical Investigations*, §§1–3, pp. 53–57. [Ed.]

theoretical science) or an art? John Stuart Mill declared this conflict one of the most needless in the history of science. In reality, though, it is otherwise.

Every normative and practical discipline presupposes one or more theoretical disciplines as its foundation. That is, a normative discipline tells us what characteristics an object must have in order to be considered positive, "good," in terms of a certain positive value, good behavior, good person, good science. Before we can decide what sort of an act, a person, or a science we shall qualify as "good," we need to have a certain knowledge of it, and that, in the case of a full, consistent knowing, means a *science* of comportment, of persons, of science as such.

If we now return to logic, the whole significance of the debate about the theoretical or the practical and normative nature of the discipline stands out. For there are authors, such as John Stuart Mill, for whom logic is *merely* a practical application of psychology, in particular of cognitive psychology.[17] There is no pure theoretical discipline that could be called logic. For their opponents, things are otherwise: logic as a practical doctrine is an application of specifically *logical* principles and laws, distinct from psychology. The supporters of the first thesis, of psychologism, raise the following argument: if we define logic as the art of thought, of judgment and proof, of knowing or striving for truth, then the objects of this practical skill which we artfully direct and regulate will always indicate something psychic, a mental, spiritual activity or its products. Thus what is psychic is the content with which logic deals practically and normatively, and psychology, which deals with the laws of spiritual, specifically mental processes, contains therefore the theoretical foundation of logic as an art. The content of logic itself confirms it: it speaks of concepts, judgments, valuations, deductions, inductions, definitions, classifications—all of that is psychology selected according to normative standpoints. Psychology is contained already in the fundamental logical concepts of truth and untruth, of affirmation and negation, of the universal and particular. At first sight, this argument is appealing and seems to be true; its opponents protest in vain that logic is to ordinary psychological thought what morality is to life, that it confronts contingent actuality with necessary laws and rules. Kant

---

17. See John Stuart Mill, *A System of Logic*, pp. 1–8. [Ed.]

and Herbart thus conjoined the autonomy of logic too closely
with its normative nature. The psychologizers do not deny normative necessity in logic: normal, normative laws of thought simply
show us how we should proceed *if we want to think validly.* To
think validly, however, means to think in harmony with the special
laws of thought, undistorted by the influence of habits, traditions,
emotional components, and so forth. For that reason a psychologizer is also not content with halfway measures such as the claim
that logic does not study real, causal connections and relations of
thought but the relations of mental configurations with respect to
truth-untruth, validity-invalidity, that the point is not physics but
ethics of thought.[18] In particular, causal connections in logic are
demonstrated by the fact that argumentation produces evidence.—Nor will the psychologizer be convinced by the common
argument that logic cannot be an application of psychology
because the construction of a psychology already presupposes the
validity of logic: for if this argument were valid, it would block the
construction of logic no less; besides, this argument fails to distinguish logical laws as the premises *from which* we reason and as
rules *according to which* we reason.

Thus at first it looks as if the psychologizers have presented a
successful argument. Actually, though, their argument shows only
that psychology *plays a part* in the theoretical construction of
logic. They do not prove that its participation is either *exclusive*
or essential. Husserl will advance the arguments of the opposition
in a form that will reveal the absurdity of the psychologistic
thesis.

First of all, it is clear that psychological laws are vague empirical
generalizations (as for instance the laws of association) whose
validity and application depend upon circumstances which cannot
be rigorously defined. In contrast, logical laws in the strong sense
of the term, at the core of logic, as logical principles, syllogistic
formulae, laws of conclusion from like to like, Bernoulli's principle
of complete induction, and others, are absolutely rigorous.

Secondly, we do not know any natural law a priori, no such law
can be justified by a direct insight into its validity, its necessity.

---

18. See Husserl, *Logical Investigations,* p. 94, where Husserl cites Theodor Lipps,
Grundzüge der Logik, §1, p. 1: "A question as to what should be done always reduces to a
question as to what must be done if a definite goal is to be reached, and this question in its
turn is equivalent to a question as to how this goal is *in fact reached.*" [Ed.]

Natural laws can be justified only inductively, and here insight is possible only into a greater or lesser *probable validity* of the law, not into the law itself. Accordingly, those logical laws and principles cited should be mere probabilities, the syllogistic mode Barbara would mean that the conclusion from the given premises is valid within the limits of a certain probability; a logical rule would be one of the possible formulae fulfilling the requirement of approaching observed facts in the matrix of possible errors of observation.—If logical laws were causal laws according to which we realize cognitions in a mental context, then such laws could only be given as probable and the results of their application could also be only probable. Even the claim that knowledge of these principles is probable would be only probable, just as the assertion of this probability, with the probability quotient naturally decreasing, seriously threatens the overall value of cognition.

Besides, what experience, what analyses, show that valid mental acts arise from pure, undistorted working of the natural laws of our thought? What does logical and what does illogical thought look like concretely, in our inner experience? How does that "undistorted working of the natural laws of thought" differ from thought considered according to the norm of logical rules?

The psychologizers blithely interchange laws in the sense of the *content* or *object* of judgment with the real processes constituted by the psychic acts of judgment themselves. Logical norms motivate the course of our thinking, we organize our ideas to conform to those norms which, for this reason, appear as if they were themselves causal factors of this process—this leads to the further confusion of law as a causal factor with law as a rule. In reality the causal laws of a real mental process wholly conforming to rules of logic are not themselves identical with the rules of logic, just as the functioning of a calculator is not governed by the rules of the mathematical laws it carries out. The psychologizers confuse an ideal law with an actual law, normative regulation with causal regulation, ideal motivation with actual motivation.

We can further cite as a serious counterargument that *logical laws have no psychological content,* but would have to have such if they were a normative version of psychological realities. However, no law of logic implies any factual reality or any matter of fact whatever, none presupposes the existence of any imaginations, judgments, or any thought processes in its content. From the fact that all *understanding* and *knowledge* of the content of the law presupposes imaginations, judgments, and other mental acts we cannot conclude that the *content* of the law itself likewise presupposes them.—Logical laws do not have the character of idealizing *fictions cum fundamento in re* like the exact laws of empirical sciences, for instance of physics. Quite the contrary, like pure mathematical theorems, they have the character of genuine laws.—Conversely, no truth that is cognized by a pure rational intuition can be a truth about facts. Truth is something essentially atemporal, thus it is no fact, no actuality, which is always in time. The laws of logic as the laws of truths are atemporal in their content; as laws of reality, they would have to be rules of the coexistence and sequence of facts.

The inability of psychologism to grasp the distinctiveness of the logical becomes evident in its explanation of logical principles, especially of the principle of contradiction. The psychologizers are so intensely devoted to their empiricistic prejudices that they do not hesitate to cite formulations—for instance concerning our inability simultaneously to believe and not to believe the same, or concerning the incompatibility of actual *acts of judgment* corresponding to contradictory *propositions*—so that it would be possible to formulate the principle of noncontradiction as "two contradictorily opposed acts of belief cannot coexist"—which not only is not a rigorous and evidently necessary law but even psychologically is at best doubtful, unproved, or erroneous: which, we need not add, refers to the exclusion of the coexistence of contradiction in the same subject at the same time, while the law of noncontradiction excludes with apodictic evidence the contradiction of two propositions and two facts corresponding to them, always and regardless of the subject. And is there not a real coexistence of contradictions, in a way even conscious, in the case of a person who is affected by ambivalent inclinations, attracted and repelled simultaneously by the same motive? Is not a person rendered unsure by skepticism simultaneously in a state of believing and not believing?—The empiricist explanation of the syllogistic process is no less perverse. It speaks of the "generation of evident givenness" in the case of the conjunction of certain premises and of the absence of evident givenness in the case of others, not sanctioned by logic. It is again as if we were dealing with real processes and as if evident givenness were a product analogous to the product of a chemical synthesis—which is not sanctioned by logic—with the difference that while in the case of a chemical reaction we can control the reagents and know their precise amounts and presence, in the case of mental processes the circumstances of the process remain vague and obscure.

To characterize the psychologistic teachings philosophically it then proves useful to introduce a new, more precise conception of *skepticism* than the ordinary. Ordinarily skepticism means doubt about the possibility of penetrating to a "true reality" behind mere appearance. Skepticism in the pregnant sense is a doctrine whose very formulation denies what is subjectively or objectively a condition of its own validity. So, for instance, a theory which holds that there is no difference between a blind and an evident judgment is skeptical in this sense—contradictory: its thesis is presented as a cognition, that is, as an evident judgment. Thus psychologism is not simply an invalid theory (with invalid premises or conclusions);[19] psychologism is a *logical* skepticism *contradicting the objective conditions of validity of all theory—for its theses and theories deny the conditions without which logical theory makes no sense at all*. Psychologism finds itself in the position of skepticism as *relativism*. Relativism is the position expressed in Protagoras' dictum that "humans are the measure of all things," that is, that all judgments, truths, propositions are relative to humans and are valid only within this relation (either individual or generic). Individual relativism proves to be a skepticism as soon as it claims to be a *justified* theory, that is, one *based objectively on reasons;* its explicit formulation denies what it tacitly assumes. However, a generic or species relativism is also skeptical, though more covertly so; its argumentation assumes that the objective content sequence of reasons to which it appeals is valid independently of any subject while its explicit formulations of it are *directed against this assumption*. Every theory presupposes the objective validity of logical ideal laws and of concepts such as truth, proposition, object, property, relation, etc.; those are not realities, least of all subjective, but are rather universal idealities, whose special instances and examples are concepts, propositions, theories we are using and formulating. Every theory that denies their ideal objectivity must therefore be labeled skeptical in the sense indicated; every relativism is such a

19. K. H. Volkmann-Schluck, "Husserl's Lehre von der Idealität der Bedeutung als metaphysiches Problem."

theory; psychologism, however, is a relativism, so that psychologism is a *skeptical relativism*. Among such skeptical theories belongs the attempt to maintain that laws of logic do not need to hold for minds with a different mental structure; such beings would, for instance, be justified in thinking in conflict with the principle of contradiction; argumentation for, giving reasons for, any such theory contradicts itself.

Psychologism as skeptical relativism can be summed up in *three prejudices* which sum up the essence of psychologism as a whole.

The *first prejudice* confuses *laws serving as norms* of cognitive activity and *laws that themselves contain the idea of such a norm,* and then asserts that "the rules by which psychic processes are governed are obviously psychologically grounded; therefore the norms of cognition must be grounded in the psychology of cognition." This prejudice forgets that laws such as the principle of noncontradiction, *modus ponens* and *tollens,* the rules of syllogism, etc., *can be used normatively* even when they do not themselves contain the idea of the norm; they can be *transformed* and *transposed* into norms which then have the psychic as their object and content. Here it then also becomes absolutely clear what was the defect of the antipsychologistic argumentation so far: that it was content with the assertion that laws of logic, unlike facts, are *norms,* while their autonomy is based on their *ideal objectivity;* it failed to see that logical laws are not norms of themselves but only *can be used as norms.*

Now it is also evident that objective idealities and laws based on them are the very content of what might be called *pure logic,* as long as we are dealing with idealities pertaining to the concepts of truth, science, and theory. In Husserl's judgment, this pure logic had up to now been for the most part a *desideratum* buried beneath an insufficiently transparent accumulation of in part normative, in part inessentially methodological formulations of logical substrates, relations, and laws.

The *second prejudice of psychologism* appeals to the factual content of logic: do not judgments, reasonings, proofs, truths, and probability, necessity, and possibility, refer to mental processes and states? Here the distinction between propositions of pure logic and normative propositions does not help; every logical proposition, be it ever so theoretical, is *eo ipso* psychological. However, already the evident consequence that even mathematics would then be pure psychology, counsels caution. Here we need only distinguish between ideal and real objectivities in order for us to see through the entire equivocation of the psychologistic argument. Even though there are no numbers without the act of counting and even though without arithmetical operations there are no arithmetic propositions and truths, numbers, their relations, etc. are nevertheless something entirely different from such operations as counting, adding, etc. Counting, summation, etc. *as real processes* are unique temporal realities for which, as with all realities, empirical laws of causation, occurrence, and sequence hold. Also unique in this way are real *conceptions* of objects, propositions, and truths of which we become aware in such conceptualizations. By contrast, the numbers 1, 2, 3 . . . , a sum, a product, etc. are not particulars in time but are rather generalities which are literally identical in all various instantiations; the number five is not my counting to five, nor someone else's counting, nor is it my or someone else's conceptualization of five; it is a *species,* a generality, an *ideality* which is *realized* or given in the individual *instance* of a class of five members. If we have such an instance before us and see in it not this particular and contingent aggregate of five members given in time but rather an *instance of the species* "five," then we are carrying out what is ordinarily called abstraction and what in no sense consists of a mere analysis of what is given in part while omitting other aspects, but has a fully positive, irreplaceable, and irreducible meaning of an experience of the general in all its significance, a seeing of the general in the particular. Acts of counting arise and perish, but it would be absurd to say of numbers, part of whose meaning is that time has no significance for them, that they are nothing individual, that they arise, exist, that they are here or there.—However, what holds true of mathematical entities can be applied without further ado to pure logic. Its concepts of conception, concept, judgment, proof, theory, necessity, and truth are likewise *ideally intended* and it is mere equivocation if we understand them as temporal psychological realities in which we happen to be aware, at a particular moment, of a certain conception, concept, or truth. As with all ideal entities, these concepts of pure logic also *have no empirical extension* and the generality they express is no empirical universality of a summary enumeration of facts but rather a wholly different, purely ideal universality which cannot be reached merely by enumerating all particulars but by an *idealizing abstraction.*

At this point we need to be aware of the following basic differences:

There is an essential, ineradicable difference between the sciences of the ideal and of the real: sciences of the ideal are a priori, those of the real are empirical. The first generate ideal, lawlike universalities in pure exactness, the latter real generalities in intuitive probability. *The extension of ideal universalities is the domain of ultimate specific differences; the extension of real generality that of individual, temporally differentiated particularities.* Therein consists also the difference between an ideal and a real law: a real law is a universal proposition about facts, an ideal law is genuine generality expressing a relation among idealities.

There is a difference between a cognitive sequence which is a real psychological process, a sequence of things cognized which constitute the object of a science, whether ideal or real, and the logical process of justification of cognitions, assertions, proofs, and truths.

The *third prejudice of psychologism* is the one to which psychologism turns once more in its *theory of evident givenness.* Even if we admit all the foregoing, the psychologizers reason, it is still the case that cognitions as such necessarily have the character of evident givenness. Evident givenness, however, is a psychological fact, it is a certain feeling, a sense of necessity that things are thus and not otherwise, and a feeling is naturally a psychological fact.—However, here, too, there is a ready answer which consists of the fundamental distinction between evidence as a particular psychic fact and the evidence of purely ideal universal relations. For just as with concepts, judgments, and other logical configurations taken as ideal generalities, universally ideal propositions also apply to evidence understood as an ideal generality characterizing ideally generally understood mental acts, that is, the general substances of our psychic acts. Logical propositions can thus be transformed, with no loss of validity, into propositions about ideal conditions of evidence; so for instance the law of excluded middle can be transformed into the proposition: evidence can be instantiated by one but only one member of a pair of contradictory judgments; modus Barbara can be transformed into the proposition that evidence can arise in an act of judgment in which the premises have a known form.

This answer to the thesis of the psychologizers concerning evident givenness has a far-reaching significance. At first sight it does

appear as if a universal ideal proposition concerning evident givenness and its necessary consequences were a psychological proposition. Yet it is not a proposition whose validity as law would be of
merely factual universality, but rather is a validity of a universal a
priori nature. It is not a proposition about the *fact* of evident
givenness but about its universal essence and its essential relations.
To speak of universal essences of psychic realities is no stranger
than to speak of a universal such as the number five, a singularity
present in many exemplifications, or of a universal tone a_1 which is
actualized whenever it is played on a violin or any other instrument. If it is possible to speak of the universal essence of a tone,
then we can surely with equal legitimacy speak of a universal such
as a particular shade of red; for we can undoubtedly distinguish it
from others yet recognize it again in a different instantiation, and
the same condition is met even in the case of those universals we
encounter in psychic acts such as perception, imagination, or
memory. The evident givenness of judgments does not depend
merely on real conditions such as attention, physical and mental
alertness, but also on ideal conditions such as those just noted:
without the fulfillment of the conditions laid down by logical laws
and structures no evident givenness is possible. To be sure, evident
givenness in this sense is no accidental feeling accompanying certain judgments as a mere fact, devoid of internal coherence. The
evident givenness to which ideal laws apply is nothing other than
the *lived experience of truth*. Truth here is *an idea (a universal)
whose individual instance is realized in the lived experience of an
evident judgment*. Here Husserl comes very close to the conception of "being known" held by Aristotle. However, he makes his
doctrine of objectivity more precise with a further indication:
there exists an *ideal lawlike regularity* according to which a mere
intention of a judgment *without evident givenness* can be transposed into an evident assertion of that judgment: there exists a
lived experience of coextension, of agreement between an opinion
and what is self-given and present, what is intended, and this
coextension is evidence; the idea of this agreement then is the idea
of truth.

Husserl believes he now has at hand all he needs to build up
his "pure logic"; that logic to which Leibniz pointed in *his* calculus and *characteristica universalis* without actually building it
up, on which Bolzano worked in the first two parts of the

Wissenschaftslehre, in fundamental theory and the theory of elements;[20] also what Kant meant by "pure logic" belongs here, even though he had a much less precise conception than Leibniz. For Leibniz's idea was that of a *"de formulis seu ordinis, similitudinis, relationis, etc., expressionibus in universum"* while Kant basically retained the traditional Aristotelean-Stoic forms.[21]

The task of pure logic is to resolve the question of the nature or ideal essence (not factual, but rather a priori) of theory as such. That presupposes the delineation and systematization of those concepts and laws which are the *ideal components of theory as such* and from which follows the order of justification, the form of explanation as a lawlike order belonging to and based on such concepts. Already in Husserl's early stage this logic had the form which Husserl will later develop systematically in his *Formal and Transcendental Logic* with respect to its objective aspect;[22] it will consist of

1. the delineation and description of those categories which belong to any logical formation, that is
   (a) pure categories of meaning such as proposition and its components, elementary syntactical particles, rules of composition and complication;
   (b) formal categories of objective content such as "something," substrate, and syntax, relation, property, number, etc.;
2. the constitution of laws and theories rooted in these concepts, that is again, on the one hand
   (a) theory of concurrent validity of meanings (such as syllogistics and other systems of logical deduction); and on the other hand
   (b) theory of individual object regions such as theory of products, numbers, etc.;

---

20. See, with respect to Leibniz's concept of a *characteristica universalis,* his *De Arte Combinatoria* (1666; esp. pp. 10–11 in *Logical Papers*), and *De Synthesi et Analysi Universali* (1679).

The reference to Bernard Bolzano, *Theory of Science (Wissenschaftslehre),* is to book 1, "Theory of Fundamentals" and book 2, "Theory of Elements." [Ed.]

21. On Leibniz's concept of logic as a science of relations, see his *De Scientia Universali seu calculo philosophico.* Kant's attitude with regard to traditional Aristotelian logical analysis can be appraised in a collection of lecture notes published in the volume *Lectures on Logic;* see also *Critique of Pure Reason,* B viii. (i.e., preface to the second edition). [Ed.]

22. See Edmund Husserl, *Formal and Transcendental Logic,* part 1: "The Structures and the Sphere of Objective Formal Logic." [Ed.]

3. theory of possible forms of theories or pure theory of multiplicity which is Husserl's *novum*—the construction of purely formal deductive systems, parallel to possible multiple abstract geometries.

Thus it is evident that the rejection of psychologism is only a part of the project of a philosophical systematics which already contains *in nuce* some of the chief motifs of phenomenology. In concluding, let us enumerate these motifs.

The construction of a pure logic on the thesis of idealities, on their nonempirical nature and the nonempirical nature of the relations anchored in them, as well as on the recognition of these relations.

Idealities are not restricted to pure logic even though the idealities of pure logic constitute a clearly delimited group among other idealities, for they are those ideal entities which belong to the essence of the object as such, of its conceptual definition, cognition, and articulation.

It is, however, already clear from the explanation of the *Prolegomena* that ideal entities are not limited to the region of pure logic—the region to which Husserl takes mathematics also to belong; there are also idealities of *contents:* essences or natures of objectivities such as a physical, extended thing; cause and effect, space, time; "quality" in its specific differentiations such as life, value, cultural entity, and so forth. Among such idealities, too, there are lawlike relations which are not given in empirical experience but rather in the (a priori) intellectual perception of ideal entities as such—and here an extensive field of research beckons.

However, it is also evident from the lawlike regularities of evidence that there is something like an essential correlation of subjective, psychic essences with the objectivities which belong to such subjective processes—not contingently but rather on the basis of essential laws. The correlation between an act of cognition and its object is not a matter of contingent empirical occurrence but is rather rooted in essential, eidetic a priori laws. Here we encounter a new set of problems, only vaguely hinted at so far, from which there will arise, after extensive reflection, phenomenology in the strict sense of the word—a nonempirical theory of the internal, ideal structure of experience in its relation to its object.

The pure logic which Husserl adumbrates at the end of the "Prolegomena to a Pure Logic"[23] is another step on the way to constituting logic as a science.

In the Platonic dialectic logic still retains in part a practical content, i.e., the striving to come to an agreement with oneself and with others as well as the clarifying of our own views, opinions. Plato conceives, as the basis of this possibility, an appertinent object of constant, consensual, and firm cognition—the ideal object to which he assigns the nature of *true being* while Aristotle's striving for a science is subjected to this true being and to theory about it, to metaphysics; logic, dialectics here remains incomplete, a mere tool of cognition even with the discovery of the idea of pure logical form—therein in Aristotle's thought, too, remains that originally "practical" meaning of logic.

In modern times the practicality of logic means something else: striving and fruitfulness, the *ars inveniendi;* and, beginning with Leibniz, the "universal mathematics" was to become the all-embracing tool, mastering reality ever more comprehensively and ever more formally.

It is evident that Husserl's "Platonism" has nothing in common with the metaphysics of ideas and forms. The point is not to ascertain "true being," the path to true being and goodness. The path that Husserl treads is that of modern science, transforming original living relations and given life into precisely manipulable idealities, transforming them by idealization into objects of a higher order.

Husserl's *Prolegomena* is a work born at the turn of the century. The concept of a pure logic sketched therein has been transcended by present-day logical practice, though to this day the fundamental thesis of that Husserlian quasi-Platonism—the impossibility of doing without ideal objectivities, without ideal relations as essentially different from empirical-individual generalizations—has not been controverted, even though we undoubtedly imagine the construction of logic in many particulars differently today than did Husserl in his time.

---

23. Husserl, *Logical Investigations,* vol. 1: "Prolegomena to Pure Logic," chapter 11, pp. 225–46.

Chapter 3

Pure Logic: The *Logical Investigations*

The characteristic orientation of all of Husserl's philosophical thought—his simultaneous concern for both the objective and the subjective, for our lived experience and that to which this experience is directed—is evident even in the pure logic sketched out by Husserl in the concluding section of the *Prolegomena*. As we have seen, pure logic breaks down into a theory of the forms of signification and its laws and a theory of purely formal objectivities such as the object in general, class, multiplicity, number, etc. Evidently the concern of the *Philosophy of Arithmetic*, combining logical studies with studies of subjectivity, was not abandoned but rather raised to a higher level.

Husserl did not simply take over the mode of logical objective research expounded and practiced by Frege. He did not arrive at a new objectivism by speculations within a purely objective region. Even his objectivism is based *on a new theory of a subjective approach to logical objectivities,* treating them as a special type of universal, ideal objectivities as such. This theory we need to explain first.

> If what we intend is *red as a type,* a red object appears before us, and in this sense we look at a red object which is not what we actually intend. Its aspect of redness comes to the foreground and in this sense we can also say that we are looking at this aspect. Yet even this aspect, this individually defined particular trait is not what we intend when, for instance, we make the

> phenomenological observation that aspects of redness in a disjunctive part of
> an area are likewise disjunctive. While what appears before us is the red object
> and the aspect of redness stressed in it, what we really intend is the *sole iden-*
> *tical redness* and we intend this redness in a new mode of awareness in which
> it becomes for us an object type rather than an individual object.[1]

The moment of redness appears twice in this text. First, as part
of the originally given red object which continues to be present in
its individuality. Out of this given object we have selected one
moment—redness. The subjective selection, the focusing of attention, has its own objective correlate—redness *stands out,* a quality
becomes central in place of the object on which our attention normally focuses because this objective center is explicated, extended
in its properties.

Now, however, comes something new, though it neither cancels
nor abolishes what preceded but rather presupposes it—the act of
intending the universal. In this act, what I have in mind (intend) is
not this individual quality of this individual object, brought to the
fore, but rather that which *makes it the kind of quality it is*—that
which does not have to become actual just here and now, for it is
independent of the here and now of the individual thing to which
it belongs as a property or, more precisely, as a *qualis.*

An act of individual intending had to come first; an intending
of a universal is not possible except *on the basis of* that act, yet it
represents something entirely new. The fact that it is possible only
as an act based upon the intending of a particular shows that we
are not dealing with a mere state of mind; the act of intending
something individual is not wholly indifferent to intending something universal; Husserl does not explicate all that is contained
herein—the awareness of the irrelevance of spatio-temporal substrate localization undoubtedly plays a role here even though the
author does not stress it specifically; that also means that the
awareness, the intending of the universal, is linked with a perception of the entire context of space and time, the entire localization
within a substrate. At times it has been asserted on the basis of
much too superficial a reading of the text cited above that the "act
of intending the universal" is identical with an unmediated grasp,
a simple seeing of the universal as such, and this insight is then
identified with a mere abstractive isolation of the moment of red-

---

1. Edmund Husserl, *Logical Investigations*, pp. 337–38 (translation Kohák following
Patočka's Czech translation).

ness, the mere *datum* of redness as such, in order to assert further, with apparent justification, that Husserl's vision of redness as such does not contain any moment of universality.[2]

Husserl, however, speaks explicitly of the act of *intending* the universal which, as such, is not yet a *grasping* of the nuance of redness in its originality. Intention only aims at it: intentionality is oriented to the distinctive content which is the identical universal as against the spatially and temporally diffused individual, but it does not yet see it, recognize it.

An interpretation of our text presupposes *the difference between the act of intending and its fulfillment* which Husserl explains in an entirely different passage of his *Logical Investigations*.[3]

Expressive acts, with whose help alone we can formulate our lived experience, play a special role among the acts of consciousness (that is, the lived experiences which become conscious and, not being directly object of reflection, can become such). Naming, judging, etc., are such acts of expression. Other lived experiences (for example, perceptions) are transposed into meanings by expressions—to be sure, meaning is determined by perception, but it is not expressed by it. An act expressing an intending, the intentional expressive act, can (although need not necessarily!) enter into a significant substantive relation to a perception: the perception can become the *fulfillment* of the mere or empty intention, the contents of the two acts can be *coextensive,* they can become identical. The unity of the expressive thought and the perception expressed by it might be static, as when I perceive a jasmine bouquet which I also intend; or it can be dynamic, as when I can subsequently see the guest, who had just rang, as he enters the door.

This difference in a static or a dynamic relation between a mere intention and its fulfillment does not, however, apply solely to the intending of an individual and to simple (or sense) perception, but is also applicable to the more complex intentionalities built up on individual intentions (founded acts) and the "intuition" corresponding to them.

With respect to intending the individual, of its parts and aspects, the intention of the universal is something fundamentally new, not derivable from the former; it is an intention aimed

2. Theodor Adorno, *Against Epistemology: Studies in Husserl and the Phenomenological Antinomies*, pp. 102–3, 110–11.

3. Husserl, *Logical Investigations,* Investigation II, chapter 2, pp. 350–61.

elsewhere, to something entirely different from the individual thing or a collection of such things. Like the intention of the individual, it aims at a unitary objective pole, at a single object in various acts; but, unlike in the case of individual intention, its object is not located in objective space-time.

The intention of the individual can reach a (static or a dynamic) fulfillment; now we need to ask what it is that fulfills the intention of the universal.

> Where general ideas reach their fulfillment in intuition, there certain new acts are built up on our percepts and other appearances of like order, acts related to our appearing object quite differently from the intuitions which constitute it. This difference in mode of relation is expressed by the obvious . . . turn, that the intuited object is not here itself what is intended but serves only as an elucidatory example of our true general meaning. Expressive acts now trace these differences and their intention does not refer to what we hold before us as seen (that is, individually) but rather refers to something universal to which perception only testifies. Where a new intention is adequately fulfilled by perception, which provides it with a foundation, there it is proving its objective possibility, or perhaps the possibility or reality of a universal.[4]

Thus it is possible and necessary to broaden the concept of perception beyond *individual* or *sense perception* to include also those objectivities which cannot themselves be perceived by the senses.

What cannot be perceived by the senses, however, includes such components of the expressed intention as for instance that something is a subject, a predicate, a member of a set or of a class, and so on. Husserl calls these objectivities "factual contents" *(Sachverhalte)* and claims that *"As the sensible object is to sense-perception so the "factual content" is to the act in which we notice it. . . . We would almost like to say in general, that is how "facts" relate to the acts in which we become aware of them."*[5] Every categorial form can "emerge" for us, be given to us *as it itself is,* only on the basis of the act which places it before our mental eye—that is the analogy with plain sense perception: Husserl feels justified in speaking of *categorial perception.*

> The essential homogeneity of the function of fulfillment, as of all the ideal relationships necessarily bound up with it, obliges us to designate as *perception* every act that is a fulfilling act in the mode of a confirming self-

4. Ibid., p. 778 (translation Kohák following Patočka's Czech translation).
5. Ibid., p. 783 (translation Kohák following Patočka's Czech translation).

presentation, and every fulfilling act whatever as an intuition and its intentional correlate as object.[6] . . . So, consistently with ordinary linguistic usage, sets, indefinite manifolds, wholes, quantities, disjunctives become "facts" and for us "objectivities," while acts in which they present themselves to us become "percepts."[7]

A categorial perception or intuition is always a complex founded act, that is, one that is based on other, simpler preceding acts. Such a higher act can be built up so that the objects of its lower founding acts enter into its intention themselves, in their own individual form (as in the case, for instance, of categorial relations such as conjunction, disjunction, judgment). On the other hand, there are cases in which the objects of the founding acts do not enter in with the intention of the founded act, as in the case of the region of *perceptions of the universal* (or *eidetic intuition*).

Abstraction takes place on the basis of primordial intuition and with it a new categorial trait of acts enters in, with which a new kind of objectivity becomes perceivable, one which can appear as really or figuratively given *only* in such founded acts. By abstraction I of course do not mean mere stressing of some nonautonomous aspect of a sense object but rather *idea-generating abstraction* wherein I become aware, in place of a nonautonomous moment, of its "idea," its universality, and in such a way that it is presently given.[8]

Thus the first text we cited contains, in a compressed form, all these ideas: the difference between an intention and a fulfillment; between static and dynamic modes of fulfillment; between simple and complex founded acts of intending; between simple and founded fulfillment; empty intention, as well as the fulfilling perception and the originary perception which presents the thing itself; between sense intuition and categorial intuition; and between the wider conception of intuition, categorial intuition, and one of its forms—the perception of the universal.

If we overlook these implications, we might easily be tempted to consider the "perception of the universal" as a direct intuition "shooting from the hip" to "hit upon the universality of a concept without passing through the range of its extension,"[9] contrary to Husserl's explicit description:

---

6. Ibid., p. 785 (translation Kohák following Patočka's Czech translation).
7. Ibid. (translation Kohák following Patočka's Czech translation).
8. Ibid., p. 800 (translation Kohák following Patočka's Czech translation).
9. Adorno, *Against Epistemology,* p. 126 (translation Kohák following Patočka's Czech translation).

For we become aware of the identity of the universal through the repeated performing of such acts (that is, abstraction) *upon a basis of several individual intuitions* (that is, extension) [J. P.'s italics], and we plainly do so in an overarching act of identification which brings *all such individual acts of abstraction into one synthesizing act of identification*. . . . In an act of abstraction, which need not necessarily take place by means of naming, the universal *is itself given to us;* we do not think it only significatively, as when we merely understand general names, but we apprehend it, *behold* it. Speaking of an intuition, and, more precisely, of a *perception* of the universal is quite justified.[10]

This passage makes it clear that an eidetic intuition *in a single instance* is neither a necessity nor a rule, but only a certain possibility which is not wholly unknown even in classical theories of abstraction.

Husserl's doctrine of the perception of the universal is something of a middle road between the classical theories of abstraction adumbrated by Plato and Aristotle. Unlike for Plato, the object given to us in the perception of the universal does not possess "true being," it is not maximally real but rather lacks reality altogether. *Eidos,* or the universal object, if considered for itself, not within the context of what is substantive *about things,* is distinguished from things in a platonic manner, though without reality.

That brings up an important aspect: because we are dealing with a nonreality, the reality of the instance is irrelevant to the *eidos* as such; thus the *eidos* can be perceived equally well in fantasy.

Fantasy can even be elevated to a method of grasping *eide* from nonessential accompanying circumstances. If we wish to grasp what is really essential for a tone as such, what cannot be lost without losing the tone as tone, we must subject its various aspects to variation, and that is possible only in fantasy which substitutes the possible for the given while preserving that which persists throughout change. *Eidos,* the essence "tone," is then that which remains invariant, the unity of mutually presupposed aspects of quality, pitch, intensity, and timbre which must always be present if we are to deal with a tone as tone—all of this quite independently of who, when, on what instrument, with what intention and purpose, produced the tone.

Does not, though, the seeking of the *eidos* of a specific significative intention of a certain word mean that in reality we are let-

---

10. Husserl, *Logical Investigations,* p. 800 (translation modified by Kohák based on Patočka's Czech translation).

ting the entire inquiry be guided by the conventional meanings of words? The claim has even been made that it is a merit of the method of the perception of the universal that it cannot be falsified by facts, for if a case occurs which deviates from a previously intended meaning, then it simply does not fall within the given *eidos:* for instance, if whiteness belongs to the being of a swan, then there can be no black swans. In fact, however, the method of perceiving the universal means just the opposite: verbal intention is merely an experimental unity, only perception shows which traits really presuppose one another, either unilaterally or reciprocally, and the concern for intelligible coherences cannot be left up to factological empirical cognition which offers not substantive, inner perceived coherences as such but only individual factual sequences.

The method of variation and the search for the invariant which Husserl stresses so much underlines the immense importance of fantasy, of that free, nonreceptive element in our comprehension of the world. General names, which experimentally designate possible essences, point to those moments in our contact with what is in which we do not merely receive it in the form of a given individual fact but where, rather, it already in mere reception shows us moments of intelligibility, of mutual connection, of mutual reference.

Modern plastic arts can offer numerous examples of the method of fantasy variation by which we reach what is essential. It shows us that the given order of the components of a face can be varied to a far greater extent than at first seems possible without the face ceasing to be a face. Quite the contrary, a mouth placed vertically or in place of the eyes stresses the facial character of the configuration that does not itself occur in common, actual experience far more than the indistinctness of the ordinary configuration, grown indifferent.

Now, having described the approach to universalities as such, let us turn once more to pure logic.

We have said several times already that pure logic has two main parts—a theory of meaning, its forms and laws, and a theory of objects in the most formal sense, that is, a theory of the meaning of existents and objectivities that must be satisfied if anything is to qualify as in any sense existent and objective.

This division again shows the double orientation of Husserl's thought—to the subjective aspect and to its objects. For meanings are naturally linked to acts of intending; these acts in turn make no sense without an object whose most basic forms logic investigates, excluding all concrete content, together with the forms of meaning.

Thus the first question of pure logic will be, what is "meaning"? We shall see that, according to Husserl, even this problem can be resolved only on the basis of a theory of empty intention and its fulfillment.

Husserl's theory of meaning[11] is one of those aspects of pure logic which remain significant to discussions of logic and semantics to this day.

It is founded on Husserl's theory of our access to the universal. We have seen that Husserl built up a theory of categorial perception and of a universal perception intended also to secure the objectivity or being of generalia. However, for Husserl, meaning is one of the most important universalia or generalia, essential for logic.

What is meaning from Husserl's perspective? Meaning is a universal whose instantiation (example) or singularization is the expressive act. Objectifying or expressive acts are capable of expressing those of our lived experiences, like percepts and feelings, which are not themselves expressive or objectifying: they are acts of naming, judging, conjoining, disjoining, etc., whose intentional act is a singularization, a singular case (or example). Objectifying or expressive acts—acts of naming, judging, conjunction, disjunction, etc.—are capable of expressing even those components of lived experience such as perceptions and feelings which themselves are not expressive or objectifying.

Meaning as an ideal objectivity plays the important role of guaranteeing the objectivity of thought, the possibility of the same being realized, that is, thought, in really different acts of thinking. Husserl's theory of meaning is thus the heart of his response of psychologism. Because this response rests on the positing of universals, the refutation of psychologism is for Husserl indissolubly linked to this thesis. That thesis, however, is for him essentially based on an argument from the realm of lived experience, the sphere of subjective being.

---

11. Ibid., Investigation I: "Expression and Meaning"; Investigation IV: "The Distinction Between Independent and Non-Independent Meanings and the Idea of Pure Grammar"; etc.

Among contemporary theories of meaning which, with Mohanty in his recent publication,[12] we can divide into sign theories and operational theories of meaning, Husserl's theory represents a third position which we could describe as synthetic. The theory of meaning as sign, that is, subjective conceptions associated with linguistic expressions which serve to evoke them, is extremely subjectivistic in that meaning is here coextensive with psychic realities; such a theory is also psychologistic, unable to account for the identity of meaning in diverse processes, unable to come to terms with the phenomenological fact that in various thought processes of our own and in those of others what we intend is *numerically the same.*—By contrast, the operational theory of meaning, elaborated particularly by Wittgenstein in his *Philosophical Investigations,* represents a radical objectivism in the theory of meaning. According to this theory, meaning is indeed linked with a certain universality. However, that universality does not lie in the object around which thought revolves and at which it aims but rather solely in the *use* of rules we learn to manipulate. Language is something like a game, a comportment within the framework of rules according to which we manipulate signs in a given situation. We have come to understand a language (that is, grasp its meaning) once we have learned to manipulate such rules, to play the language game. Thus language is a form of life (life understood entirely as a regulated activity, a practical behavior). Evidently, we are dealing basically with a behavioristic theory and for that reason we speak of it as an extreme objectivism.

The operational theory consistently follows the nominalistic themes used already by British empiricism. The British empiricists, Berkeley and Hume, also sought to reduce universals to the rules of use of certain signs, that is, ultimately to reduce the universal to action and will, replacing the theoretical conception of the universal as object with a practical conception of it as a rule of behavior.

In the operational conception of meaning the problem of how to conceive the relation between an expression and a reality assumes a great importance; for even if an expression makes no sense in the sense of *meanings* which it intends, it must *name,* point to something real; in the case of a meaningful rather than a

12. J. N. Mohanty, *Husserl's Theory of Meaning.*

meaningless expression there must always be some reality on which it is based, differentiating it from a pointless combination of words. Nominalist or nominalistically inclined authors have to discuss at great length "objective reference" or the objectivity of meaningful expressions. So for instance Bertrand Russell was led by his concern about objective reference to the distinction between names and what he called descriptions;[13] others, such as Strawson, for the same reason distinguish the content of a linguistic expression (meaning proper) from its use which alone gives the expression a real objective relation, a relation to objective reality.[14]

Precisely this problem of objective reference makes it evident how easily the extreme logical objectivism defended by Frege, for whom logical objectivities were something no less objective than hills, lakes, and seas, even though it may set out from an affirmation of the objectivity of such objectivities as concepts, classes, and relations among their members, passes over into a nominalism with its no less objectivistic inclination to claim that the subject in its experience of the universal has no real reference and content, is no access to what is.[15]

The operational theory of meaning contains some important themes. Language is, as Wittgenstein claims, undoubtedly a "way of life," a game whose rules must be mastered. Meanings are not independent of our practice and will. The only question is whether this praxis is not at the same time a grasping of something that is in its way objective; whether our practice does not bear within it a certain *light on things* intrinsic to regulated activity.

Regulated activity, regulated behavior—behavior that is *subjectively* regulated in such a way that the regulation takes place *within us*, not merely *upon us*—has as its correlate precisely also a meaningful, typical world, schematized in universals.

Thus the art, the skill of using signs according to rules is at the same time an art of moving about among meanings and so dealing with the content and style of our world, a content and style which are not given and at hand simply as contingent on our presence but as individual things and processes.

---

13. See Bertrand Russell's "On Denoting," as well as "The Philosophy of Logical Atomism," in *Logic and Knowledge*, pp. 200–201. [Ed.]

14. See P. F. Strawson's "On Referring," in *Logico-Linguistic Papers*, esp. pp. 7–11. [Ed.]

15. See Gottlob Frege, "On Sense and Reference"; also the collection of essays under the title *Funktion, Begriffe, Bedeutung*. [Ed.]

Among the rules of verbal usage some have the special significance of saving us the need to refer back to perception, to the realization of whatever a linguistic expression presupposes as its meaning correlate. The theory of linguistic meaning as a *mere* operation stems from this derivative, secondary phenomenon, from the rules governing meaning drained of intuition so that the intended correlate is almost wholly absent from them. It is as with the nominalist theory of arithmetical concepts worked out by Helmholtz and Kronecker; the operations have obscured the meaning of that with which we are operating.

Mohanty asks, if meaning is an operation, that is, something extended in time, why do we understand an expression statically, at a stroke, and not gradually, as an operation should require—we do, after all, know what we want to say at once, in an unexplicated form, and do not have to wait for the actual operation.

Husserl's theory of meaning bridges the gap between extreme subjectivism and extreme objectivism.

Meaning is objective as that which is common to various subjective actual acts of intending. It is, however, common to the fact of regulated comportment as subjective, not as objective merely. Meaning can never be simply objectively noted and described, as Wittgenstein's theory would have it.

Because meaning is an expression of a mere intention, the object of reference, the objective situation it names or judges, is in no sense essential to it. What is essential to meaning is only the unity on which the repeatability of an ideally identical intention is based. For that reason, the problems of objective correlate, of "descriptions" or of the distinction between content and use, are not fatal for Husserl's theory. Husserl can recognize even absurdities as genuine meaning structures, repeatable, though of course not realizable, in various intentional acts.

On the basis of his theory of meaning Husserl can now construct the first discipline of pure logic—so called pure logical grammar.

Pure logical grammar is a science of the forms of meaning regardless of the idea of mutual systematic agreement. It is sustained solely by the idea of meaning elements and of their linkage. It separates meanings into basic types—simple and complex, individual and joint meanings, and so forth. Pure logical grammar seeks essentially to capture the essence, the *eidos* of language—that which makes a language a language, that without which language cannot exist; also that which makes it possible for the same meaning to appear in diverse linguistic garbs, that is, that which makes possible translation, the transference of meaning from one language into another.

The idea of a pure logical grammar is not new. The medievals were familiar with the "linguistic logic" of the tracts *de modi significandi*.[16] The thinkers of the sixteenth and seventeenth century, especially in the Lullean tradition, strove for a parallelization of concepts, words (and things).[17] In the eighteenth century, especially in France, the concept of a *grammaire raisonnée*, the grammar of a logically constructed language whose formations correspond to the structure of meaning, was quite widespread.[18] The historicist and romantic conceptions, however, introduced new themes which brought to the fore the multiplicity of linguistic forms, the contingency of the means of expression of a language and the variability of its structures.[19] There arose the problem of the extent to which the so-called inner forms of a given language, the linguistic schemata within which the formation of an expression is carried out, actually correspond to meaning-contents. This distinction occupied particularly the linguistic philosophy of the independent Brentanian Anton Marty.[20] Husserl could in many respects build on Marty's attempt at constructing a universal linguistic theory of concepts. The conception of a pure logical grammar has its dangers, the chief of which is the overestimation of the universality of certain forms central to Indo-European languages as fundamental to logic in general—for instance the schema of subject-predicate and its nominalized version which, following the

---

16. Examples of proponents of the "speculative logic" of the *modi significandi* include Martin and Boethius of Darcia (see bibliography); for an overview of this tradition, see chapter 13 of *The Cambridge History of Later Medieval Philosophy* entitled "Speculative Grammar." [Ed.]

17. I.e., the tradition stemming from the thought of the French philosopher and missionary Raymond Lull (1235–1315), whose *Ars Magna* inspired Leibniz's notion of a *characteristica universalis,* which could be described as an "alphabet of thought." [Ed.]

18. See the so-called Port-Royal Logic of Antoine Arnauld (1612–1694), Jansenist theologian and philosopher, and Pierre Nicole (1625–1695), *The Art of Thinking,* as well as Arnauld's *A General and Rational Grammar (Grammaire générale et raisonné,* 1660). [Ed.]

19. See Johann Gottfried Herder, "Essay on the Origin of Language" as well as his *Reflections on the Philosophy of the History of Mankind.* Also, as an example of an important early influence on Herder, the *Sturm und Drang* movement in general as well as the Romanticism of the early nineteenth century, especially with regard to the question of language, see Johann Georg Hamann, *Vom Magus im Norden und der Verwegenheit des Geistes.* [Ed.]

20. See Anton Marty, "Über das Verhältnis von Grammatik und Logik." [Ed.]

Greek/Aristotelian model, translates judgments into the form of *A is B.* I do not mean to suggest that the form of the Indo-European sentence belongs merely to its "inner form" and has no logical significance, only to warn against the identification, common in the west-European tradition, of the logic of our language with logic as such.

The Indo-European propositional structure has a logical foundation elaborated in great part already by Aristotle on the basis of linguistic metaphoric schemata (subject as agent or as object of action) up to the skeletal meaning structure (S is P). This structure, however, itself presupposes aspects of a particular world view, chief among them being the assumption that meaning is constructed gradually out of basic elements as out of bricks. This synthetic view of meaning is logically flawless, though not necessarily the only one possible or even fundamental. For individual meaning undoubtedly presupposes a meaningful whole into which it fits and which is thus more primordial, and in this respect the Indo-European schema of building up meaning is a linguistic latecomer; an impersonal meaning-schema which proceeds analytically from the whole to the part, starting from the *state of the world* rather than from *things in the world,* might be more primordial.

Here, however, it is also evident that traditional (as well as modern mathematical) logic leaves us bereft in fundamental questions concerning the essence of meaning because it is a formalization of a certain overall mode of its thematization which has its historically relative presuppositions. We can arrive at those presuppositions *philosophically* along the path of reflection about the way in which meaning is built up in our experience, the path of analysis of meaning and of its presuppositions. Logical grammar as an objective system is insufficient, pointing to something more basic; yet thus far we are not philosophically prepared to analyze this deeper dimension.

The next chapter of pure logic is the theory of pure analytic agreement of apophantic, predicative meanings with each other, the theory of their noncontradiction. All of the theory of entailment, traditional as well as modern theory of the forms of joint validity and invalidity, all that we usually subsume under the theory of judgment, belongs in this chapter.

Pure logical grammar and analytics are thus the proper segments of a logical theory of meaning. Theory of meaning has no fundamental concept other than meaning. However, it is essentially

a part of the idea of meaning that it intends, means *something*. As
we have seen in the preceding chapter, already the *Philosophy of
Arithmetic* dealt with the purely objectively formal concept
"something" or "one." "Something," "object in general," became
the point of departure for a further chapter of pure logic, one
which lets us rediscover the problems of the *Philosophy of Arithmetic* in a broader context. We have seen how in this work Husserl
generated the concepts of multiplicity and quantity on the basis of
the concept of "something" and of colligatory acts. To the basic
concepts of this region Husserl now adds other concepts as well,
notably class and relation, thus broadening the region of concepts
for which "something in general" (irrespective of the difference
between thing, property, relation, etc.) is a necessary foundation.
Thus to pure logic there belongs necessarily, as a correlate of
meaning, this objective aspect as well, though in a purely formal
sense. The object under consideration here is not a concept at
which we arrive by a mere abstraction of traits, it is not a *summum
genus,* a "category" in the traditional sense of classical metaphysics. It is obtained by "formalization" (a common procedure
favored especially by modern mathematics) which consists of iso-
lating the network of relations capable of being realized by various
"models," various representatives of a more concrete nature. In
this way we arrive at concepts and relations whose validity is prior
to that of the "categories" in the traditional sense, and it turns out
that mathematical concepts have, in scholastic terms, a "transcendental" validity of this kind, that is, that mathematics, strictly
speaking, is not a mere science of quantity (something Leibniz
had already suspected), but a formal "ontology" which in turn is a
part of pure logic. This distinctive Husserlian "logicism" does not
mean, as we have just seen, a reduction of mathematics to logic, as
the logicism of Frege and of Bertrand Russell in the period of
Principia mathematica. Husserl is not interested in reducing
mathematics to something more elementary, to derive the actual
content of mathematical disciplines, in particular numerical concepts, from mere logical concepts, such as, traditionally, the concept of class. For Husserl logical concepts in the narrow sense are
meaning concepts while class belongs to formal ontology; formal
ontology does then belong to logic, though in a special wider
sense, and its terms cannot be derived from a theory of meaning
alone.

As against the *Philosophy of Arithmetic,* we can now see the true source of those "entities" whose radical "genesis" the earlier work followed: that it is the "categorial intuition" by which we need to widen the traditional experiential basis, the traditional delimitation of the sources of our contact with what there is.—At the same time, it becomes evident how wide the region of those "psychic relations" of which the first work spoke is, the region of those relations which do not have necessary objective foundations so that the objects which constitute their foundation can be imagined also without them; this includes not only arithmetic but all of logic, the entire region of the forms of thought; just like number, quantity is an extrinsic form with respect to numbered things, so also the forms of subject, predicate, syntax, disjunction, and conjunction are extrinsic with respect to what enters such forms, becoming thereby an elementary meaning or a meaning of a higher order.

We have not analyzed Husserl's theory of pure logic in its systematic completeness. Our only concern was to show how Husserl used this conception to face the criticisms which charged his first work with a lack of clarity in the subjective foundation from which he intended to offer a clarification of basic arithmetical processes, an ambiguity which could lead to a confusion between psychology and logic. We have tried to show that it was the conception of categorial intuition which offered a possibility for a solution. That conception, however, contained still other, no less rich potentials than those that led to the constitution of pure logic.

Chapter 4

The Concept of *Phenomenon*

In the preceding chapters, devoted to the development of a pure logic, we have seen that its construction was not to be a parting of the ways with subjectivity, with the problems of the subjective demonstration of principles, but that, on the contrary, for Husserl pure logic itself depends on widening the problem of building a bridge from the subject to the objectivity of knowledge, that is, to the object known, unitary for every subject through all its diverse thought acts, and no less so for all rational, thinking subjects. Pure logic, the theory of ideal generalities (meanings and formal objects in general), makes sense only if such universalities are not pure fictions and, secondly, if our mental life is capable of convincing us of them, if it is so formed as to have access to them. That means that from the beginning it must include an ability to go beyond pure processes which can be only objectively noted and, as the real process unfolds, to step up to the objectivity which this life has in view, to which it is ordered.

Traditionally, the orientation of the psychic to an object and its character of a real process tended to be parceled out between theory of cognition and psychology. The result was that the theory of cognition lost touch with inner experience while psychology ended up in an empiricistic psychologism.

In Husserl's younger years, two main versions of psychology seemed relevant to him: an empirical psychology inspired by the sensualism and associationism of eighteenth- and nineteenth-century British thought and Brentano's intentional psychology.

Empirical psychology proceeded unhesitatingly without any differentiation between real psychic processes and their object and so not only incited to psychologism but was itself essentially a psychologism. Ultimately, it reduced all objects and objective processes to their "image" in the stream of consciousness. Thus it was fundamentally incapable of measuring up to the task which Husserl had set for himself.

In contrast, Brentano's psychology began with a conception of the object as "in-existing" in the act of consciousness. Brentano, Husserl's teacher in Vienna, also wanted to be an empiricist in psychology, but his empiricism was not inspired simply by nominalism, as British empiricism, but by the Aristotelean-scholastic tradition in a broader sense. The conception of an intentional or mental "in-existence" was a scholastic notion that persisted in some modern thinkers such as Descartes and the Scottish thinkers (Hamilton)—on all of whom Brentano built.[1]

Brentano's distinction between physical and psychic phenomena, on which his psychology is based, is essentially a replay of Descartes' dualism in the *Meditations* extended by the Lockean motif of reflection.[2]

Psychic phenomena constitute the proper field of psychological study. They are phenomena representing a genus wholly different from physical phenomena (basically, sense data and their images in memory and imagination). The highest genus characterizing a psychic phenomenon is the intentional or mental "in-existence" (of an object, of a content); that is, psychic phenomena are those in which we imagine something, assert or deny something, love or hate something. Physical phenomena can, to be sure, be the content (object) of psychic phenomena, but not their part or component, so that psychic phenomena cannot be characterized in terms of a composition nor any kind of derivation from physical phenomena. Here it is important to recall the Cartesian distinction between the self-certitude of consciousness and the dubitability of all other "ideas" of our mind. Not even a hyperbolic skepticism can make me doubt that I imagine something, posit something, love something, when these processes in fact unfold within me.

---

1. See the article on "intentio" in *Historisches Wörterbuch der Philosophie*, vol. 4, pp. 466–74, for a brief history of the concept in the Middle Ages; also, with respect to the use of the concept in William Hamilton (1788–1856), see lecture 18 of his *Lectures on Metaphysics and Logic*. [Ed.]

2. See Franz Brentano, *Psychology from an Empirical Standpoint*, book 2, chapter 1: "The Distinction Between Mental and Physical Phenomena," pp. 77–100. [Ed.]

Thus psychic phenomena are marked by an *evident givenness of their existence* which physical phenomena lack. Thus the common trait of all intentional acts (representations, judgments, love/hate) is the evident givenness of inner perception, of the internal givenness of these acts, which differentiates them sharply from physical phenomena which lack such givenness, and that quite apart of any metaphysical presuppositions concerning physical or mental *being,* wholly empirically; on such an empirical character we can unhesitatingly base a science.

Thus Brentano did not introduce the concept of the psychic phenomenon in order to assure contact between the subjective and the objective, to show how the subjective can and does reach objectivity (which was Husserl's project at the time of his *Logical Investigations),* but, quite the contrary, intended to prove the total separateness, independent autonomy, of psychic phenomena so that they could thereafter be treated in their own way, as independent sequences of real processes. Thus the problems of the theory of knowledge are foreign to the Brentanian conception of intentional "in-existence" (with the exception of the problem of evident givenness which he takes for a direct, realistically understood immanent self-prehension), his problem being, rather, psychology as an autonomous science. By differentiating sharply between psychic, intentional phenomena and physical, nonintentional phenomena, Brentano fundamentally distantiated his psychology from the then-dominant sensualism, and that was his chief concern.

Alas, the concept of the evident existence of the phenomena of inner perception is, naturally, itself a noetic one and so exposed to all the difficulties of this Cartesian starting point. Notably, Descartes himself did not manage to work out a conception of a pure inner phenomenon, substituting for it an interpretation that has recourse to the concept of a psychic substance in interactive unity with physical substance. This metaphysical presupposition is then, for Descartes, guaranteed by the proof of God's existence which thereafter justifies all further objective evidence by the argument of *veracitas Dei.* Without this metaphysical foundation it would be impossible to start from the form of *"ego-cogito-cogitatum"* in such a way that the *"ego"* could be interpreted as a finite spirit integrated into the objective world of nature by its connection with a corporeal foundation.

Brentano's psychology passes over this entire metaphysical situation, implicitly taking over that dualistic interpretation of psychic, inner, and external phenomena as something self-evident. For Brentano also accepts, without any critique, the fact that the natural sciences take as the basis of their interpretations only a certain region of "physical" phenomena (phenomena of normal external perception) and subject these phenomena to an explication based on mechanistic concepts (that is, the whole metaphysics of mathematical mechanism), and presupposes in his psychological starting point an interpretation of a "phenomenon," but his psychology lacks concepts which would enable it to grasp and describe this interpretation and to identify its nature.

In particular, the fact that Brentano's intentional acts never have the *same,* strictly identical, object but only *like* objects, of same species, shows that Brentano's intentional psychology lacks concepts which could master the fundamental concept of *conception,* of *interpretation,* which in turn must have a *phenomenal foundation* that cannot be bypassed by appealing to metaphysics; evidently the object is, for Brentano, still in a certain sense drawn into the *reality* of the mental process so that Brentano's intentional psychology never transcended the limits of psychologism. However, this retreat before the identity of the object onto the grounds of a real psychic process is in vain, failing to resolve the problem of the intentional relation of the subject to the object, for *sometime and somewhere* we do need to arrive at the identical object without a conception of which all our cognition in all the diversity of its acts remains nonsensical, and on what other grounds could that be if not those of consciousness and its continuous experience?

By contrast, Husserl was inevitably led to these problems by the logico-noetic problems we sought to present in the preceding chapters.

There we saw how *"the same"* appeared to him in *various* modes of presentation, in mere intention and in intuition or perhaps in originary intuition; we saw how precisely *the same* moments could become the basis for varied acts of intuition of *"the diverse,"* for instance the same moment of redness could in one case represent this red roof, in another a shade of redness as such. With the concept of *comprehension,* of apperception, interpretation thus became inseparably close to the concept of intentional meaning as such, that is, of psychic "activity" (composition of the psychic of acts) which is oriented to objects.

Were this appearance of a strictly identical object in various subjective processes not possible and intelligible, then there would be no sense in speaking on the one hand of the "Pythagorean theorem," of the "law of contradiction," or on the other hand of "the planet Mars," "the city of Prague," "Aristotle of Stagira." Neither the individually identical object nor objectivity in general would be accessible to us through and in the "flux of subjective phenomena." For Brentano, however, if two persons presentify to themselves the greenness of a leaf, then each of them necessarily has a different object, a different physical phenomenon, a different sense impression of green; and there is no way of passing from these subjective phenomena to an objective unity *on the basis of the phenomena themselves.*

Thus Brentano deviates from that fundamental direct experience for which a "phenomenon" is nothing other than the thing itself appearing in its *hic et nunc,* as it is given in its own appearance, the thing which is itself present here; or at least the thing given in a "quasi-experience" such as remembrance or fantasy. This thing *qua cogitatum,* as the object of experience, is no less certain than the lived experience of the perception *in which* it presents itself to me. On the other hand, a toothache (which I can feel in a healthy tooth), the strains experienced in amputated limbs, the fatigue that marks us directly as corporeal subjects, are all clearly psychic phenomena which are no more "indubitable" than the "physical" phenomenon of a given hue of red, of a nuance of smell, or of a melody.

Thus, Husserl insists,[3] there is no marked noetic difference between outer and inner intuition—such that, as Brentano assures us, outer intuition would be devoid of evident givenness, dubitable, while inner intuition would guarantee, with absolute evident givenness, the existence of its object. The point Husserl wants to make with that is that external intuition is also certain— *qua cogitatum.* Inner intuition is also dubitable insofar as it contains an "apperception" or a "comprehension" of its *cogitatum* (as a thing integrated in the world as a causally produced component).

Were we to object that in inner phenomena we need to differentiate between *apperception* and *perception,* we would be no

---

3. Husserl, *Logical Investigations,* vol. 2, appendix: "External and Internal Perception: Physical and Psychical Phenomena," p. 852.

closer to the truth. For just as apperception plays an important role in outer intuition, it undoubtedly does likewise in inner intuition. "Apperception" is only a word which we need to transform into its actual content equivalent. What does "apperception" mean other than that component of our lived experience, eminently present in perception itself, on whose basis there is present to me something more, something other than lived experience as such, namely the *object* of this lived experience? It is apperception, comprehension, that brings it about that I do not see green blotches but rather the leaves of a tree, that the blue line on the horizon *is* the mountains, that the spotted gray of this surface *is* the printed page of a book.

Accordingly, Husserl recognizes three conceptions of the phenomenon while in Brentano such distinctions become fused with each other.

First of all, the phenomenon is the *entire lived experience of perceiving* with all of its components. (This total lived experience is that towards which we need to aim the view of reflection and grasp it in evident inner perception, providing we purge it of all objective apperception, of all objective conceptions.)

The second concept of the phenomenon is phenomenon as *thing,* the *object* which appears in lived experience with all its qualities, moments, and relations: the table on which I write, the lamp giving light, the landscape I see through the window.

The third concept of the phenomenon is that of the "representant," the component of my lived experience—for instance the *impression* of red, green, etc.—that serves as the pivot of my apprehension in its orientation to the object. Such impressional, subjective, representative moments are not themselves aspects of the thing—they are not properties of the lamp, qualities of the landscape, etc., but are, rather, components of my own lived experience; objective qualities can in a certain respect be considered analogues of things, yet not identical with them. It is precisely this "representant" that Brentano in most cases calls the "physical phenomenon," failing to distinguish it adequately from the phenomenon in the sense of the object. For if this differentiation is to be really sharp, then the object must be conceived as an objectival and "transcendent" unity which is not a real *(reell)* component of lived experience as against the real *(reell)* components and parts, a distinction which does not occur in Brentano.

Now the situation is becoming clear. It turns out that Husserl did not abandon the Cartesian thesis of the self-evident givenness of consciousness for itself. He does not, however, believe that this self-evidence is simply given; rather, in his view, it must be reached by a purification of *all* objectifying conceptions which, in the naive view, confuse givenness and apprehension. Lived experiences thus purified can then be the object of an adequate intuition. The objects of this adequate intuition will not then be only *acts* but also, and no less so, all those sense contents as such which Brentano had qualified as physical phenomena, and these sense contents will be no less evidently guaranteed. It will then be not only so called "external" objects that will be intuited nonadequately but also we ourselves, as long as we are apperceived as a part of nature. Both outer objects and our own interiority will be nonadequately intuited *insofar as they are things and objectival moments.*

The threefold conception of the phenomenon which Husserl notes allows us to go further still. It shows us how consciousness itself functions, by what means it reaches the object or, better, in what way *it is a reaching for* the object. That is, adumbrated in global lived experience we find (1) the direction of the intention, (2) the moments which orient it, and (3) the orientation itself. The direction in which consciousness is directed is toward the object as such, which is not a real *(reell)* part of the consciousness that intends it. Orienting moments are impressions, those components of lived experience which themselves are not the intending, aiming, pointing apprehension that transcends the experience itself and points beyond it. Most important are those intending and pointing moments, those intentional acts by which the orienting moments, the representants, become that in which transcendent objectivities, standing outside consciousness proper, appear, are shown.

Thus the basis of a polemic with Brentano brought about a new conception of the phenomenon as well as a new conception of the intentional relation. Intentional acts are not the same as psychic phenomena. The psychic and the internal are not the same as intentionality. It begins to make sense to speak not of the intentional inexistence of the object in the act of consciousness but rather of intentionality as a special dynamic synthetic trait which not only already always *has* but rather in a certain sense *constitutes,* realizes (or fails to realize) a relation to the object. The intentional act is a part of the intentionality of consciousness in general, of an activity which aimed at a certain *achievement,* which is the *appearing object.*

From this we can see the basic schema according to which the intentional component of consciousness progresses. Intentionality is that unifying bond thanks to which the experience of consciousness is not a rhapsody of impressions and other phenomena but rather a unitary meaningful process. This process brings together temporally disparate sequences; it induces relations of similarity and difference; it fuses, interpretatively, impressions into synthetic wholes, letting unity emerge in them; it intends, by verbal expression, units of meaning to which it can return as identical, under certain circumstances transposing meaning into an intuition which fulfills it or disappoints it—all of which presupposes a synthetic bond among individual acts, a bond constituted by the pointing, intentional activity. Through all this, consciousness holds onto impressions, though also "animating" these impressions with its objectival intentions, not stopping but rather "passing through" them to the object and its qualities. "Animation" or "apprehension," the interpretation of impressions, brings it about that what appears to us is an object, whether individual or ideal, whether a particular fact or a universal. For what we intend, the theme of our objectival experience, is not our impressions but the thing, for instance this lamp here with its colors, shape, utility—though those are not *parts,* moments, or qualities of our lived experience but its *object correlates.* While on the one hand there unfolds the real *(reell)* process of the emergence of impressions, with their animating synthesis and comprehension, "on the other hand" there emerges, as an "intentional correlate," an object of such and such a type with all the richness of its qualities and relations.

Note that the "animating" activity of consciousness has essentially a synthetic character. That means that the erstwhile problematic of the *Philosophy of Arithmetic,* the problem of the origin of number in colligation, has undergone a vast generalization. Not only number, that special categorial object, but all objectivity of whatever type becomes the correlate of a certain synthetic activity of a special kind, always lawlike and true to type. The synthetic process of "apprehension," of conception, is responsible for this excess of the consciousness of an object over mere impressional "representants" in the real *(reell)* process of consciousness; it is responsible for the appearance proper of the object.

This comprehension now ceases to be a mere empirical, factual coherence. It is not a mere fact that an individual material object can only be given in a one-sided, nonadequate perception which points beyond itself to the perception of other aspects. From the example of the perspectival givenness of a spatial shape (and consequently of the material object) I can see clearly that no variation can change anything here: it is an eidetic cognition, and all cognitions having to do with the reciprocal lawlike subsumption of lived experiential real *(reell)* processes to the objectivities emerging in them are eidetic. The correlation of object and lived experience, which assigns to a certain type of lived experience and manifestation an objectivity that shows itself and appears in a typical manner, is thus a great field of eidetic laws. Intentionality is a region of a priori investigation.

Thus intentionality proves to be at the root of appearance, of the manifestation of the object. It becomes possible to trace its "genesis," its "constitution," because the object is not merely intentionally *given* but *constructed* in the intentional activity. This is an unexpected result, opening up an entirely new perspective. Intentionality appears to us as an active process of which we have no inkling in ordinary experience because there we rest content with bare results, always already in some sense complete and fixated. Since intentionality aims essentially at the object and does not normally pause at lived experience, there follows from this quite logically the tendency of our lived experience to overlook itself, not to see itself in *how* and often even *that* it is at all. If we are to live in things and with things, we must not live in ourselves and in our comprehension of ourselves—an aspect of the activity of lived experience from which Heidegger and Sartre will later deduce an insurmountable "existential" tendency of life to avoid its most authentic tasks, to avoid itself in its preoccupation with things which are in their entire nature different from the human mode of being, the tendency of lived experience to be rid of itself, to alienate, externalize, and reify itself—an experiential approach to the phenomenon of alienation. In the theme of intentionality, as it is thematized (noematically) by Husserl, the potential for such an interpretation is present, though Husserl himself does not follow that path; once more showing that the concrete problems of description and analysis begin to transcend the limits of his systematics, that something new is forcing its way through all the openings in the system—openings that are precisely those descriptions and analyses freed of preconceptions—loosening the system and transcending it. An "existential" interpretation will in any case become possible only when "comprehending oneself and living with and in oneself" are no longer understood as "living in reflection, in an awareness of the lived experience as such, purified of all alien interpretations," but rather as an essentially nonobjective mode of being which uses objectification only to reach its limits and thereby to reaffirm itself.

By contrast, Husserl will follow the path of the grand systematics that opens up in the correlative theme. It is, as we have noted, primarily the field of eidetic laws which determine the relation between typical constellations of intentional synthetic acts on the one hand and, on the other, the typical objectivities which manifest themselves therein, suggested, intuitively illustrated, or originally present. That spreads out before the philosopher's eyes the vast theme of "constitution," of the lawlike manifestation of all possible objectivities in subjective processes which only thereby reach their true significance: they are that in which the clarity, the uncovering of things is brought about, the access of beings to beings, contact in general; it is only here, on this ground which is fundamentally *oriented,* aiming, precisely intentional (which is not the same as voluntary or deliberate), that we can begin to clarify the mystery of meaning and significance, of the *inner* coherence of what is, that is, of the inner connection and of mutual reference.

Noetic orientation proves to be a fundamental trait of intentionality as Husserl thematizes it. Relation to an object, as intention, as intuitive illustration, as self-presence, as adequation, as well as opposites in syntheses, as adequation and nonadequation, as fulfillment and disappointment, all lead him to extensive analyses. Thus it appears that reflection as such is not yet the method which would guarantee the grasping of what is reflexively given; on the one hand the occurrence of the concept of intentionality in Brentano and his predecessors deep into scholasticism shows that the objective orientation of internal life cannot escape the view of reflection, but on the other hand the proper significance and content of intentionality is not yet uncovered thereby. Intentionalities do not lie on the surface of conscious life, exposed to view like props on a stage. We first need to gain a general access to them, to understand their self-transcending, "transcendental" character to render them visible in the proper sense of the term. Thus it is inaccurate to charge Husserl's efforts at a description of inten-

tional life with positivistic factology. The facts described had first
to be "prepared," freed up (like a slide for a microscope) by an
understanding from the objectifying tendency of intentionality so
that the object itself could serve as the guide for uncovering of the
implied subjective achievements, concealed in obscurity, ever more
concealed and remote.

Husserl's intentionality is thus a conception of a consciousness
capable of grasping and comprehending itself, as Husserl hopes, in
an adequate mode, yet on the other hand this conscious lived
experience is ever accompanied by a dark, nonconscious aspect
and with it also access to the problem of the unconscious, subcon-
scious, and nonconscious.

Husserl's conception of intentionality was to play an immensely
significant role both in his phenomenology and in the thought of
an entire generation of philosophers that followed. For all that, we
need to note that the dialogue with Brentano and with his conception of physical and psychical phenomena, presented in the
appendix to the last volume of the *Logical Investigations,* does not
appear to us to be completely closed by the distinctions, proposed
by Husserl, among three concepts of phenomena.

Husserl's idea of the "representant" of the impressional component of lived experience is not free of equivocation. On the one
hand, such an orienting component pointing to further experiences certainly does exist in sense experience, yet it is not at all
certain that it is for that reason a real *(reell)* component of the act
of consciousness. We cannot exclude the possibility that, in this
respect, Husserl's whole doctrine is not altogether free of all rem-
nants of psychologism. We shall explain this in more detail in
chapter 6.

For now, we might still add the following schema:

Brentano distinguishes an (immanent) psychic phenomenon,
guaranteed by the evident givenness of inner experience, which is
throughout a "consciousness of . . . ," from the (transcendent)
physical phenomenon, the phenomenon of the object, whose transcendent existence is not guaranteed and is often even evidently
impossible; this phenomenon is that *of which* we are conscious in
the psychic phenomenon. Physical phenomena can be, indiffer-
ently, objects of memory, fantasy, as well as perception.

Husserl distinguishes the immanent, pure phenomenon guaranteed by the evident givenness of inner perception (in the sense
that its existence cannot be doubted as long as it is perceived)

from transcendent phenomena, among which belong psychic entities in the psychological sense no less than physical objects, all of
this having only presumptive evident givenness.

Now he is forced to label *a part of what Brentano considers
physical phenomena* as likewise immanent because it is guaranteed:
these are the presentations as such, the "hyletic data" in their pure
presence, the "nonintentional components" of lived experience.
They are equally as guaranteed by inner perception as the intentional component.[4]

Does not, however, Brentano's conception of the psychic as
intentional provide, after all, a very clear criterion and distinction
of two types of being, which are differentiated in terms of content
and not only by extrinsic denomination like the evident givenness
of the existence of an object of the appropriate phenomenon?

A truly nonintentional real *(reell)* component (that is, a part)
of lived experience means that this nonintentional component
belongs to the I, that we can speak of it as a part of the I. *How,*
though, is it to be a part of the I? As the I's impression, one might
say, as something indistinguishable from the I—for instance, the
gray color of one's eyes. Yet "gray eyes" surely is not the I, it is
not a *perception* of gray eyes; "impression" is an ambiguous term
which means on the one hand the consciousness of a presence
and on the other hand the presented as such; we cannot assert
that the two are indistinguishable, coextensive, or else consciousness itself would (in our example) have to be a quality of grayness
or entirely gray. Thus the concept of "impression" only obscures
the problem.

Husserl has to search for a nonintentional component of the
act so that, for one, he could bring those "physical phenomena"
which in their *presence* are no less guaranteed than the subjective,
intentional psychic domain they reflect under the same heading,
and at the same time so that he could be free of the possible
objection that something that is not evidently guaranteed is nevertheless present to reflection.

---

4. There are a number of places in Husserl's works where one can find reflections on
the concept of *hyle:* see, for example, *Ding und Raum Vorlesungen,* Hua XVI, §§14–17;
Ideas I, §§85–86; as well as the third part of *Analysen zur passiven Synthesis,* Hua XI.
Patočka is not alone in his criticism of this concept—both Merleau-Ponty and Sartre
authored thoroughgoing, sharp criticisms of Husserl's use of hyle. As illustrative, see Sartre,
Being and Nothingness, pp. 314ff. For a more positive appropriation of the term, see
Immanuel Levinas, *The Theory of Intuition in Husserl's Phenomenology,* pp. 76–85, 88ff.
[Ed.]

It is indeed easy to object that to extend evidence to a "physical phenomenon" means to guarantee the existence of something that need not exist—for instance the color impressions of the color-blind, hallucinatory impressions, the illusions of amputees. . . . A nonintentional component of an act would exclude all that but in turn codifies a distinction between an objectival color and a color impression and so on.—That is a distinction which is, in a way, phenomenally justified, for in truth color as a property of a thing and "free redness" which is not yet predicated of anything are two different things; still, that does not yet make "free redness" something internal as it would have to be if it were a nonintentional component of a lived experience.

Actually, there could be a third conception to which Husserl never resorted because it was only his theory that generated the presuppositions for it.

Such a solution might run as follows: there is a *part* of Brentano's "physical phenomena" which, though not essentially internal, guarantees its "object" as long as it is active, the same way that reflection guarantees its content. This part is the perceptual impression as such (that is, not the lived experience but the impressional content). Such impressions together with their traits are no less certain, no less a presentive being than that which "inner intuition" presents in reflection.

The guarantee of such impressions stems from nothing other than reflection itself: if reflection guarantees its object, then it guarantees a being which is essentially related to another; in the cases in which this consciousness is one of a living presence it guarantees *eo ipso* the present as present.[5]

To be sure, it guarantees nothing more: it does not guarantee the present impression as a *rose,* as a *blue inscription on a white background,* as the *whistle of a locomotive* on its way through the countryside, because all those are temporal syntheses and as such extend beyond the present. What the present impression gives and guarantees, however, is the presence of an impressional field in its current now-phase (and, of course, also with the structure of extension into a temporal and spatial depth, into the indefinite—a structure which is a part of the constitution of the living present, of impression; an impression is something essentially temporal,

---

5. Compare to Husserl, *Ding und Raum,* §§27–31; Beilagen XIII and XIV. [Ed.]

always already integrated *in concreto* in an interpretative process of a continuing synthesis of an objectival sense, but this process is no longer guaranteed by its results).

That means simply that the world is not merely an *object,* an objectival synthesis, but, thanks to the object, a *perceptual field.* This open perceptual field is contemporaneous with our actual lived experiences, immanent in the same present, yet not subjective! Thus further distinctions are needed besides those which Husserl offers. Apart from subjective immanence we need to distinguish a presentational immanence which is not coextensive with the subjective. Not all that is immanent in the present is subjectively immanent, though all that is presentationally immanent is guaranteed in the sense that its givenness as present is at the same time a guarantee of existence; for it is here, in person, so that we cannot imagine any greater accessibility or presence. Thus any attempt to declare something an illusion is applicable only to constituted meaning outside presence, not to the phenomenon of objectival givenness as such.

Thus we have (1) a guaranteed presentational immanence, divided into subjective immanence and subjective transcendence; and (2) an unguaranteed presentational transcendence which is always at the same time a subjective immanence.

Chapter 5

Pure Logic and the Problem of the Grounding of Experience

Logical Investigations set the problems of *Philosophy of Arithmetic* in a new light by enriching the conception of psychic relations, on which the idea of demonstrating primary arithmetical concepts in the first work had been based, by the instance of categorial intuition, that is, of intuition which is a correlate of spontaneous, free mental activities in which objective formations common to diverse real mental processes yet "originate."

That way *Logical Investigations* also dealt with the possibility of being mistaken for a psychologism that recognizes only individual psychic realities and empirical laws governing their occurrence.

However, categorial intuition and its special form, the intuition of the universal, are not simply the basis for a reform of logic which, according to Husserl, would make logic a systematic theoretical science for the first time. *Philosophy of Arithmetic* deals with the philosophical problems of a special discipline; *Logical Investigations* moves on to a higher level of generality inasmuch as logic, as a theory of science, is the foundation of all the special sciences. Now, however, setting out from a conception of intentionality as subjectively reflexive, yet conceived with respect to the object, Husserl begins to penetrate to the problems of philosophy as such, specifically to the problem of *philosophy as a science* which seeks not simply to gain objective knowledge but to justify such objectivity.

In the first part of his new work, *Ideas Pertaining to a Pure Phenomenology and to a Phenomenological Philosophy* (volume 1, published in 1913, though summing up much older reflections), Husserl contrasts fact and *eidos (Wesen* or "essence")[1] in order to define the nature of philosophy in general, delimiting its scope and determining its method.

He starts with "natural knowledge and natural experience" which he characterizes as experience *within the horizon of the world*.[2] True being, reality, that is, real being, is here taken to mean the same as "being in the world," being as part of the world.

Being in the world presents itself in its original form, that is, as what it itself truly is (and not in a mere representation) in perception. We are conscious in an originary way of physical things in external perception and of ourselves in inner perception. With respect to the mental life of others, empathy gives us an insight of their psychic life, though not an originary one. Our knowledge of the world is mediated in a systematic form by the sciences, some of which (natural sciences) are based on external perception; others (human sciences) on both inner and outer. Both of these kinds of science are experiential sciences of the world. Their foundation is *fact,* that is, experiences, which here count as ultimate proof, showing things as they are, positing the experienced *individually* as what actually is at this place in space and time. Individual being, however, is contingent: that is, it could be at another time, in another place, in another way. Natural laws do not change that: they, too, are only rules of facts derived from observing individually contingent facts.

Yet this fact, that we understand the contingency of facts as such, that is, that we understand them *as* facts, holds an important recognition within it. Facts for us are facts in relation to something that is not factual. We call the nonfactual *eidos (Wesen* or "essence") and understand it as the obverse of fact: as that which does not change with the place, time, and other circumstances of occurrence, as that which is independent of all that. Over against

---

1. This chapter is a detailed discussion of "Matter of Fact and Essence," the first chapter of part 1 of Husserl's *Ideas I*. [Ed.]
2. See ibid., p. 5. [Ed.]

the contingency of fact there stands the *necessity* of *eidos (Wesen* or "essence").[3]

Eidos (Wesen or "essence") is originally nothing but the necessary *"whatness"* contained in individual, factual being.

> An individual object is not merely an individual object as such, a "This here," an object never repeatable; as qualified *"in itself"* thus and so, it has its *own specific character,* its stock of *essential* predicables which must belong to it (as an "existent such as it is in itself") if other, secondary, relative determinations can belong to it (as to "a being as it is in itself" [J. P. insert; Tr.]) [. . .] *Everything belonging to the essence of the individuum another individuum can have too;* and *highest* eidetic universalities of the sort just indicated in our examples delimit *"regions"* or *"categories" of individua.*[4]

Every eidetic *whatness* can be "transposed into an idea"[5] so that the intuition of the individual passes over into an intuition of an *eidos,* that is, of something universal. This assertion itself is not a factual but rather an eidetic law, just like the law of the mutual relation of fact and *eidos.* The intuition of *eidos* (in light of the indifference of *eidos* with respect to the opposition between imagination and reality, to speak of perception would be useless) can now be adequate or inadequate. It can be inadequate with respect to clarity, but also with regard to completeness—for there are ideas, such as the idea of the thing, that can never be perceived in all its aspects simultaneously, and even some which can never be exhausted in perception. Inadequacy cannot be an objection to the intuition of *eidos* because it would apply no less to the intuition of individualities.

Ideal *eide (Wesen* or "essences") are unconditional universals; unconditional because they do not contain a single thesis relative to facts, to actualities. Eidetic cognition undoubtedly applies to realities, but no assertion, no positing of any fact has any significance for the region of eidetic truths: one cannot argue with facts in the eidetic sphere:[6] in geometry, circles and lines drawn on a blackboard are not arguments but only ancillary aides to proofs. (There are, to be sure, permissible operations for translating

---

3. See ibid., p. 7: "But the sense of this contingency which is called factualness, is limited in that it is correlative to a *necessity* which does not signify the mere *de facto* existence of an obtaining rule of coordination among spatiotemporal matters of fact but rather has the character of *eidetic necessity* and with this a relation to *eidetic universality.*" [Ed.]

4. Husserl, *Ideas I,* pp. 7–8.

5. Ibid., p. 8. [Ed.]

6. See ibid., p. 11. [Ed.]

judgments concerning ideal unities into judgments concerning cases, instances subsumed under such *eide,* and to "illustrate" or schematize those in a diagram.)—What falls within an *eidos* as its instantiation or particular realization has the character of *eidetic necessity.* Necessity is distinct from universality, though the two are closely correlated: necessity is a relation between the more general and that which falls under it, whether as its ideal extension or as its realization.[7] Such, then, is fundamentally the relation between fact and *eidos:* facts realize eidetic, ideal universalities, contexts, and lawlike regularities.

Every eidetic unity has its place on a scale of eidetic generality. This scale extends from eidetic *singularity*—universals to which nothing further is subordinate—up to the highest genus. Since Husserl reserves the term "category" for the semantic domain (the sphere of meanings), he employs the concept "region" in its ordinary sense to designate the highest genus.[8]

Eidetic universality is of two kinds which cannot be reduced to one another.[9] On the one hand there is the universality of material or content *eide* which retain the fundamental content-definitions of all the individuals in their region. These include, for example, the eidetic singularity of the tone A_1 or C within the highest or regional genus of "the acoustic as such," while a sulfur crystal or a chair have as their highest region "material object." Higher determinations of identity constitute a part of the lower so that their relation can be considered a mode of the relation of part to whole.[10]—In addition there is the region of *formal eide* at which we do not arrive by variations that reveal a common invariant, stressing common traits, but rather by the *draining away all content traits.* In the first case we are dealing with an abstraction of a wholly different type than in the second; the abstraction by stressing common content is different from an emptying abstraction.[11]

---

7. See ibid., §6, pp. 14–15. [Ed.]

8. See ibid., p. 22: ". . . one must set the signification-categories apart as a group by themselves and contrast them with the others [i.e., formal essences] as the *formal objective categories* in the pregnant sense." See also §9, pp. 18–20, and §12, pp. 24–25. [Ed.]

9. See ibid., §12–13, pp. 24–27. [Ed.]

10. See ibid., p. 25. [Ed.]

11. See ibid., p. 26. Husserl makes this point by contrasting "generalization," i.e., the process of logical variation that establishes the "hierarchy of generality and specificity" (p. 25), and "the essentially heterogeneous relationships belonging, on the one hand, to the *universalization of something materially filled into the formal in the sense of pure logic* and, on the other hand, to the converse: the *materialization* of something logically formal" i.e., "formalization" and "deformalization," respectively. [Ed.]

An emptying abstraction does not end up with nothing but rather with the form of *object in general* which is not a highest genus but rather the mere form of a possible object while all content objectivities are its fulfillment.[12] Thus there is still another generality "above" such categories, above them not as a higher genus but in the sense of the form which is prior to its content. *Object as such,* as a formal *eidos,* has its specifications in its turn; for example, substrate objects, relations, sets whose singularities are, for instance, *eidos* as such, equality, three, four.[13]—Meaning categories, too, are not attained through variation but through formalization, and categories such as substrate meaning, predicate, syntax, and *apophansis* are likewise purely formal *eide.*

Consequently, we have two kinds of substrates, that is, of those eidetic formations of which further determinations hold as of ultimate subjects: on the side of content it is "the ultimate content *eidos*" or eidetic content singularity; on the formal side it is "this-here" *(tode ti)* or the pure individuality to which they point with no further determinations.[14]

A further important distinction within the eidetic region is that between independent and dependent objects.[15] Dependent objects are those which necessarily point to others, for instance a syntactic form which points to a substrate, form in general to some content on which it imposes form, the form *"Wesen, eidos"* to determinate content *eide*. However, this distinction of independent-dependent applies even within the region of content (or material) *eide* themselves: here, too, we must make the important distinction between those that can be thought only in conjunction with others and those which can be thought independently; perhaps we could also say that those which can be thought only as parts, as moments, must be distinguished from those which are thought as wholes of such parts. That is particularly important with respect to ultimate substrates because it is the ultimate material substrates which, by their eidetic regularity, define for us what in the region of facts

---

12. See ibid., p. 26. [Ed.]

13. See ibid., p. 28: "The latter class [variants of the empty Something] is itself by no means empty or poverty stricken; it is determined, that is to say, as the totality of the predicatively formed affair-complexes belonging to the realm of pure logic as *mathesis universalis,* with all the categorial objectivities out of which they are constructed." [Ed.]

14. See ibid., p. 28. [Ed.]

15. See ibid., §15, pp. 28–30. Husserl's expression is "selbstständige und unselbstständige Objekten" which Kersten translates as "self-sufficient and non-self-sufficient objects." Cf. chapter 1 of Investigation III, vol. 2 of *Logical Investigations.* [Ed.]

actually is and what is not—for they determine what an individual is and therewith the meaning of the expression "individual fact" (that is, something belonging to an individual). Dependence, "the partial character" of certain *eide,* can be finely illustrated by the relation between color and extension—one cannot be without the other, they mutually "found" one another, gradation is possible only together with quality while quality, especially in some of its differences (such as tone), is not possible without a definite degree of intensity;[16] a lived experience is not possible without a relation to something experienced.—By contrast, a thing which encloses within itself all of the dependent moments as a whole, is a *concretum.* Here we have to distinguish *regions of concreta* which include diverse dependent aspects such as extension, temporal location, quality, intensity, etc. from the fundamentally different concretization of a region into a singularity which contains, as an addition, the specifications of all such dependent aspects. Singularity, which is thus doubly a whole, as an "instance" to which we can point in the form of "this here," is an *individual.* A "this here" whose material *eidos* is a *concretum* is what we call an individual.[17]

Now a regional *Wesen (eidos)* determines the mode in which certain abstract essences are necessarily conjoined within a particular *concretum,* and *this mode is evidently nonreducible to relations in the purely formal objectival region.* However, as we have seen, formal objectival relations constitute the region of mathematics in the broadest sense of a *mathesis universalis.* If we now define the formal region, with Leibniz, as the region of pure analytic relations, that is, of such that their highest principle is the principle of noncontradiction, we thus attain a rigorous definition of the difference between formal and material a priori or, in other words, *between analytic and synthetic a priori* whose mutual relation Kant (according to Husserl) had never correctly defined, even though the difference between analytic and synthetic can be defined on the basis of eidetic intuition.[18]

Thus considerations of pure logic show their relevance for fundamental philosophical questions.

They are especially necessary for the considerations of the philosophy of science since they show how the empirical sciences—

---

16. See ibid., p. 29. [Ed.]
17. Ibid.
18. See ibid., pp. 31–32; also p. 21 for the definition of "formal region" as "analytic." [Ed.]

sciences of fact which had also been defined as sciences of the world, dependent upon the positing of this given factual world—depend on the sciences of *eidos* which need posit no facts, because in them such a positing means nothing, cannot serve as an argument within them.[19]

Since in the eidetic realm we have already made the pivotal distinction, the appropriate classification in the region of eidetic sciences basically follows as a series of consequences of what preceded.

The fundamental distinction in the region of eidetic, that is, of a priori sciences is the distinction between the formal and material disciplines. Formal disciplines deal with formal essences which are of two kinds—categorial and objectival, and which ultimately constitute, in a theory of forms of possible theories, the most general mathematical concept, *mathesis universalis.*[20]

The material disciplines are defined by the highest appropriate region and because regions are either regions of *abstracta* or of *concreta,*[21] material (or content) eidetic disciplines in turn divide into material disciplines on the one hand and abstract ones on the other. Among the abstract belongs what we might call, in an inaccurate analogy to Kant's corresponding theory, a "pure aesthetics," a theory of eidetic relations in the region of purely objectively conceived "sense qualities" such as colors, tones, etc. Geometry also belongs here as a theory of the extension and form of contents (and not merely relational schemata). Among the concrete disciplines belong, for example, the theory of the material thing, of the conscious living being as regions of *concreta.* As such, philosophical anthropology would be a material eidetic discipline belonging to this last region.

It is, of course, necessary to respect the fundamental law according to which no material region is without its appropriate form so that this correlation must apply in appropriate eidetic disciplines as well.

There are material eidetic disciplines in which formal regularities play the foremost role with respect to the theory of science. Here material eidetic intuition figures basically only in foundational questions, with initial concepts and relations resting on it,

---

19. See ibid., §8, pp. 17–18. [Ed.]

20. See ibid., p. 17; also, on the idea of pure logic as a *mathesis universalis,* see §§60–61, and the whole of chapter 11 in the Prolegomena, vol. 1, *Logical Investigations.* [Ed.]

21. See ibid., p. 30. [Ed.]

while the most important discoveries are then deduced from them by formal analytic means.

That is so especially in disciplines based on "exact" *eide,* that is, those whose content can be enclosed in rigorous definitions and fundamental postulates. Such exact *eide* can be derived from what had been originally presented to us in experience only by special operations which exclude from them all that is not appropriate, operations of so-called idealization which are themselves based on eidetic laws.

Disciplines such as elementary plane geometry as it is presented in the first books of Euclid's *Elements* are such exact eidetic theories. The region of their discoveries is exhausted by a finite number of primary concepts and relations: Husserl calls such a region a definitive diversity, so that we can say that disciplines such as elementary geometry of plane or spatial formations are exact definitive eidetic disciplines.—Therefore in them formal reasoning and construction play an incomparably more important role than the intuition of *eide* and of eidetic relations.

By contrast, there are eidetic disciplines in which the opposite is the case, where eidetic intuition is nearly everything and where formal and deductive reasoning are limited to occasional controlling and generally ordering nature. That is especially the case when we are not dealing with exact *eide* which we could enclose by a simple procedure in appropriate definitions, *eide* which resist idealization and where there may be so many intuitions accessible through similarities and differences that with respect to the thing we have to abandon the idea of exhausting the entire region in a finite number of basic concepts added to primordial ideal intuitions. For example, Husserl believes that this is the case in all eidetic disciplines dealing with the eidetic structure of lived experience, for what is most important in this discipline is the lived intuition of all relevant differences, of new original relations and qualities (though we need to add that such a discipline does not yet exist in a systematic form).

It is precisely here that we encounter another fruitful aspect of reflections about the philosophy of science on the basis of universal intuition—on these grounds it is possible and necessary not only to characterize and describe already historically constituted a priori disciplines but also to postulate new ones which have not been constituted thus far.

Such disciplines include not only an eidetic theory of lived experience as such with its a priori, eidetic, nonfactual regularities but, according to Husserl, even eidetic disciplines of material nature are yet to be worked out, insofar as they deal with aspects irreducible to the pure mathematical garb of natural scientific conceptualizations, to the mathematized disciplines appertaining to the concrete *eidos* "material thing" (for example, materiality as such). Furthermore, qualitative aspects of the material thing have also been neglected with respect to *eidos;* likewise an eidetic theory of movement, despite its exact mathematization in mechanics, has not been developed systematically enough, so that the meaning of this mathematization remains for the most part obscure.

Evidently, in the first chapter of Husserl's *Ideas,* pure logic undertook the task of providing a basis for empirical knowledge, of grounding experience in a universal a priori.

According to Husserl, it is *eidos* as unconditioned universality, presupposing no fact, that is to fulfill the task of providing an a priori foundation for empirical knowledge.

We have already examined Husserl's theory of the universal based on a special intuition which is irreducible to the empirical intuition of the particular. We have traced the origin of an intention other than that of particular realities and then, in some cases, the possibility of fulfilling a universal intention without positing a particular fact. In all this, universal intention was presented as a special kind of experience. Now, however, it does not claim only to be a special kind of experience but aspires to the role of grounding, of justifying all factual experience. What is the basis for this claim of eidetic intuition?

The need for a grounding, for a justification, of the empirical makes itself felt with the awareness of the difference between fact and *eidos.* With that the factual as such is *eo ipso* identified as contingent. This contingency of the factual is something we have known before, it is a priori, and it implies that a fact as such is possible only within the framework of a prevenient knowledge; purely factological knowledge, knowledge of facts *alone,* is not possible.

That experience contains no isolated contents, nothing that is not interrelated, is for Husserl no mere fact explicable in terms of factual psychological regularity (as the laws of association). Just as those collective formations known as quantities arise on the basis of the psychic relation of colligation, so the intention of the universal arises on the basis of a "psychic," that is, free, relation which is not determined by the mere contents of a thing or, better, by the activity of examining and grasping particulars, of coextension of individual moments of these particularities—simply, activities oriented a priori to colligation in diversity, to synthesis and unity. Association is possible only because experience strives throughout for unity, for the coextension of the common.

This intention of the universal is then fulfilled in various ways. The universal can remain unthematized, giving rise only to an awareness of common traits among particularities. Or it can be specifically thematized, giving rise to the concepts of the common, the typical. The most common concepts of this type are empirical types such as "flower," "dog," "tree"—common traits given by the senses here ground no more than a certain type which in itself tells us nothing about the inner nature of things, at the most pointing to it as symptoms. An analysis of such an empirical type shows that we are dealing with a richly complex construct out of parts which in turn have their own typology while the coherence among them is for the most part one of an empirical kind; for instance the coherence between a dog's teeth and its other anatomical properties. Such an analysis could then continue indefinitely; we could, on the basis of it, make corrections of classifications based on superficial sensory similarities, thereby uncovering deeper, structurally causal relations. This gives rise to the idea of the universal to which, in addition to the familiar commonalities, belongs an indefinitely open horizon of hitherto unknown specifications, the idea of an empirical universal[22] and, correlatively, systems of such universals in any given field.

Husserl, however, believes that in addition to such empirical types which fulfill the idea of an empirical universal we necessarily must have also those pure universals which signify what is necessarily common in all possible experience as such, universals of which we are not aware merely as one possible type among others but where the universal is necessary a priori. That means that it is a universal capable of prescribing a priori rules to all empirical particulars. Thus for every empirical tone it holds that it includes quality, pitch, timbre, intensity; for every material thing it holds that it must be a spatiotemporal-qualitative and process-substrative unity. In the case of empirical concepts things are such that an

---

22. Husserl, *Experience and Judgment: Investigations in the Genealogy of Logic*, p. 340.

ongoing experience can always, on the basis of encountering ever more particulars about ever more individuals belonging to a type, lead ever again to corrections of the concrete conception of the structure of the type; by contrast, in the case of pure *Wesen—eide*—something of this sort is evidently impossible: "this infinity of actually being-able-to-continue (in experience through all variations) is given with self-evidence, precisely because, before all experience, these concepts prescribe rules for its later course and, consequently, rule out a sudden change, a cancellation."[23] When we are dealing with genera of *concreta*, such rules defining universals are regional concepts: material thing, living being, thinking being. In other words, we can have experiences only of instances which realize singularities of such regional genera, that is, of things (with all the processes this implies), of living and thinking beings (with their aggregates), and this limitation *is no mere fact*, it is not the necessity of mere empirical typology as in the case of a mineral, a dog, or a flower.

In their role as rules of experience, regional genera, especially genera of *concreta*, also serve as guidelines for concrete inquiry, determining its concrete logic: which means that they are not mere content entities, intuited once and for all, but are rather law-like regulating guides guaranteeing an unlimited unity of the style of experience.

Thus a regional genus such as "material thing" does not manifest itself simply as an abstract *eidos* such as "tone" or "sense quality," by simple coextension of individual contents (with which differentiation goes hand in hand). It requires us to take into account the various aspects and relations in which a thing manifests itself (for example, normal sensibility within the community of subjects; movement and rest; inner and outer causal relations); all such relations are nothing merely empirical but rather belong to the inner, eidetic structure of the thing which cannot be in any way other than as a unity within such relativities. Thus a genus is nothing other than a unitary coherence of objective mutual references unfolding within the evident givenness of a potentially ever ongoing process of science.

Pure eidetic concepts, free from facticity, can only be reached by letting go not only of all observed realities in the world, but even of the restriction to this our world. For a pure *eidos* stands

---

23. Ibid.

higher than the factual world, a regional concept has as its extension the *universum* of all possibilities, that is, not only our factual world but the totality of all possible worlds. With respect to this, there is a double differentiation of regional genera, a free, discontinuous differentiation within pure possibility without mutual dependence and differentiation within the framework of a single temporal continuity, that is, within the framework of a unitary (not necessarily actual) world. Thus eidetic structures prove to be the form of any possible world as such, they are world structures.

In this way Husserl means to carry out at one stroke both the task of *grounding experience on a priori knowledge* and of *constituting a science of the eide of things a priori*—an ontology, as it used to be called in the rationalist epoch. Husserl aims, we might say, at a synthesis of Kant and Leibniz.

Some critical comments might be in order already at this juncture.

Husserl understands the problem of grounding experience—of facts which require grounding, justification—from the standpoint of the contingency of fact as against the necessity of eidetic universality.

However, eidetic universality is, for Husserl, something at which we arrive in similar fashion as we did at number: the mind, on the basis of the free activity of comparison, gathers objects into a relation, one which in itself may be objective and nonarbitrary but in such a way that only this particular activity opens up access to it. The mind is oriented a priori to unity, coherence, and adequation. Where, on the basis of the mutual coextension of certain typical traits, it uncovers in gradual analysis the inner connections of traits in an ongoing horizon of possible corrections, there emerges before us empirical universalities; where we have an evident consciousness of the possibility of reaching ever further towards a material coextension among diverse variations represented by actual or imagined individuals and then even specific examples, we gain pure a priori universals, *eide* or ideas.

Experiential knowledge is justified a priori insofar as a necessity reveals itself at the base of its contingency. This necessity is an eidetic one for necessity is precisely the relation between the universal and its instantiation.

However, as Lothar Eley[24] has shown, Husserl reduces the relation between fact and *eidos* to a relation within the framework of the *eidos* itself: a subordination of the individual to the *eidos*, that is, to an eidetic singularity. Husserl then sees nothing more in the fact, in the given, than in the *eidos* itself, merely its "content" as one of the possibilities lodged in eidetic necessity.

Strictly speaking, *facticity as contingency* is nothing other than the consideration of facts from the standpoint of *eidos*, as an instantiation of *eidos*. For eidetic necessity is the enclosure of the genus in the species as well as of the species in particular cases. The obverse of this necessity is the contingency of the difference with respect to the genus, of individual instantiation with respect to the kind. For the difference as such is not necessarily posited together with the *genus*, as the differentiation of lower genera and kinds shows. If the problem of grounding experience is posed as a quest for the necessity at the base of the contingency of facts, then it is clearly already posited exclusively on the level of *eidos* so that facticity inevitably becomes one of the possible, coordinated instantiations within a general framework of "pure a priori possibilities."

It is questionable whether facticity as contingency is the proper form in which to pose the question of justification, of the grounding of facticity.

The second question is whether the concept of universal or categorial perception which Husserl justified on the grounds that it is required by the objectivity of the mental process and by the possibility of verifying it might be limited to the material extension and the differentiation based on it and to the correlative conception of form.

We might ask whether Husserl did not at this point succumb to the prejudice of the given derived from contemporary positivism: that whatever is to be, to be valid, must be capable of being "given" by some positive content. Perhaps that is why Husserl also insists that a difference is possible only on the basis of a common content, that is, that there is not something like an absolute, pure difference.[25]

---

24. Lothar Eley, *Die Krise des Apriori in der transzendentalen Phänomenologie Edmund Husserls*, pp. 38, 54–55.

25. Husserl, *Experience and Judgment*, p. 340.

What, then, of the pure positing of being in which the "this here" presents itself? Here there is undoubtedly no content which we could compare; being is not a real predicate; this thesis, however—not as a subjective act of acknowledgment but rather as an absolute *actus essendi*—can be described as different from all its contents, precisely different as other, not coextensive with a content.

The relation of difference, however, is also synthetic, like the relation of adequation, and can be no less an original synthetic relation. A grounding justification of givenness as such cannot be carried out along the lines of material coextension, but rather along the lines of this radical difference. Radical difference does not preclude mutuality but rather might still conjoin where coextension does not reach. For difference, one not being the other, is common to two members of this relation even where a wholly radical difference prevails; that is rooted in the symmetry of the relation of differentiation, of diversity.

The grounding of experience in its facticity is not the same as grounding it in its contingency. This grounding in facticity does not proceed within the immanent realm of thoughts and imaginations but rather represents thought transcending its immanent domain, beyond the contents that are subject to our free variation together with the emphasis on what is coextensive. In such grounding, thought aspires to the means with whose aid it can move even beyond its inmost immanent domain. The point here is to think the radically other, the different, and yet not make it a mere matter of thought. The object must not become a mere object of imagination and thought, and yet it must be thought. In this sense, the relation of mind to facticity is not merely the relation of the necessary to the contingent within which the necessary is contained as in one of its possibilities.

Perhaps we need to think the relation to fact most of all inversely as well: it is *fact* as such, in its radical irreducibility to the universal of whatever content, that presents the mind with the stimulus and opportunity to unfold its *factual freedom* of breaking free of *mere givenness as such*. This factical freedom, the possibility of not being content with present givenness, of not being bound to it, then unfolds in the activity of comparison, into the access to ideas, in the "constitution" of idealities which in reality are thus always bound to their factical foundation.

That is, this detachment from the given always presupposes the given and can never be so complete that it could fly over it and get an overview of all its structures and concealments. We are not reaching the material from which worlds are formed, the possibilities from which a creator selects, but rather are freeing ourselves from the particular for its cohesion, its unity, its coherence; we construe and project the nongiven on the basis of the given.

Thus while we accept Husserl's idea of a universal perception [*Wesensschau*] of its object, the *eidos,* we do not thereby mean to accept all the consequences Husserl derives from it, while on the other hand we also believe that in some respects Husserl does not take the idea as far as he could.

Husserl did not carry the categorial perception to dialectical relations, that is, to those relations in which the *joint linking* the diversity of ideas is not a *common content,* a coextensive object, aspect, or structure, but where the linkage takes place without it, and consequently is not the bond of the positive but of diversity and negation. For this reason, the conflicted problems of grounding experience, of the relation between mind and fact, of radical externality which is yet to be internalized, is not posed dialectically in Husserl's thought.

On the other hand, precisely because he enclosed *eidos* within immanence, Husserl reveals a tendency to make everything immanent, understood as one of the eidetic possibilities. On this terrain we cannot follow him in spite of all the remarkable achievements, material and formal, of the method of variation, comprehension, and coextension, whose result is the identity *eidos.* It is a simple consequence of the preceding that we shall not call the respective eidetic disciplines "ontologies."

Chapter 6

The First Explanation of the Phenomenological Reduction

In chapter 4 we saw that in *Logical Investigations,* in addition to purely logical considerations, a new conception of subjectivity emerges, oriented in principle to the object—the conception of intentional subjectivity. Hand in hand with that, we noted, in the critique of Brentano's conception of psychic phenomena as putatively wholly immanent and evident in their immanence, there arises the problem of the "pure phenomena," purged of all objective positing and so truly guaranteed in its givenness—the basic problem of the pure phenomenology to come.

At the time of the first publication of *Logical Investigations,* Husserl appears to have believed that this problem of the ultimate ground of pure logic, as well as the problem of its reflective and radical, wholly primordial philosophical foundation, could be resolved by a proposed new eidetic discipline—by eidetic, that is, nonempirical psychology.

It could not, however, escape Husserl's notice that the relation between intentional acts and their objects is of a special type, incapable of being compared or reduced to purely objectival eidetic relations. It is not a relation of either a reciprocal or a one-sided grounding, for the act and the object do not constitute a whole of which both would be a part. Similarly, "fusing" or "joining," relations emphasized in the region of eidetic nature and *eidos* by other phenomenologists (for instance, Héring and Ingarden), will not do because they, too, are special ways of grounding.[1] Even less appropriate in this case is the objective law of eidetic exclusion. Here we have a relation of necessary mutual belonging without the components constituting a real unity, that is, something that forces us to go beyond all schemata of purely objectively oriented formal ontology. However, it is not just that this relation is not reducible to any other eidetic relation; we might actually say that all eidetic relations are somehow based upon this relation, as we can see in the effort of *Logical Investigations,* noticeable from the start, "to build a bridge between subjective experiencing and the objectivity of cognition," that hidden mainspring of Husserl's entire intellectual development thus far. Thus already these considerations make it quite evident that an eidetic discipline which would meet these new demands could not be just one among others but would need to stand above them in at least some aspects.

In addition, we also need to take into consideration the way we think of the psychic, both in life and, for the most part, in psychology and philosophy (even though in these disciplines, especially in the transcendental branches of philosophical thought, we encounter hints anticipating a different viewpoint). The psychic tends to be viewed as an aspect of a human being who is an object within nature, bound to the rest of natural being by the unifying bond of real time and causal efficacy. Thus the way we know and in general think about such a being does not fundamentally differ from the way we know and think about natural objects in general, even though it surely has its specific traits as well. However, the eidetic, a priori relation between thematizing and cognizing subjective acts and corresponding objectivities must hold here as well. Thus we would have a discipline which would reflect on the relation of *all* objects to the subject's lived experience, including the subject as a part of the totality of what there is, who, as such, would be also an object for the subject. Such a discipline would require a clarification of the concept of subject, for if the subject in the sense of the foundation of all experiential acts and the subject in the sense of a special object were the same, then this discipline,

---

1. See Jean Héring, "Bemerkungen über das Wesen, die Wesenheit und die Idee," in *Jahrbuch für Philosophie und phänomenologische Forschung* 4 (1921), and Roman Ingarden, "Essentiale Fragen. Ein Beitrag zu den Wesensproblem," *Jahrbuch für Philosophie und phänomenologische Forschung* 7 (1925). [Ed.]

as an eidetic theory of the subject, would also be at the same time
the whole and a part, that which justifies and that which is justified. That something like that would be unthinkable made itself
felt already when Husserl, in the supplement to his sixth *Logical
Investigation,* criticized Brentano's distinction between psychic
and physical phenomena, for hidden behind this criticism there is
already the future distinction between "pure phenomena" and
mere "real immanence" characteristics of the psychic as psychology understands it.

The first consistent attempt to arrive at a "pure phenomenon"
and so at a radical resolution of the philosophical task of grounding our cognition in general, posed in the reflective attitude, is
contained, after earlier starts, in the 1907 lecture, *The Idea of
Phenomenology* (Husserliana vol. 2, published in 1958).

Here the procedure of arriving at the pure phenomenon is
presented in three stages. Reaching the pure phenomenon is the
procedure which Husserl designates as the "phenomenological
reduction" (to pure immanence).

The first stage presents the idea of a critique of cognition and
of philosophy as this critique. Thus philosophy is located on a
wholly different level than objective cognition, which approaches
things in a direct, objectival posture and includes all scientific disciplines, both empirical and a priori. Husserl builds up the distinction between the two on the Cartesian methodic doubt which suspends even those judgments which there is no practical need to
doubt, as soon as they show they might be less than perfectly certain, even if only theoretically. Husserl, however, replaces the
Cartesian *skepticism* with a mere *critical suspension of judgment
(epoché),* a suspension of the validity of such judgments for the critique of cognition which may not derive from them any knowledge, any premises for its knowing, but must restrict itself to what
is truly indubitable, evident, in the Cartesian *cogito*—the perception of lived experience in the course of such experience in simple
awareness. Thus *mere perception* is to become the absolute, self-
certifying source of cognition, drawing on nothing else, sustaining
itself solely from itself, in *pure immanence.*

Thus precisely transcendence now becomes the basic philosophical problem which cannot be resolved in the direct stance to
which objects are already preveniently given as preexistent, as tran-
scendents: transcendence as that which is somehow present in
lived experience yet at the same time goes beyond the limits of

being absolutely contained within it, that which cannot be given apart from lived experience and yet is not a part of it. The question can also be framed thus: how can cognition, from itself alone, that is, as a lived experience, discover something in lived experience that is itself not lived experience? Already the formulation of the problem itself shows clearly that it cannot be resolved by any of the special sciences, however rigorous and extensive, since every such science already presupposes the givenness of the object and so operates on the level of transcendence; thus it cannot undertake the task of tracing its origin, its nature, and its structure.

If this structure, nature, and origin are really to be studied on the level of pure immanence, then we need to distinguish various conceptions of *immanence;*[2] ordinarily we mean by it *real* immanence, that is, the fact that the lived experience of knowing, which is an actual reality, also contains an object of knowledge; we tend to take it for granted that an act of cognition can find its object and simultaneously take it into itself; the immanent is what is within me, the transcendent is what is outside me. A real immanence is thus an immanence of the object in the subject which is itself a reality among other realities of the world.

Over against such real immanence there is real transcendence which posits objects as existing and claims that in cognition it can grasp facts which are not given in cognition "in the true sense of the word," which are not "immanent."

Transcendence, however, is an ambiguous term. On the one hand, it can mean *reell transcendence,* that is, the fact that the object of cognition is not a part, a *reell* component or a moment, of the process of experiencing. Whatever is in that sense a part or component of that process, we call *reell*ly immanent. Transcendence here is the opposite of *reell* immanence and mutually exclusive with it: what is *reell*ly immanent cannot be transcendent, and vice versa.

On the other hand, however, transcendence also means an *absolute and clear givenness, self-givenness in an absolute sense.* This givenness, precluding any reasonable doubt, is a fully immediate perception and grasping of the intended objectivity as it itself is, the *originary evident givenness* as distinct from cognition which intends or posits a thing but does not perceive it; in this givenness we always go beyond the limits of what is given, strictly speaking,

2. Husserl, *The Idea of Phenomenology,* pp. 2–4, 27–28.

what can be directly perceived and grasped. Here transcendence and immanence in no sense exclude each other: what is transcendent, what is not before us in the full sense of the word, perceivable and graspable, might still be immanent in a sense (as the objectival meaning of a certain cognizing act).

Reell components of the act of intuition (*reell*ly immanent) are sense impressions (of red, of acoustical sensation, etc.) and intentions which "animate" them, as we explained earlier (see chapter 4 above). By contrast, red as a quality of the tile roof of the house over there, across the street, or a tone A_1, are certainly *reell*ly transcendent but in spite of that can be immanent, at least partially, *in the sense of being self-given.*

We can now formulate two questions, one pertaining to the *reell,* the other to the self-given immanence and transcendence: (1) How can cognition go beyond what is *reell*ly immanent to it? (2) How can cognition posit as existing something that is not really and directly given in it?

These two questions now define the problem of the phenomenological reduction: it is on the one hand a reduction of transcendence to immanence, but, seen from the other side, it is the *genesis of transcendence in immanence.*

The second stage of Husserl's exposition of the concept of reduction can be described as a progression from the exclusion of real transcendence to the exclusion of transcendence altogether.

Here it is first of all necessary to carry out a modification of the Cartesian *cogitatio.* Descartes' turn from dubitable transcendence to indubitable immanence is a turn to real immanence, to immanence within a finite mental substance linked to the things of the physical world by a real interaction in the same objective time. Descartes' immanence thus became the starting point of modern psychology. But humans in the world, mental substance as the ultimate *subjectum* of all *cogitationes,* are not themselves *cogitationes,* are not absolute givens to which alone we wish to or need to restrict ourselves. That is what distinguishes psychological reflection from the reflection on pure phenomenon, from phenomenological reflection. *Psychological* reflection accepts the validity of the equation I = subject *cogitatio* = psychophysical reality. *Pure* reflection is a reflection on *cogitatio* purely as such. Psychological reflection passes from the object to the psychophysical subject, thus it is a transition from real transcendence to real immanence. Phenomenological reflection reduces even this real immanence, first to pure *reell* immanence, to whatever is simply and purely a component of the lived experience of *cogitatio* as such. (Husserl here distinguishes pure and psychological reflection also by noting that the first is the awareness that there is cogitatio, the other the awareness that there is *my cogitatio,* that *cogitans sum,* thus positing a subject transcendent to various *cogitationes;* later he will distinguish sharply between the subject of *cogitationes* as a person, a thing in the world, and as an I, the phenomenon of "transcendence in immanence" which appertains to the meaning of every *cogitatio.*)[3] So it turns out that to every psychic lived experience there corresponds, after the phenomenological reduction, a pure phenomenon which is nothing other than *an absolute givenness of the immanent eidos* of the psychological phenomenon. This absolute givenness is precisely what manifests itself in the absolute self-certainty of perception, in pure intuition.

Now how can we make this absolute givenness an object of science? Is not givenness a Heraclitean flux from which we cannot step out, which changes at every moment so that while it is always absolutely given, it is given differently in each instance? Does not every science by contrast seek to posit an objectivity identical with itself, an objectivity identical for the various phases of the stream of various subjects, and so to transcendence? Then is not phenomenology as a science a contradiction?

The task of phenomenology is not to eliminate all objectivity but to ground objectivity itself in immanence, to demonstrate the birth of transcendence in immanence. There is surely a point in doubting a phenomenon which intends something not contained in itself; there is, however, no point in doubting what is contained with full evidence in a phenomenon, what I see as presently given in it. That is how a conscious lived experience is presently given in consciousness, as a part of awareness, *reell*ly contained in it, both constituting a unity—if we are aware of our perception, then awareness seizes perception in the act, perception does not cease perceiving, only something more, something additional is present, namely, perception aware of itself. Thus the grasping of lived experience is itself an absolute cognition, an absolute givenness, and therewith also all that such grasping involves, that is, judging and comparing in purely present givenness—judgments about presently grasped lived experiences; however, if I observe an intu-

---

3. See Husserl, *Ideas I,* §§37, 80.

itive judgment reflexively, then I note also that it is based on intuitions and imaginings, and this recognition is again an evident, absolute recognition in pure intuition. Generally, then, a part of this intuitive grasping is a seeing of a universal eidetic nature in a singular experience in its singularity, seeing the difference of perception and conception, of a judgment and its moments, of fantasy, of mere intention, of the real and quasi-real, and so forth . . . But for this possibility, the phenomenologist would really drown in the Heraclitean stream. For what reaches intuition, absolute reflective self-givenness, is not merely some singular presence but correlatively also the eidetic nature, the *eidos* of lived experiencing as such.

Individual experiences do differ in their nature in their intentional eidetic nature, the intentional meaning they have, or, in other words, in what is immanent to them. Thus the intentionality of consciousness conjoined with eidetic intuition leads on beyond the mere givenness of the immanent.

Here the third stage begins, from absolute immanence to the discovery of transcendence in immanence.

Reflection concerning eidetic nature, pure *eidos,* appears as the most suitable example of how to demonstrate transcendence within immanence itself. Does not the universal as such—the object of *Wesensschau,* of ideational perception—transcend the *reell,* temporal stream of cognition? Such a universal, after all, is not contained within that stream as its part or moment. Nonetheless the givenness of the universal is not a givenness in the sense of *cognitive transcendence* in the sense that the known would here be only the beginning, a challenge to go on to something further, something deeper and something that might revise what is known thus far; rather, in perceiving the universal we seize everything that can be present before us in perception; no further cognition about it is possible, and there is no point in seeking it—consequently we have here again a certain immanence, that is, *the immanence of self-givenness. Reell* transcendence thus need not yet be transcendence as such—*reell* transcendence can also be *an immanence of self-givenness.*

Transcendence thus is not something that phenomenology can or need fear and avoid altogether, but rather only when it is not the transcendence of eidetic self-givenness. However, since in essential self-givenness we shall be able to grasp *all lived experiences and their* eide, the fundamental problem of phenomenology will also be within our reach, namely the *nature of cognition,* the *eidos* of the process of lived experience in which in mere opinion, in hints, in symbol, in representative perception, in analogy, the object itself is ultimately given. All relations, all mutual references, all conjunctions, all harmony, all purposiveness of cognitive processes in their mutuality, all these will not be ultimately *beyond* reach of phenomenological reflection but rather will become accessible to it. The meaning of experiential processes tracing the possibility of the *thing itself* presenting itself to our view can be thus immanently grasped. That will then resolve the problem posed: that of presenting a critical foundation of science and of cognition generally, clarifying the nature of transcendence and the meaning of objectivity. The example of eidetic intuition or perception thus shows that a certain objectivity belongs to the meaning of certain cognitive acts, an objectivity which itself is not a part of such acts as either a concrete or an abstract component, but which on the basis of them is nonetheless corporeally present to us in the original, not in mere representation only, and that in such a way that it evidently cannot be accessible in any other fuller or more adequate manner.

It is not only perception or fantasy as the basis for grasping of the universal *eidos* that can serve as an example of immanent transcendence. An immediate memory (retention), in which a just-past phase of a lived experience is given, likewise opens up such a transcendence in immanence, a transcendence which is *given* with full evident givenness and without which speaking of a past would be meaningless; so that in this retention, together with a vivid awareness of the present, the meaning of the past is constituted, a past opens up, a temporal horizon, and so, too, the possibility of understanding individual objects, because individual beings are objects in a single, really objective temporal stream. A temporal sequence, a temporal extension, is not contained in "lived time" as its component, and yet it is accessible to us only on the basis of it.

The earliest stage was the *evidence of the cogitatio.* Here it seemed at first that we were on solid ground, in *pure being.* That here it would be enough to touch and observe, then with respect to such givens compare and distinguish, point out specific universals and so arrive at substantive judgments—anyone would readily agree to all that. But now it turns out that such pure being, *cogitatio,* is, on closer inspection, not so simple, that *different types* of objectivity are "constituted" even within the Cartesian sphere itself and this constituting means that the immanent givens are not simply contained in consciousness as things but that in every instance they present themselves in something like "appearances" which themselves are not object nor contain objects *reel*ly, but which rather in their shifting, most remarkable construction somehow give rise to objects for the I—as long as just those kinds of appearance and configuration are appropriate so that what we call "givenness" would be present before us.[4]

On this basis, Husserl proceeds to examine various types of objectivities, from individual real objects to universals, *eide,* to abstract conceptual configurations, facts, and meanings, to values, etc., in order to observe that throughout the meaning of objectivity opens up in a correlative study of lived experience and of its objectivities, "transcendent," yet accessible to it alone, and concludes:

> It is only in a cognition that the essence of objectivity can be studied in all its basic forms. . . . This *evident "seeing"* itself is truly *cognition in the fullest sense* and objectivity is not a thing contained in cognition as in a sack . . . but rather in givenness we see that the *object is constituted in cognition.* . . . Cognitive acts . . . are not discontinuous particulars . . . but rather fundamentally interrelated, belonging teleologically together and manifesting a continuity of content, corroboration, verification, and of their opposites.[5]

So in the end the reduction did not lead to a lessening, a narrowing, of the content of human cognition but rather to its deepening to the very nature of cognition and of reason as such.

Such is the first description of the phenomenological reduction and of its philosophical meaning, particularly significant in its conciseness—the discovery of Reason as such at the foundation of human reflective cognition, the discovery of infinite consciousness at the foundation of our empirically finite cognitive acts.

As it is presented in *The Idea of Phenomenology,* it is clearly evident that the object is constituted in cognition and that it is thus relative to the lived experience which is given absolutely. Here, however, that double mode of givenness does not yet lead to the conclusion of a dual, fundamentally different mode of being. In that sense we can say that the exposition in *The Idea of Phenomenology* does not yet wholly fulfill Husserl's speculative intention of justifying an idealism of a special kind (as it is formulated, for instance, in the conclusion of *Ideas I* and in *Cartesian Meditations*), an idealism asserting that the meaning of the being of the

4. Husserl, *The Idea of Phenomenology,* pp. 55–56.
5. *Ibid.,* pp. 59–60.

world is only that it is the intentional formation of "transcendental subjectivity."[6]

For it is evident that if *The Idea of Phenomenology* is supposed to present to the eyes of the philosopher the *genesis of transcendence,* then the task has not been fulfilled. Though it is evident that transcendence is relative to immanence, that immanence itself contains transcendence within it as an inseparable trait, it has not been shown that immanence is more original, more basic: both are equally original. While transcendence may not be possible without immanence, it has not been demonstrated that immanence might be possible without transcendence. The "genesis" of transcendence refers to the forms, the degrees, and the varieties of transcendent objectivities, leading one to another, step by step, rather than to real components making up transcendence; quite the contrary, even though objectivity is the correlate of a process, it is said to be present in this correlation *at a stroke.* Thus transcendence is not *deduced* but *presupposed.* The correlation of the object and the structure of lived experience would entail a derivative nature of the object only if the structure of lived experience were understood as a productive activity, yet while the constitution of which Husserl speaks does have a synthetic and so an active and creative character on the side of the subject, on the object side there is no indication of any reference to having been constituted. If we interpret the creative character of constitution on analogy with mathematical and logical objectivities, then we might object that one could defend the objectivity of the relevant entities even here and that in no case is the *truth value* of mathematical truths based on spontaneous constitution but rather on the objective aspect of mathematical entities.—The idea of constitution means essentially that *a transcendence of self-givenness is compatible with reell immanence of the eidetic nature of lived experience,* which in this respect can also be considered *a kind of immanence,* a transcendence in immanence.

Thus if it is to be shown that the absolute givenness of reflexive consciousness really entails the primacy of subjective being to the objective, then this primacy must be justified still more closely. The description of the reduction presented in *Ideas I* is devoted to

---

6. "Author's Preface to the English Edition of Ideas," [in *Husserl: Shorter Works,* p. 48—Ed.]: "The world as an intentional formation of transcendental subjectivity" here apparently means the product of transcendental subjectivity. Thus it is relative, dependent on the primary, nonrelative being of consciousness (because its being is ever presumptive).

this justification. Only from their standpoint can we also understand why Husserl devotes so much space to describing the idea of the world and of the dependence of this idea on the regional *eidos* of the material object, of material nature.

So now in *Ideas I* Husserl prefaces the explanation of the reduction with a systematic explanation of mundane, experiential sciences and with a theory of the *eidos* and of the eidetic foundation of knowledge.[7] We have seen that the point of the theory of *eidos* is a projected schema of eidetic disciplines, of regional ontologies which, together with formal ontology, adumbrate an analytic and a synthetic a priori, for all the projected mundane scientific disciplines, that is, for sciences "within the natural standpoint," characterized by a *belief in the world* (the general thesis of the natural standpoint). This a priori, as we have seen, is a priori for all possible worlds, for all conceivable universes, and so stands above all factical contingency. (It might seem that the evidence we cite, derived from *Experience and Judgment,* does not apply to *Ideas I;* however, the sections concerning the origin of universals and eidetic perception in this work agree strongly with *Ideas III,*[8] and have certain parallels even in "Idee der Philosophie," where we read of the principal significance of categories, meaning regional concepts which set down the rule for experience.) The chief significance of the extended exposition of the theory of the *eidos* in this work, we believe, is to call attention to the a priori character of appearance, of knowability, which belongs to the *eidos of worldly being,* of worldly objectivity.

Consistently with the foregoing, the conceptual pair transcendence-immanence, prominent in *The Idea of Phenomenology* and overtly pointing to the Cartesian motif of certitude as the point which kindled Husserl's own speculations (though, as we shall see, with a different motivation), is upstaged by the conceptual pair which covers the same opposition with a new cloak, the pair worldly-transcendental, the being of the world—the being of transcendental consciousness.

How does Husserl explain the concept of the world in *Ideas I?* The world is presented as the *context of material nature,* extending endlessly in space and time, assumed as pregiven. The givenness of

---

7. See Husserl, *Ideas I,* §§56, 59. [Ed.]

8. Compare Husserl, *Ideas Pertaining to a Phenomenology and to a Phenomenological Philosophy. Book Three: Phenomenology and the Foundations of the Sciences,* §§7–8, pp. 22–46, to *Experience and Judgment,* §§84–89. [Ed.]

the world is centered on what is perceptually present but is not restricted to it, a circle of the more or less certainly conscious is essentially co-present with it, surrounded finally by a dimly conscious horizon of indefinite reality whose givenness is an eidetic necessity—that precisely is the root of the endlessness of the world's givenness. The temporal extension is, in contrast with this spatial extension, stressed only secondarily, practical traits are treated from the viewpoint of the polarity of a purely objective world as against the world of values, possessions, practice; fellow humans and animalia are perceived basically as material bodies.— The "ideal" context, that is, mathematical objects, etc., is treated in a correlation with *spontaneous activities of consciousness* so that it is not given "preveniently" as a constant horizon.—What is true for me in my context holds, as I know, for other subjects as well— and that, too, is a part of my subjective context. All that can be summed up in the "general thesis of the natural standpoint," that the world as reality is always already present, at most here and there different than I had thought so that I have to cancel some "appearances" by replacing them with other reality which is always to some extent hypothetical and constantly being verified.[9]

This general thesis is no specific particular act, such as a judgment concerning the existence of the world, but rather belongs to our *natural standpoint* as its *constant correlate*. Every particular we perceive is already placed within the modifier "given," "present," "already before," preveniently here. That is our way of grasping, predicatively and after the fact, a trait which is nonpredicatively, nonconsciously present already in the original experience.

Now Husserl insists that *whether it is explicit or not, this general thesis can be set aside just like the explicit thesis of a judgment.*[10] We can treat it as we treat particular cognitions which can be suspended, as Descartes' experiment with methodological skepticism shows. Such an attempt to doubt is a matter of our complete freedom. It is that much more possible to carry out a modified version of this experiment, one which does not simply cancel, deny the existence of the world, as Descartes recommends, but *simply suspends its validity for our philosophical purposes,* a suspension which Husserl calls *epoché.* Husserl does not undertake it for the same purpose as Descartes, to gain absolutely certain premises for the sciences of the world, which would then be constructed in com-

---

9. See Husserl, *Ideas I,* §§27–30, pp. 51–57. [Ed.]
10. See ibid., §§31–32, pp. 57–62. [Ed.]

plete indubitability. Husserl stresses explicitly that his purpose is wholly different from that of working out an absolutely indubitable sphere of (worldly) being.[11] Not a region of indubitability within mundane being, but a new, wholly indubitable region of being, never noted before and never delineated, is the purpose of this new modified Cartesian approach.

Every being presents itself originally, as it is in itself, in perception, that is, in the mode in which it is itself present, in the original, before the view of the perceiver.

Lived experience, in the sense of a pure, phenomenologically reduced lived experience, presents itself in such a way that the object (reflexively perceived lived experience) is *reell*ly *contained* therein,[12] so that perceiving can be only abstractively distinguished from its object, only as a dependent moment of the object itself. A lived experience can constitute a *reell* unity, on the basis of it distinctive *eidos,* only with other components of the same stream of experience, never with transcendent objects.

What, on the other hand, is the self-givenness of a material thing, the perception of it, the way in which it presents itself as present in the original? A material thing ultimately demonstrated by sense perception (which applies also for physical things whose nature and structure are in other respects subject to reduction), cannot in principle, for eidetic reasons, ever be *given or perceived immanently.*

That leads to another point (about which it is at first not clear whether Husserl considers it equivalent to the first or as something additional). Every material thing is given, and can be given, only *in perspectives.* No perspective presents it as a whole; each points to further and other possible ones. What is more, the thing itself is accessible to me only in perspective; I can never approach it except through perspectives. By contrast, a lived experience is not given *through* perspectives but in itself.

> The eidetic nature of specially constructed *modes of lived experience*— more precisely, of specially constructed perceptions—is such that what they intend enters consciousness as a thing in space; to its eidetic nature there belongs the ideal possibility of passing over into certain ordered, continually

---

11. Ibid., p. 58: "One procedure, possible at any time, is the *attempt to doubt universally* which *Descartes* carried out for an entirely different purpose with a view toward bringing out a sphere of absolutely indubitable being." [Ed.]

12. Ibid., pp. 79–80: "Here the perceiving includes its Object in itself in such a manner that it only can be separated abstractively, only as an *essentially non-self-sufficient [unselbstständige]* moment, from its Object." [Ed.]

consistent perceptual variations which can go ever on and which are therefore never closed off.[13]

According to Husserl this distinction is not one between incomplete and full givenness; not even a lived experience is ever complete, being always given only as a phase in a flow, but this incompleteness or inadequacy is in principle different from that with which a material object is given.

> While the eidetic nature of being given by means of appearances is such that none of them gives the thing as something absolute rather than in a one-sided presentation, the eidetic nature of immanent givenness is such that it presents precisely something absolute which simply cannot be presented from various sides and perspectives, something that proves itself something that cannot be canceled.[14]

It is clear, Husserl says, that the sense contents in which things appear are not themselves given perspectively and that, as experienced, they are beyond all doubt in an absolute sense, while the things in which they appear are not.[15] The difference between the way a thing and a lived experience are given is not one of fullness and completeness, of temporal extension and temporal immediacy; it is, rather, a difference of the immediate (experiential) and of the mediate (objective), between what gives itself and what is given on the basis of something else.

That leads to something else as well. For all its incompleteness, a lived experience as such is indubitable; it makes absolutely no sense to imagine that our I, in its lived experiencing, would have only fantasies about itself, constantly feigning its past, etc.—for even if it were to feign the objects of its past, its lived experience of what it feigns will be real and can be grasped by an absolute reflection such as grasps what is. (To be sure, our own physical corporeality does not belong to what is thus experientially, absolutely grasped: that is no less transcendent than every other thing.) By contrast, *objective existence is never an existence which*

13. Husserl, *Ideen I*, Hua III, p. 97, lines 33–39 (translation Kohák following Patočka's Czech translation).
14. Ibid., p. 102, lines 31–36 (translation Kohák following Patočka's Czech translation).
15. Husserl, *Ideas I*, p. 97: "It is indeed evident also that the adumbrative sensation-contents themselves, which really inherently belong to the mental process of perceiving a physical thing, function, more particularly, as adumbrations of something but are not themselves given in turn by adumbrations." [Ed.]

givenness demands as necessary—givenness, bodily presence, never guarantees it, it is always possible that all that is present will prove to be an illusion, a hallucination, a continuous dream, etc.

> Everything that exists for me at all in the world of things, the world of realities, is in principle only a presumptive reality; by contrast I myself . . . or, rather, my lived experiential actuality, is an *absolute* reality, given unconditionally in an absolutely incontrovertible positing.[16]

Now, however, Husserl presents a shorthand consequence— that the positing of the world, which is "contingent," stands against the positing of my I and the life of my I, which are "necessary," absolutely indubitable.

> Everything bodily, *in persona,* self-given in the objective realm, might also not be, no self-given lived experience can not be.[17]

This eidetic law rests on presuppositions which Husserl does not formulate explicitly but which it is important to point out. They are

(1) that all givenness of the world is either a perception of a thing or is based on a perception of a thing; and
(2) that the thing, this reality solely in a synthetically transcendent, mediate givenness, is not only a form of contingency, of our real world, but rather belongs to the form of any world whatever, for it is not only a regional concept but rather the regional concept which is the guide and rule of all possible experience.

These unspoken assumptions, especially the second one, also explain why, in *Ideas I,* the theory of the *eidos,* as a necessary a priori structure which is the eidetic foundation of all knowledge of contingent facts, precedes the philosophical theory proper, the theory of the phenomenological reduction, the winning of pure immanence, of absolute being and of reason as such. For Husserl, this continuity was so self-evident that, in presenting the doctrine of *eidos,* he even forgot to call to attention that the basic concretely regional concept "thing" is a structure of a world or, better, of the world, doing it only as an afterthought in a critical supplement published in his *Nachlaß.* There he himself objects against himself that *eidos* as it is presented here ignores the fact

---

16. Husserl, *Ideen I,* Hua III, p. 108, lines 28–36 (translation Kohák following Patočka's Czech translation).
17. Ibid., p. 109, lines 1–6 (translation Kohák following Patočka's Czech translation).

that the world as a unitary *universum* (a *universum* of compossible possibilities) had not been explained earlier so that the regional concepts are not presented as universal structures of the world. As a result, it is not clear that all being must really fit within regional concepts as they are presented in the first chapter of *Ideas I;* in addition to regions known to us there might very well exist others, possibly ones wholly inaccessible to us.

The difference between the relative, mediate, contingent, presumptive, *reell*ly transcendent being of the world and the absolute, immediate, necessary, certain, *reell*ly immanent being of lived experience is what *Ideas I* seeks to elaborate and what is not yet contained in the presentation of the reduction in *The Idea of Phenomenology.*

Only this difference then fully justifies Husserl's "phenomenological idealism": it is philosophically unthinkable to imagine an independent existence of things, that is, to think things absolutely, to think absolutely what by its eidetic nature is not and cannot be absolute, lived experience. In light of this difference, then, transcendence really becomes the product of immanence on which all that is transcendent depends by the very nature of its being. The constitution of objectivities becomes really a *production* of objects in consciousness.

The theory of reduction, as it is presented in *Ideas I,* then inevitably leads to an immanentization of the object in spite of the transcendence of its self-givenness. If we reduce all conscious reality to absolute, pure phenomena, then, after the reduction, transcendence does not disappear; it is not crossed off and destroyed, but rather continues to belong to immanence, though no longer as *real transcendence* but as the *phenomenon of transcendence,* as the objective correlate of what is purely, *reell*ly immanent, that is, of lived experience as such. This objective correlate remaining after the reduction, a correlate of which it no longer makes sense to ask about existence or nonexistence, is what Husserl calls *noema,* while the pure, *reell*ly immanent lived experience with its components and moments he calls *noesis,* translating the problem of the eidetic correlation of experiential and objective eidetic structures into that of the eidetic relation of the *noesis* and the *noema* in absolute, nonrelative being itself.

That is how Husserl seeks to demonstrate that the objectivity of the object is thinkable only if we start out from the subjectivity of the subject; it is possible to find the object in the subject but never the subject in the object (for instance, mind in nature). Here Husserl revives Fichte's attempt at understanding the world from the mind and its own essential structure which brings it about that the mind identifies itself with its product, forgetting its own eidetic nature, its primacy or freedom, and makes itself an object, that is, alienates itself from itself.[18] The phenomenological reduction is thus an act of absolute freedom in which the alienated mind/spirit returns to itself, discovering its absolute essence, its absolute being.

To be sure, the method which Husserl follows in his attempt at uncovering the absolute being of the subject is fundamentally different from Fichte's in that it does not *construct* the individual stages of alienation but rather studies various forms of objectivity in correlation with relevant subjective structures, *empirically,* in pure reflection. Husserl's distrust of conceptual constructs, which led to the demand for a fully intuitive method, lies at the basis of the phenomenological conception of the absolute consciousness which cannot be studied as an object, *eidos,* idea, or an objective or structural regularity, however conceived.

Phenomenology so conceived is a purely intuitive study of noetico-noematic structures. Its field is all reality as constituted in subjective lived experience and the study of its constitution: either of constitution as a study of the *foundation,* primarily one-sided, of lived experiences and their layering and structuring, or a genetic constitution, a study of their essential temporal structure. For the moment we will not deal with all that, postponing it for later chapters in which we shall present several views of the constitution of time, body, and community.

In this chapter, we shall now add an attempt at a critique of the phenomenological reduction. Later we shall return to Husserl's further attempts to present it more clearly and profoundly.

Husserl's conception of two types of being, a difference which the reduction uncovers, is doubtful.

---

18. Cf. part 1 of J. G. Fichte's *Science of Knowledge (Wissenschaftslehre);* Patočka himself, however, has elsewhere voiced reservations about this comparison, pointing out that Husserl's idealism arises not so much out of the idea of the ego as a pure conditioning *principle* (i.e., one that is itself unconditioned) grasped in an "intellectual intuition," as out of the Cartesian notion of self-consciousness as an *object* given in pure, indubitable evidence. See Patočka, "Der Subjektivismus der Husserlschen und die Möglichkeit einer a-subjektiven Phänomenolgie." [Ed.]

Everything that is self-given corporeally, *in persona*, in the objective
realm, might not be, no self-given experience can not be.[19]

From that we can deduce the derivative, nonevident nature of
the world only if we identify the givenness of the world with the
givenness of objects in the world, of things. Things certainly might
not be because they are always anticipated, they are synthetic unities. What, though, about the world as a whole? The world as a
whole is no empty intention which could be translated into an adequate perception, which we could anticipate as a thing and verify on
the basis of ongoing experience whether it is or not, whether it is
this or that. The world as a whole is not a presumptive reality that
can be gradually verified in the syntheses of its individual aspects.

To that we could, of course, reply that the world as a whole is
nothing self-given: it is things in the world that are self-given; only
its *components* are here in the original. That, however, holds only if
we identify the world as a whole with the sum of things, and precisely that thesis is doubtful. The whole, the sum of all things,
cannot be given except as a *present* memory; and yet a memory is a
mode of being given, of the givenness of the *past* as *past,* and not
merely an empty intention.

That at the same time removes the objection that we might
after all be dealing with a *mere anticipation.* Undoubtedly, the
world is anticipated, but this anticipation has at the same time the
character of something that cannot be present except in its prevenient form. The world as a whole is never verified but is rather
always the presupposition of all verification. From that it follows
that the givenness of the world as a whole is not less indubitable
than the givenness of lived experience in its self-givenness.

From that it would again seem to follow that if the reduction
proves to be one to indubitable being which is indubitable because
it is self-given, then the givenness of the world as a whole is as ultimate and unshakable as the givenness of lived experience as such.
The being of the world as a whole is thus as unshaken by the reduction as the being of lived experience. Hence it follows that transcendence as such, given in that transcendence of the world as a whole,
is not reducible, deducible from anything else, that it therefore cannot be somehow deduced, "constituted," from pure immanence.

19. Husserl, *Ideen I,* Beilage VI, pp. 389–90 (translation Kohák following Patočka's
Czech translation).

The world as a whole is ever-present, present as a horizon; this horizonal givenness is something original. For the horizon is neither a particular perspective nor an anticipation. Perspectives and anticipations are possible only on the basis of it.

Hence it might be possible to deduce that though consciousness is a constant anticipation, it can carry out this anticipatory role only on condition that it *accepts* something like a global givenness of the world which is prevenient, is not exhausted in anticipations nor reducible to the verification of the particular. There is no reason that could shake this givenness if, as a horizon, the world itself is *unverifiable* and yet the condition of all verification.

We might still object that the world, upon verification, might cease to be an *ordered world,* could dissolve into chaos. A chaos, though, is something different than *no world at all;* it is precisely an *un-ordered world.* An un-ordered world does not mean the nonexistence of the whole, only the nonexistence of the whole of a *certain type.*

The world as a whole, however, clearly means something that is present and certain in presence but that does not in principle reduce to any givenness of a particular, so that its thesis can never be excluded by suspending the theses of such particulars. Certainly, I can "exclude" this thesis as well, but only by not being interested in it, not caring about it, not making it an object of my theoretical interest. That, however, in no way relativizes the being to which the thesis refers because, as soon as I begin to analyze particular beings in the structure of their givenness, I must again take this thesis as a basis.

The transcendence of the world as a whole consists precisely in that the whole is present, given as a whole, that is, that it can never appear as a particular, that I can never have it "before me" as a particular object but rather can only have all objects, all individual realities, only within its framework. The world is in principle something containing, never something contained. All knowledge involves the possibility of knowing oneself, of self-reflection and adequate self-grasping, as well as grasping that essential "interiority" within which it moves together with other particulars. That, however, also means that consciousness of this whole, prevenient in this thesis, together with its necessity and unshakable certainty, transcends itself. The reduction cannot ascertain anything other than that this thesis of the whole is *my thesis*. It cannot, though, go beyond it, it cannot construct it, constitute it out of other, more elementary theses; it cannot relativize it with a hypothetical application of nonbeing. This thesis would gain no greater transparency by being translated to my *reell* immanence, to mere subjective structure: quite the contrary, the attempt to translate it into a mere thesis without an objective correlate *has no justification,* there is no reason for it, while it deprives the thesis of its objective content—which is something at which we do not arrive from any philosophically grounded argumentation but rather *from the prejudice about the primacy of subjective being.*

Chapter 7

Analysis of Internal Time Consciousness

Even before the systematic presentation of the phenomenological reduction, Husserl and others had already applied methodological principles for building up a philosophy consistent with its formulations. That shows most clearly how deeply the problem of the reduction is embedded in all of Husserl's earlier efforts: (1) in the way in which the correlation between intentional structures and their objects, later assumed to be universally valid for all objectivity as such, emerged for him in abstract numerical and eidetic entities; (2) in the aporia of the whole and the part which is a necessary consequence of a subject that is on the one hand the bearer of *all* objective structures while, on the other hand, it is one of them, one of the structures whose bearer it itself is.

For that reason, the lectures on internal time consciousness of 1905, presented two years before the *Ding-Vorlesung* whose introduction is *The Idea of Phenomenology*,[1] offer the reader an example of an examination of the constitution of basic outlines of objectival quality of a thing without which no individual real object is conceivable.

Husserl starts out by explaining wherein his examination of the experience, the lived experience of temporality, differs from an inquiry into objective, real time;[2] phenomenology sets that time

---

1. Edmund Husserl, *Ding und Raum Vorlesungen 1907*, Hua XVI; the five lectures that make up *The Idea of Phenomenology*, published in a separate volume of *Husserliana*, were an introduction to the lecture course published in *Ding und Raum*. [Ed.]

2. Edmund Husserl, *On the Phenomenology of the Consciousness of Internal Time*, §2, p. 10. [Ed.]

aside as a premise from which it would start and which it would use, though it retains it as a phenomenon which it will analyze in its correlation with mental processes whose being is guaranteed by their givenness. Husserl believes that just as in the perception of objectival qualities there is a difference between sense data and the "conception" which animates them, so, analogously, there are also temporal traits, temporal intentions which first constitute certain givens as a temporal sequence.

Thus the examination of internal time consciousness represents an inquiry within the *epoché,* with the confidence in objective temporal relations suspended; whatever relations may be *objectively* involved in the succession or in the contemporaneousness of two lived processes, the lived experience is here taken purely as it is lived, in pure perceptual evidence with those noematic correlates which intentionally belong to it with eidetic necessity.

In this the investigation of temporal consciousness is analogous with the exploration of the subjective relation to space. Space, extension, are given in changing but regular perspectives; identical distances and shapes appear successively in different ways; the appearance (phenomenon) of the same is not always the same. Husserl expresses this by saying that "the appearance of the house is not something next to the real house or above it"; "it makes no sense to ask about the distance of the field of vision from my table"; etc. (Such images, we believe, need be taken with a grain of salt, for "the appearance of a house" is not the object in perceiving a house, nor is "the perceptual field" in perceiving a table.) There is a difference between a given perspectival view of a table and a perceptual field—a perspectival view is in one sense the thing itself, even though only partially; the perceptual field is never that.[3]

Now the principal question is this: what is the *origin* of time, the origin of temporal succession and temporal relations?[4] We already know that we must not interpret this question psychologically, that is, as a question of the *causal origin,* of the natural, objective factors which cause its appearance in experience, so also not for instance as a question of nativism against empiricism, as the psychologists speak of it (because there the point is whether

---

3. See Husserl, *Ding und Raum,* §6, p. 17: "Assertions about Perceptions and Assertions about Perceptual Objects: Real [*reelle*] Constitutive Elements of Perception." [Ed.]
4. See Husserl, *On the Phenomenology of the Consciousness of Internal Time,* §2, p. 9. [Ed.]

the decisive factor in the emergence of the idea of time is an innate ability, an inner factor, or externally caused sense data).— The question about the origin of time, as Husserl here formulates it, is a question about the *data and the characteristics of intentional apprehension* on the basis of which temporal sequences and other temporal relations appear to us. The word "constitution" does not yet appear in these introductory explanations, yet the matter is already explained: *reell* moments of lived experience, data, and characteristics, some nonintentional, others intentional, are the constitutive elements of a temporal phenomenon.

Husserl's presentation here is divided into three main parts: (1) establishing continuity with Brentano's theory of temporal modes; (2) an analysis of temporal intentionality; and (3) the constitution of time and of temporal objects.

(1) A persisting consciousness is not yet a consciousness of persistence, successive states of consciousness are not yet a consciousness of succession. Retaining in consciousness, conscious retention, is not a retention of the same consciousness: otherwise a melody would not differ from a harmonic coexistence of tones; a consciousness of movement in its successive phases would not be possible but rather would be identical with a consciousness of the successive filling of the space through which a body passes. Those were the reasons which led Brentano to his conception of a fantasy modification of a sense impression in temporal modes.[5] If the consciousness of succession is not itself a sense impression, it must have a different source, and what could that be other than that autonomous activity of the reproductive ability we call fantasy? Besides, Brentano insists, here we have the sole instance when fantasy proves genuinely creative—because a modified reproduction of an impression that is no longer present is something that never does and never can occur in sense experience.

Still, Husserl subjects this Brentanian conception to a severe critique, even though the perceptive analysis it contains first allowed him to pose the intentional problem clearly.[6] The temporal modification by which we constitute an object or preserve it in imagination, even though it is no longer present in perception,

---

5. Husserl's presentation and criticism of the concept of phantasy modification is based on an unpublished text of Brentano's; for a more detailed presentation of Brentano's position on the nature of time consciousness, see Franz Brentano, *Philosophische Untersuchungen zur Raum, Zeit, und Kontinuum.* [Ed.]

6. Husserl, *On the Phenomenology of the Consciousness of Internal Time,* §§3–6, pp. 16–20. [Ed.]

means that A, which is no longer corporeally present, has not passed, but is again here, even though modified. Thus the temporal moment linked to that weakened A is again a present one. For that reason, too, from this new modification we do not learn anything about A *having been* present. The presence of A in consciousness, even with the added moment, the modifier "past," does not account for the transcending consciousness that A has passed, even if we label this added moment "past A." For that we lack the explanation that what is currently in my consciousness is identical with what had already been there previously, even though it is no longer in a present, perceptual phase. What, after all, are the "moments of original association"? Are they times or "temporal indices," analogous to Lotze's "locational indices"?[7] If they are times, then we have a series of contemporaneous times, which is absurd; but, if they are indices, how can they lead us to real time? (Brentano likewise cannot tell us why the index "past" is ir*reell* when all the moments of the original fantasy or association are components of *reell* presence, that is, the very opposite of all that is ir*reell*.—We cannot explain a temporal sequence simply in terms of ever new moments added on to what is given; temporal form is not identical with its content, the form here exceeds its content, while in Brentano temporal indices are essentially only new contents tacked on to the sensory ones. So though Brentano did call attention to the difference between sense content and the apperceiving temporal traits, he never analyzed it.)

In spite of this sharp criticism it would be hard not to notice that one of the most basic traits which distinguishes Husserl's analyses of time consciousness from other contemporary approaches (at the time, around 1900, thanks to James and Bergson,[8] the analysis of inner time was very fashionable) is derived precisely from Brentano; namely, that Husserl undertakes it from an intentional standpoint or, perhaps, from the viewpoint of his modified, dynamic conception of an intentionality striving for a unitary object amid the manifold of lived experience. Thus

---

7. Patočka is apparently referring to the principle Husserl traces to Lotze and which, he asserts, lies behind Brentano's use of phantasy as the origin of the sense of time—i.e., the principle that, in order to be able to be conscious of the difference between the present and the past, thus between a point in time that is "earlier" or "later" than another, a "timeless" knowing [*Wissen*] must be presupposed within which the contrast can be drawn. See Hermann Lotze, *Metaphysic*, pp. 262–63. [Ed.]

8. See William James, *Principles of Psychology;* Henri Bergson, *Time and Free Will.* [Ed.]

Husserl takes over Brentano's suggestion in order to transform it into something wholly original that has no parallel in the literature dealing with time consciousness at the time, enabling him to overcome just those shortcomings which he points out in Brentano—the inability to distinguish the noematic correlate of the lived experience of time from its *reell* components, the failure to notice the essential concern for the unity of the object characterizing also temporal intentionality. It also allows him to consider his own theory immune to those objections which modern philosophers and psychologists at the time (Husserl cites Stern,[9] though he could have with equal justification cited James and Bergson) raised against other psychologies, represented by Herbart or Lotze, objections which apply to Brentano as well: Husserl's conception of the self-constitution of the stream of consciousness raises his views above the "dogma of the instantaneousness of the unity of consciousness"[10] which asserts that, if a sequence of events is to become conscious, it must simultaneously become the object of a relational consciousness which fuses events into a unity. To this Stern opposed his "presentational time" [*Präsenzzeit;* Ed.] which covers the entire objectively temporal interval: in a melody, tones are components of the same presentational act, even though they are successive. In one sense, Stern uses this term to designate the same thing as Husserl's "living presence." However, the idea of presentational time remains unclear. It fails to distinguish with appropriate clarity the objectival temporal sequence, which presupposes a consciousness of the successive phases through which an object or an objective event passes, and the internal self-unification of consciousness itself, which is always already presupposed in the consciousness of successive objective phases. For while it is true that a perceived duration is something other than an enduring perception, it is also true that the perceived duration *presupposes* a duration of the perceived. What, though, does a duration of perception mean? Every duration has an actual and a nonactual phase. Can there be something like a nonactual perception? All this calls for clarification. Will we not fall back into Brentano's aporia which analyzes a perception into present temporal atoms and moments of fantasizing association which first constitutes time as a phenomenal continuum?

9. See William Stern, "Psychische Präsenzzeit." [Ed.]
10. Ibid., pp. 330ff. [Ed.]

(2) These questions already lead us over to analyses of temporal characteristics. This is the most important part of the entire exposition.

Consider an enduring tone. It begins (point 0) and lasts into the present, then it ends and its entire duration flows into an ever more removed past, just as its individual phases had earlier. In this flow I still "retain" the tone (hence the term "retention" for the appropriate intentional moment which accounts for it) and, as long as retention endures, the tone has its own duration, constant in various temporal distances from the actual present.

The tone and the duration it fills become conscious in a "constant flow," in a continuity of "modes of consciousness." The beginning of a tone means that the first phase of the duration of the tone is in the mode of actual presence, in the mode "now." Continuous with it are further phases and as long as some phase of the tone, whose content is made conscious in a continuous coextension, in identity, is present in the mode "now," the tone endures. If some other phase of the tone is "now," then other phases are "before," "formerly," while between the beginning and the "now" stretches the spent duration, the past interval, while "the rest" is yet to become conscious. "In the end," however, we become conscious of the entire tone as past when no phase of the identical enduring tone, continuous in all phases, is any longer contained in the phase "now." The tone is made conscious as the same throughout its duration, lasting through this entire *now* time. As long as some phase of the tone is "now," the entire tone is "live," thereafter it will be "dead," no longer animated by any creative, present "now." Yet even a dead tone continues to be modified: it sinks "into the void."[11]

Objectively, there are, amid all that passes, enduring, that is, more or less fluctuating objects and processes characterized by "modes of passage" [*Objekt im Ablaufsmodus;* Ed.]: present, past, more distant past . . . On the subjective side we have the "phenomenon of flow" [*Ablaufsphänomenon;* Ed.] which is a continuity of continuous changes, constituting an indivisible unity: it cannot be divided into intervals, into phases which could be of themselves, which could be repeated like tones or other temporal objects.[12] There can be parts only as abstract moments of an indi-

---

11. See Husserl, *On the Phenomenology of the Consciousness of Internal Time*, §8, p. 26. [Ed.]

12. Ibid., §§9–10, pp. 27–30. [Ed.]

visible whole. The starting point is the "primordial impression," the point of origination which changes constantly: the corporeal "now" is constantly passing into the past; ever new points of origination replace ones that pass into "retentional" modification, a consciousness of the past, while this modification itself is actually present. Actual retention is not an actual tone but an actual consciousness of a tone that has been. Every actual "now" is subject to the law of modification: retention changes into a retention of retention, etc. In the continuum of retentions every further point is a retention of every earlier one. If we follow a series of successive impressions, we have together with them also a series of retentions belonging to the same beginning. However, because it belongs to the present, each of these retentional points is itself retentionally modified in turn. Thus every later retention bears with it at the same time the heritage of its point of origin and a mark of that original impression which belongs to the same actuality.[13]

Thus we have here a double continuum—an objectival one whose individual phases (points) mutually exclude one another, and a continuum of the flow phenomenon which is a part of the same actuality and has essentially always the same form—a primordial impression with a "tail" of retentions.

With the streaming of ever new "nows" the present phase is transformed into a past one and the entire continuity, objective on the one side, continuity of process modes on the other, sinks uniformly into the depth of the past.

So something we might call a temporal diagram suggests itself.[14] If O is the first point of a given objective process (the start of a tone), P one of its previous phases, T the present time "now," then the line OPT represents the continuum of objectival temporal phases; a line intersecting OT at point T represents the flow continuum in which individual points can receive their intentional indices (of what they retain of the objective series and so make its being or differentiation possible), that is, Tp . . . To. We might say that this continuum is a series of *retained "nows"*; though they are not a presence of an actual phenomenon, they nonetheless "now" actually presentify [*Vorstellen;* Ed.] a nonactual "now" and thereby also their own presentificational phases, etc. If we now connect Tp with P and To with O, as well as any other point of either

13. Ibid., pp. 30–32; 34–36. [Ed.]
14. Ibid., §10, p. 29. [Ed.]

continuum with the corresponding point of the other, we will have the hypotenuse of a triangle which represents the sinking of the objectival phase into the past.

The double continuum of which we have just spoken constitutes in its reference a *field of presence* to which there belongs, in addition to the objective continuum and the continuum of mutually implied retentions, also a limit which may be indefinite but not devoid of content: without it both continua would extend to infinity in a backward direction. This infinity is, in the case of the field of presence, replaced by an *indefiniteness* into which the field of presence passes gradually insofar as each older impression is not only weaker, less distinct than the preceding, but is precisely less definite, less fulfilled with respect to content, becoming in the end a mere "et cetera" in its indefiniteness. The extent of the presentational field is variable, though a horizon of the indefinite always surrounds it; the range of presence depends on objectival orientation: it can embrace a single tone, a melody, a composition, and so depends on the synthetic unification of what we have objectively before us. Even the most diffuse perceptual lived experience which is, so to speak, at the mercy of the impressions that attract us in individual sense regions is nonetheless such that in it passivity represents only the minimal level of active unification, of the active presence of the same I, that is, of the element which fuses impressions into a stream. A synthesis without I-hood is thus impossible; to imagine time consciousness as an impersonal stream in which impressions fuse into some indefinite mixture contradicts its structural character, the very form of temporal experiencing. (In one of his early works, Jean-Paul Sartre attempted just such an impersonal characterization of the original temporal stream, giving his work a strong Bergsonian cast.)[15] As Held emphasizes, a relation to the I, to personal identity, to the self-unifying activity, is already contained in the terms "retention," "lingering," etc., with which we designate the transition from the primordial impersonal presence to the past.[16] The present does not merely sink away but rather escapes *me* and *I* retain it, and that means that I keep it alive by bestowing upon it something of the strength of my own continuity, of my own identical I-ness.

---

15. Jean-Paul Sartre, in his *The Transcendence of the Ego,* actually attributes this approach to Husserl himself. See pp. 39–42. [Ed.]

16. See Klaus Held, *Lebendige Gegenwart,* part 3. [Ed.]

So what appears to us as original presence is a *field*, not a point-like "now," not that notorious "now" of the entire tradition stemming from Aristotle's conception of time as wholly objective, which thematized time as a homogenous unidimensional continuum of objective sequences in which punctile "nows" function as limits. Husserl's method, his *epoché* of the belief in objective time, uncovered at a stroke, in a wholly distinctive manner, the derivative nature of the objective temporal schema and the primacy, the prevenience of an entirely different temporal structure in our lived experience: the original *nonpunctile presence* (which is a temporal field made up of a limiting presentational phase and a living retention, or better, a series of intentional implications animated by a presentational phase belonging to the same objectively unified whole) with the *nonliving horizon of the past.* To that corresponds, on the other side, the horizon of the future which opens another intentional mode, different from retention and symmetrical with it—something of a reverse retention, an immediate anticipation which Husserl also calls *protention.*[17] The symmetry between retention and protention holds only when taken with a grain of salt: protention is not a dimension of what sinks from actuality into ever more remote and indefinite nonactuality; it does not have the structure of gradual transition into actuality from a nonactual horizon; it is not a retaining-releasing to which we are passively subjected—rather, protention means exposing oneself to the world, a *curiosity about the world* which, though it is not a matter of our arbitrary will to do it or to refrain, is yet far closer to and continuous with our forward oriented activity than with retention.—In place of the traditionally objective orientation we thus find in Husserl, with respect to the problematic of time, a focus on the subjectival temporal structures which are unthinkable without an "I," a field of presence with horizons of inactuality which correspond to each other in some aspects but are not in everything symmetrical along a presentational axis.

Without engaging in metaphysical speculations about the difference between spatial quantity and temporal qualitativeness, between spatial repetition and inner temporal fusion, *Husserl, applying the epoché, grasps the difference between original and derivative time;* a distinction similar in this respect to that at which

---

17. See Husserl, *On the Phenomenology of the Consciousness of Internal Time*, §24, pp. 54–55. [Ed.]

Bergson and James were aiming with their conceptions of *durée* and stream of consciousness. The difference between the perspective of the primary temporal consciousness in Husserl and in the two authors cited stems for the most part from the fact that Husserl here consistently applies an intentional standpoint, that is, analyzes temporal consciousness as a lawlike form of object consciousness so that it is not for him a matter of an irrational, undistantiated fusion with the experiential stream within which we would not be able to distinguish content and form, but is rather itself the basis for all *access to objectivity*, a form without which the *constitution* of objects as such would be unthinkable.

Here we first need to point out the various roles of temporal elements with respect to objectivity. It is clear, first of all, that the primary *field of presence* is itself made up of a protentional horizon, a presentational phase and living retentions—therefore, what we call the act of perception (in the sense of sensory perception) involves *this entire field of presence* in which actual presentations represent only a limiting concept. The perception of a temporal object, whether enduring or changing, is always within it; we perceive *the present as well as the immediately past.*

Retention, on which we must focus again (since, according to Husserl, it is retention that primarily constitutes the temporal field), is something quite distinct from an echo of a fading impression. Such fading is an impressional moment while retention essentially *is not* an impression.[18] The preserved tone *is not reell*ly present in retention.

Retention is not a thematization, it is not a consciousness of the object past. Retention does not make the past into an object but rather preserves it nonthematically, just by-the-way; while we live in the present and in anticipation, it emptily retains or, better, de-realizes what is just past. If we ask about the mode of its intentionality, it is an empty nonthematizing intention. Retention is no *act*, no unity of inner lived experience enduring in itself. In spite of that, retention is the indispensable originary consciousness without which we could have no access to the nonactual and so to the past. When Husserl in one place calls it "seeing the past,"[19] it is so only in this sense, otherwise retention is more like a reaching into the void left behind by the impression that has ceased to be,

---

18. Ibid., §12, pp. 33–34. [Ed.]
19. Husserl, *On the Phenomenology of the Consciousness of Internal Time*, p. 33: "The intuition of the past cannot itself be a pictorialization. It is an original consciousness."

replaced by another. Thus there cannot be a moment of seeing in retention, it cannot be an "image" of the past except as an empty consciousness. (Thus it also has no "hyletic moment.")—Retention is a subjective achievement yet is, so to speak, entirely passive; we are not free to retain or not, retentional phases follow automatically upon the original impression. The paradox of retention is that, though it is automatic, as if given, it is yet a subjective accomplishment; though empty, unfilled, it is yet an originary consciousness—an originary consciousness of the nonactual, the presence of the nonpresent.

On the other hand, to retention as an empty consciousness of the nonactual there corresponds the *fulfilled consciousness* of this nonactuality, namely a reflection on retention, making conscious its intention and its object, possibly bringing up again what is intended in retention—a secondary memory [*sekundäre Erinnerung;* Ed.][20] These acts of reflection and memory are possible only because the nonactual, the past, is already present in retention. It is only this memory that makes the past as such an object; here there is a thematization of the past and a real act, a real presentation which, as a real unity, also has a definite duration, and which as an act is a free act—entering the horizon of the past; as free, dependent on my spontaneity, this act also has an "unfinished" aspect—not simply in that everything in it is in the mode of "as if, apparently present" but rather in that the course of memory, of its flow, etc., which presents itself as a reproduction of that former present, is dependent upon a subjective free will and is always tinged with it: incompleteness, vagueness, subjectiveness are inevitable here. And yet even secondary memory is an *original consciousness:* mere retention would never give us the past as past because it belongs to the consciousness of the present—"having the phase which has expired within reach, I live the present, 'add it on' thanks to retention, and orient toward the future."[21] For that reason it may be true that an enduring, temporally extended perception takes place as a presentatification [*Gegenwärtigung;* Ed.] in the automatic workings of the impression and its intentions. However, the object as such an enduring unity, identical in the present and the past so that I can return to it ever again in diverse acts, requires memory in the strict sense; so that for it secondary memory is an originary consciousness.

20. Ibid., §14, pp. 37–38. [Ed.]
21. Ibid., p. 122.

Both retention and secondary memory are thus originary consciousness which cannot be replaced by anything else so that they present their object—a nonactual, decaying, and recallable past—in a maximally immediate, unsurpassable way, and if they do not present it in live presence, it is because it is no longer present-as-lived, because they are presenting it in the only way it is and can still be present.—Protention, likewise, is an original consciousness which cannot be replaced by or reduced to anything else.

Now, as we noted above, through protention, presentation, retention, and memory passes a constant stream intending, amid changes of temporal elements (anticipation, givenness in its retaining release into the ever distant past), what is *objectively the same.*

We need to stress that what is objectively identical are not merely passing, enduring, and ceasing processes and things themselves. What is objectively identical is their entry into the presentational field, animated by the wellspring of the "now." This entry, transformed immediately into a retained past, is likewise retained as identical in all the subsequent process and because the presentational field is present in constant flux, that is, in carrying out ongoing retention in a newly flowing actual presence, the result of this streaming is, on the objective side, likewise an unrepeatable continuum of exclusive presences, of those contacts which can be "live" only once but are subsequently preserved in nonactuality as mutually distinct "nows." The objective series of exclusive temporal places and points is thus merely a result and an objective correlate of the fact that the continuum of internal acts of retention is in constant flux, that it is creatively unique at every moment—while having the same form, a live impression with a tail of retentions, it yet has an ever different content—as we said earlier, it can neither repeat itself nor endure. (Thus the relation of objective time to the subjective flow is comparable to the relation of number to the colligatory act in *Philosophy of Arithmetic:* it is possible only on the basis of and as a result of a "psychic relation," a subjective activity, though here it is an activity without spontaneity, similar to the nonthematic retention of a past impression.) Objective time then expands through lived experience as the access to objectivity in general: "immanent" temporal objects become phenomena of temporal objects in individual experiences, then become intersubjective objects and objects claiming universal validity (physical objects); intersubjectivity extends the objective temporal form so that it becomes universal; for the movement of flowing into the past, which we first follow in our presentational field, we subsequently come to understand as a universal form which characterizes each experiential moment, even the most remote—for even the most remote experiential moment accessible to memory is a certain "now" sinking into the past and is preceded by moments capable of being experienced by others, by our ancestors, etc.—until "objective time" becomes (apparently) completely detached from all subjectivity whatever and becomes a mere physical parameter about whose own objectively transcendent nature various conjectures are possible; in any case, however, even this completely objectified time presupposes a universal temporal form as phenomenon, as an all-embracing continuum arising from the entry of an objective event into the continuum of an indivisible global progression which is our lived internal time consciousness. The basis of all experience of time is thus the structure of our presence, of the living present which is presupposed in all further, more complex and nonpresent time structures, expanding within them, objectifying and extending beyond its most original field, though in such a way that in all such extensions it is the key without which they become incomprehensible and which in turn gives them their inner evident givenness. For even behind the ultimate temporal point, beyond the reach of any extrapolation of subjective experience, there lies the meaning, not explicitly stated but ascertainable in phenomenological reflection, that the *past "now"* and every now, however distant, refers to a form of presence ever horizonally present to us as it flows off; from it follows precisely that the movement of flowing off, even beyond the limit of clarity, cannot but continue indefinitely by a mere shifting of the present, by the accretion of present phases which occasion the sinking of the preceding ones into nonpresence.

Now for that reason the objective temporal form, the form of those phases which are continually passing through the ever new actual present, is of fundamental significance for the definition of reality. There is no reality which would not have a temporal location or locations. The beginning and the end of a reality are at the same time the beginning and the end of its phases, of its temporal location and, consequently, the continuity of time is at the same time the law of the being of realities: the individually same cannot exist in a temporally discontinuous form.

For this reason the objective temporal form, the form of those phases which are constantly passing through the ever new actual present, is of a basic importance for the definition of reality, its constitution is at the root of the constitution of individual objects. Individual reality is a reality within the matrix of objectival time into whose continual diversity of phases all other realities fit in a uniform manner. Where a consciousness of a universal temporal form has not developed, there might be a consciousness of reality as something given, present, but there is no possibility here of going beyond the limits of the present and even less of distinguishing individual objectivity from empirical type. The differentiation of presence, going into the past in active recollection, and the constitution of universal temporal forms are for that reason also important steps in the constitution of reality.[22]

(3) Thus the next task is to describe the progressive constitution of temporal formations. In *On the Phenomenology of the Consciousness of Internal Time,* Husserl articulates it as follows (we are inverting his order):[23]

(a) the absolute flow or stream of consciousness which constitutes itself simultaneously with time;

(b) the constitutive phenomenal manifolds [*Erscheinungsmannifaltigkeiten;* Ed.] of various levels, immanent unities in pre-empirical time (that is, enduring but not yet integrated into a common objective temporal form);

(c) experiential entities in objective time, and those at various levels: the experiential thing of the individual subject, the intersubjectively identical thing, the thing of physics.

For our purposes—an introduction to phenomenology—we need not develop fully this task at which we have hinted earlier, especially since Husserl himself only adumbrated it.

We do, though, need to make some basic observations. First of all, it is evident that Husserl does not consider time as a special object among others but rather in relation to objects of all types. Every object has its own distinctive mode of being in time, its mode of "temporalizing" (except for temporal elements them-

---

22. Patočka's discussion in the last few paragraphs has, to be sure, followed a path of thinking that goes beyond the ground that Husserl actually covers in §§15–33 of *On the Phenomenology of the Consciousness of Internal Time.* For a further development of these ideas on Husserl's part, see the lectures and Beilagen assembled in Hua XI under the title *Analysen zur passiven Synthesis;* see also the essay by Ludwig Landgrebe on these issues, "Passive Constitution." [Ed.]

23. See Husserl, *On the Phenomenology of the Consciousness of Internal Time,* §34, p. 77. [Ed.]

selves).[24] We could say that anything that we can consider to be has its mode of temporality, its place in the order of temporal structures. This order is a continuum defined by two extremes— from that which is primary in all constitution, constituting without being constituted, all the way to objective time, which is a constituted form of reality, and to the ideal unities which are constituted with respect to the totality of everything that is objectively temporal and so are characterized by an omnitemporality [*Allzeitlichkeit;* Ed.].[25] Thus though he does not note it explicitly, time acquires for Husserl a special significance in its relation to what is. Clarifying, explaining the genesis of time becomes a question of the approach to all that is in the world; the origin of time becomes at the same time the origin of the access to the world and to things in the world.

Secondly, it is evident that the entire system of what is constituted, in whatever temporal structures, depends on what originally constitutes, and only this consciousness, originally constituting all objectivities (including its own), can be truly called absolute.[26] Even the "stream of consciousness" on which we reflect and which is constituted in an entirely different orientation than that to the objective and to objectival unities, is already something constituted, for as a stream it surely goes beyond the sphere of presence and is not identical with its reflective moment. In this sense we need to pose further questions, examining especially this unity in which our own living is constituted, our simultaneously nonobjective, subjective, and yet always to some extent "objective" life stream, and this investigation will present phenomenology with its most difficult problems, placing in question the apparently most evident principles and evident givens on which phenomenology depended at its start.

In the sections of *On the Phenomenology of the Consciousness of Internal Time* where he deals with the difference between constituted unities and the constituting stream,[27] Husserl first sets down anew the distinction we have already mentioned: every phase of an objectival change can be transposed into a static duration, every

---

24. Ibid., §35, p. 78. [Ed.]
25. Ibid., §45, pp. 101–3; also, for a reconstruction of Husserl's treatment of the constitution of the *"Allzeitlichkeit"* of ideal objects in the unpublished manuscripts, see Held, *Lebendige Gegenwart,* pp. 49–57. [Ed.]
26. Husserl, *On the Phenomenology of the Consciousness of Internal Time,* §36, p. 79. [Ed.]
27. Ibid., §§35–36, pp. 77–79.

enduring phase into change—while in the "flow" we have a continuity of phases which in principle run through uniformly—a
stream of continuous "change" which has the "absurd" characteristic that it only runs as "fast" as it does, that it cannot be either
accelerated or retarded; furthermore, it is a "change" devoid of
something that changes, and so also of all duration.

Thus the phenomena which make up, constitute time are
entirely different "objectivities" than those which constitute themselves and persist in time. They are not individual objects, they do
not have a place in objective time, and so they also cannot have
the predicates of such objects. Thus it makes no sense to say of
them that they are "now" or that they were earlier, that they followed one another in time, that they are contemporaneous, etc.
We have to say that a continuum of phenomena which is a phase
of the constitutive stream belongs to the "now" which it constitutes, another one to that "earlier" for which it is the constitutive
presupposition. Is not, though, the "stream" also something
sequential? Husserl says that we call it that on the basis of a constituted objective temporal sequentiality; accordingly, we speak, with
respect to it, of actual and nonactual phases; but all that is nothing
temporally "objective," objectival. In the actual present we have
the original source and a continuum of echoing moments—but all
those are metaphors; we have no explicit expressions for it.

So it turns out that the philosophy which set out from the
search for the absolute, apodictic (unchanging) evident givenness
of things themselves, from a wish for the gaze in which they give
themselves in themselves, finds itself, precisely where it uncovers
the primordial origin of all givenness, among such "things" for
which we lack terms and apperceptive schemata, where clear seeing ceases because distinguishability is absent—"we lack words for
all that," Husserl tells us.[28]

Yet that indomitable defender of perception does not give up:
he examines the intentionality of retention which is responsible
not only for the constitution of objectival duration but also for the
constitution of the "immanent flow," that is, the unity of retention itself—retention is not just a retention of the past actual
phase but together with that also a retention of the retention

---

28. Ibid., §36, p. 79: "It is *absolute subjectivity* and has the absolute properties of something to be designated *metaphorically* as a 'flow'; of something that originates in a point of
actuality, in a primal source point, 'the now,' and so on. . . . For all this, we lack names."
[Ed.]

belonging to that phase. Retention thus has a "double intentional-ity," one intersecting and one longitudinal—the former has to do with persisting units, the latter with the nonpersisting flow itself, so that a kind of coextension of itself with itself is implied in it after all.

> Conjointly with the first retention, however, a new "now," a new primal sen-sation, is present and is joined continuously but momentarily with the first retention, so that the second phase of the flux is a primal sensation of the new now and a retention of an earlier one. The third phase, again, is a new primal sensation with retention of the second primal sensation and a reten-tion of the retention of the first, and so on. Here we must take into account that retention of a retention has intentionality not only with reference to what is immediately retained but also with reference to what is retained in the retaining of the second level and finally with reference to the primal datum.[29]

Thus the unity of the stream itself is constituted in the stream of consciousness as a unidimensional, quasi-temporal order. When I reflect upon this special stream, I must first grasp that retentional "before-simultaneously" which is contained in the present phase, that is, the impressionally retentional phase continuum; after that I can go back along its implications and so discover in the constant "and so on" ever further implications which transcend the frame-work of the momentary present. Here the stream captures and constitutes simultaneously itself as well as objectivities other than itself. It is not an infinite regress.

Apparently, the problem is solved: even the stream is consti-tuted, by itself in itself. The stream of consciousness of which James spoke, Bergson's *durée pure*,[30] is not the ultimate datum, but rather itself demands a transition to a more original datum; but that—paradoxically—must in some sense be the same as what is derived from it or, in other words, it must itself *make* itself what it is, a quasi-object, a phase continuum of an ownness, a personal

---

29. Ibid., §39, pp. 85–86.

30. Let us note that Husserl's term *"Dauer"* ["duration"] means something quite dif-ferent from Bergson's *durée*. Though *durée* in Bergson's sense is not quite coextensive with Husserl's phase continuum of retentions, it is nevertheless the conception in Husserl that comes closest to it. However, Husserl does not transpose the continuing increment of internal change directly to qualitative cumulation, as Bergson does, but rather leaves it for the moment as a problem towards whose further constitutive clarification he strives. To be sure, the problem of time whose core for Husserl, just as for Bergson (and James), is inter-nal time consciousness is a problem of *the whole that is happening* which makes possible in it individualities, parts (that is, lived experience of the partial and the particular). [see Berg-son, *Time and Free Will*, pp. 75–139; and James, *Principles of Psychology*, pp. 225–90.— Ed.]

life. (We shall yet show concretely that this self-making, this self-constitution, is no aseity.)

Even though the constituting "is" is the same as the constituted, it certainly cannot be both constituting and constituted *in the same respect,* and if it is so, then the question is what about it makes this peculiar disparateness possible, what makes possible this dual function of the I, without the I breaking up?

Husserl did not deal with this question in any special work but only in working manuscripts. Ludwig Landgrebe, Eugen Fink, and Walter Biemel mention that Husserl was working on it. Gerd Brand and Klaus Held have distilled it systematically from manuscripts.[31]

Already in the sixth supplement to *The Phenomenology of the Consciousness of Internal Time,*[32] Husserl recognized a fourfold concept of perception: perception of a transcendent object; objective perception of an immanent object (not the tone of the whistle but rather a mere enduring tone in its coextensive phases); the perception of temporal consciousness in the "now"; and the perception of the temporality of the present itself (with its phase continuum).—This phase continuum itself, however, is in turn extended, pointing to a quasi-temporal order, even though it is not an order of persisting events. Each such order in which something unfolds in a continuity of perspectives is, however, *eo ipso* already an objectification which again requires a reflection on its foundation, on what makes it possible. Reflection always grasps an object, not the source itself which is at work in it; and yet it inevitably points to just such a source.

All of Husserl's efforts thus far consisted in seeking to show that for the universe of objects, be they material or psychological, in whatever way grounded in what preceded, there is such an inevitable foundation without which it is not possible to understand what their givenness means and thus to place on solid ground, free of the danger of skepticism (that is, scientifically), all knowledge of them—the correlative consciousness of the subject purified with the help of the *epoché* from disruptive transcendent premises.

31. See Ludwig Landgrebe, *Der Weg der Phänomenologie: Das Problem einer ursprünglichen Erfahrung,* pp. 23, 59, 182; Eugen Fink, "Die Spätphilosophie Husserls in der Freiburger Zeit"; Watler Biemel, "Husserl's *Encyclopedia Britannica* Article and Heidegger's Remarks Thereon"; Gerd Brand, *Welt, Ich, und Zeit: Nach unveröffentlichten Manuskripten Edmund Husserls;* and Klaus Held, *Lebendige Gegenwart.*
32. Husserl, *On the Phenomenology of the Consciousness of Internal Time,* p. 117.

Now, however, as we have seen, we encounter the danger of infinite regress which is only apparently removed by the double intentionality of retention, for if retention constitutes both the object in its own sense and the inner subjective stream, it is nonetheless true that even this flow is, in its extension, in a certain sense an object.

> Even if reflection is not carried out *ad infinitum* and if, in general, no reflection is necessary, still that which makes this reflection possible and, in principle (or so it seems, at least) possible *ad infinitum, must be given*. And here lies the problem.[33]

The principle of evident givenness, of the presence of things in the original, requires that the ultimate foundation be before us in the mode of an object.[34] This ultimate foundation, however, is concealed, escaping our gaze, as precisely time consciousness demonstrates. What our glance grasps of it is always already a phase in a stream and that means that it is always already somehow objectified.

If this problem is to be solvable, we must grasp what is most subjective about the subject; we have seen above that the entire identity, the identitive continuity of the personal I (which, here, faces the future, entering into the present phase, and "adds" to it its inactuality) rests in time consciousness, in the living of the present, and that such identity *unfolds in presencing* [*Gegenwärtigung;* Ed.]. We thus need to grasp presencing as such in which the very nature of being-an-I must become manifest.

For that purpose we need now to carry out another reduction within the matrix of the subjective stream, a reduction of transcendental subjectivity itself whose noetic-noematic structure is to be exhibited as the foundation to which the being of objectivity points. If we are to uncover as something given that which makes reflection on this subjectivity and its constitution possible, we cannot take as a premise anything that is constituted: thus we must set aside the stream itself. What we then receive cannot be in any sense temporally extended, not even in the metaphoric sense in which it can be said of the flow of internal temporal phases.

---

33. Ibid., p. 119.

34. Here, Patočka evidently means "in the mode of an object" in the sense of something that is *given,* and which can in turn be *thematized* in general, an object of reflection—thus "object" in the sense of "an empty X" given in perspectives, to the senses, etc. is not meant here. [Ed.]

What will now remain after this maximally radicalized reduction? Nothing other than the *I-in-the-now*, the *present I* with whatever is necessary for it to be I. Husserl calls this protophenomenon the *nunc stans* [*Nuncstelle;* Ed.]. This "standing now" is evidently something of a contradiction or a paradox. "Now" is something that is essentially passing; to call it stationary appears to run against everything evident.

Now this "present I" is to be the basis of every reflection, every self-capturing in the stream. Here, though, the question arises as to whether it can itself be given in reflection. The answer is affirmative to the extent that the reflected I will be undoubtedly the same as the one that reflects, as long as we are dealing with its self-reflection. The question, though, is whether it will be grasped *in its functioning*, in its role of the reflecting I rather than of the I that is reflected upon. And here it appears that the I so grasped is inevitably always also an I which is in some sense alienated from itself. Even when it is the same as the reflected one, something already must have placed itself between the reflecting I and its vision of itself so that it could see itself; it is even clear what interposes itself between the two—the retention of the unreflected, "now"-acting I.

Thus a pure I without any retention whatever is unthinkable. The presupposition of possible reflection is retention, which "prereflexively" generates a distance between the agent I and the I grasped in reflection—or, better, capable of being so grasped, though in such a way that in spite of that distance it does not become something other. At a distance or, as Held puts it, in "ontification," the I remains the same I. The retention which distantiates is thus at the same time one that bridges. Present reflection already explicitly grasps this possibility.

However, if the prereflective ground of reflection lies in *retention*, then how can we avoid a relapse into process, into the flux of internal phases of temporal characters? How can we avoid the monolithic retentionality due to which the whole of our life and so also all of its noematic correlates are, in a way, involved in each of its individual moments, so that our conscious life becomes the *life of a monad*[35] (as Husserl puts it, in a transparent historical

---

35. There are a number of texts where Husserl speaks of "monads"; see especially the *Cartesian Meditations*, pp. 120–30. Phenomenology as a monadology, however, is an idea that Husserl appears to have entertained at least since 1902—a preoccupation which can be traced in the three *Husserliana* volumes dedicated to unpublished manuscripts on intersubjectivity: see *Zur Phänomenologie der Intersubjektivität*, Hua XIII, XIV, XV. [Ed.]

reference) which is a "mirror of the universe," containing, in a sense, *all?*

Husserl's *nunc stans* is called upon to resolve precisely this difficult situation. The philosopher should neither fall into the ontified stream nor, on the other hand, leap out of the reflection which shows that its condition is retentionality. *Nunc stans* is a formulation of this problem which also contains its solution: it is not this nor that concrete "now" and its retention with all its concrete process, but rather the *I-in-the-now in general, with retentionality in general,* is what functions in every moment as the basis of all reflection.

At first sight this does look as if we have reached the ultimate surd in which what we reflect upon presents itself in person before reflection's gaze. It would seem that the requirement of a phenomenological grounding of all knowledge had been definitively satisfied. However, as Klaus Held has shown,[36] all we have done is to petrify the peculiar circumstance that the I cannot be grasped *in its functioning as subject.* The I can be seized reflectively only in its "self-alienation" (Brand), in its "ontification." *Nunc stans,* functioning at the base of the temporalization and the modalization of the stream of consciousness, means that we can think of this foundational I as an idea of a foundation that is constant, functioning identically in all life and manifesting itself to objectival reflection only in its temporalization. This foundation is not a *mere substrate,* a mere bearer, but rather an agent—therein it is fundamentally different from other "unities in plurality." Yet precisely its functioning as such, considered apart from the self-alienation inseparable from it, is not accessible to us without objectification. And yet objectification refers to the objectified, demanding its priority; reflection really presupposes, *needs* this putative *nunc stans.* The I which grasps itself only in retrospective objectification is at the same time marked by the idea of an antecedent foundation or, as Held puts it, "lives in its protention." The I as ultimately functioning is thus *ever future.*

Now it is evident why Husserl at times speaks of the *nunc stans* as "preexistent" as well as why he insists that this ultimate I is not individual. Since in no way is it in time but only *perennially in transition into time,* and since time is the condition of all individuality as well as of all being as it is ordinarily there for us, not only

---

36. Held, *Lebendige Gegenwart,* pp. 148–50.

in the world but also on the first level of transcendental reflection, we cannot predicate either being or individuality of the *nunc stans*. That of course does not yet mean that we could identify the *nunc stans*, concretely functioning in our life, with Spinoza's *intellectus Dei infinitus* or with Kant's transcendental apperception. While it contains nothing individualized, neither is it "solipsistic" and functions in an individual stream or, better, in individual life streams.

*   *   *

In the reflection about time we have before us one of the examples of the concrete analyses of the given in which Husserl's philosophical systematics simultaneously fulfills its program and goes beyond itself.

In his *Logical Investigations,* Husserl started out from the analysis of logical acts which relate to facts in the world; subsequently he supplemented them with analyses of what is sensorily given, with analyses of the region of sense perceptions and their objective correlates. We have seen above [chapter 6] that even the concept of the world introduced in *Ideas I* was oriented by this point of departure: the world in its original sense was our thing context.

In his temporal analyses Husserl penetrated deeper. Time came to appear to him not only as an entity, not only as a special kind of objectivity but as that which makes it possible to transcend the limit of immediate contact with individual beings and establish contact with entire universal spheres and ultimately with the whole of all that is. Time, whose origin in lived experience he investigated, became for him the *world horizon* itself. Here the first great step beyond the original system took place. Though Husserl does not say so explicitly, the original concept of the world, the concept of a horizon and of a horizonal intentionality (since horizons do not mean something purely objective), is hereby transcended and rendered problematic. If on the one hand we have the conception of an aggregate of all existing things and on the other that of a universal horizon within which things count as *existing* things, then there inevitably arises the problem of the relation between the two, their mutual precedence or antecedence, their mutual containment or excess over the other—all questions to which Husserl's ideas and concepts led both him and his immediate and mediate successors.

We have already pointed out the important role of the plurality of temporal levels, that is, of the various modes of the temporalization of time which, as we have stressed repeatedly, for Husserl is no longer a mere object among others but, rather, is in each mode of its temporalizing always the horizon of an entire order of being.

The way that Husserl carries out these ideas in his systematics leads to an immanentization, that is, a subjectivization of being. Husserl's striving for such an immanentization of being seems to culminate precisely in the reduction not only of all objective being to a constitutive stream of transcendental subjectivity but even of this flowing transcendental life to the antecedent I of the "absolute" *nunc stans.*

Actually, we could observe already in the explanation of the concept of time, as earlier in some of the shortcomings of the conception of the reduction to subjective immanence, that Husserl's conception, taken in its concrete content and not in its systematic intent, does not lead to that extreme subjectivism which would follow from Husserl's attempt to base philosophy rigorously on the absolutely evident givenness of a purified Cartesian *cogito.*

In the preceding chapter we sought to give reasons for the claim that the idea of a nonintentional component of lived experience is a remnant of psychologism in Husserl's descriptive conception. Every perceptual givenness points to a perceptual originality which cannot be relativized, whose givenness cannot be identified with subjectival immanence. Certainly, all objectively transcendent content of this givenness, *all that is given in it* and appears in it both as natural and instrumental entities, landscapes, animals, already transcends givenness as such *in a temporal manner.* All ordered reality, all of the ordered, that is, enduring, world is present as transcendent and all experience of it is a gradual and presumptive verification. That is in no way altered by the fact that we can strike out from the world as an illusion only that which we can replace, so that the world as a whole retains its validity: when we explicate the world as a presumption of an order, borne out by practice, we are only testifying to the strength of the belief in the world. That means that our belief in the world is a belief in an *ordered world* and not only in a *given* world that is forced on us. That does not mean that a world devoid of order and yet *given* (assuming that were objectively possible) would be a *mere* illusion, a *mere* dream. After all, not even a dream is a *merely subjective* reality, it is not a *mere* capricious imagining but rather has its own elements of givenness on which imagination builds, even if it is only that somehow negative impression of corporeal passivity which assumes the mask of a perceptual presence of the objects of dream imagination without effort and realization. Even if continuous imagination can present an entire possible and continuous world, it does not yet mean anything more than that *imagining* can detach itself from the foundation to which, as *imagining*, it points to such an extent that, for the one who imagines, the real givenness, on whose basis alone it is possible, drops out entirely; in particular we can deduce from it nothing with respect to the given world in which something else is added to the continuity which is in any case presumptive and dependent on ongoing verification. A *given* world would be a real world even if nothing were verified within it, even if, for imagination, it were a chaos. Just as a given order is no proof of its own reality, so chaos is no proof to the contrary. Even if the idea of a "destruction of the world" were consistently thinkable, it would not prove the possibility of a purely imaginative world;[37] rather, it might be an objectively transcendent world purposefully constructed so as to make possible intending subjects though not the fulfillment of their intentions.

Thus the idea of the destruction of the world cannot shake the subjectival transcendence of the presently given. It is, however, an effective means of distilling from the presently given all the reminiscences and anticipations implied therein. The content of the present is not merely subjectively transcendent but is also full of presentival transcendences. The *world order* can never present itself except through transcendence, specifically temporal transcendence. Temporal transcendence, however, is only possible through internal time consciousness. Thus an orderly world is relative to internal time consciousness, cannot be grasped and verified except on the basis of temporal consciousness (even if with individual corrections *ad infinitum*). Thus it is temporal consciousness that opens up understanding to the order of the world.

The dependence of all understanding of the world order on temporal consciousness does not yet imply that the order of the world is constituted within that consciousness; Husserl derives this

---

37. Patočka is here making reference to Husserl's doctrine of *nulla "re" indiget ad existendum*. See *Ideas I*, p. 110: ". . . *no real being*, no being which is presented and legitimated in consciousness by appearances, *is necessary to the being of consciousness itself.*" However, the reverse is the case: the being of the real world is relative to consciousness. See also Husserl's argument, in §55, pp. 128–30, that this relativity of the world to the sense-bestowal of consciousness is not a "subjective idealism." [Ed.]

dependence from his conception of *being* as a constituted unity, an intentional pole. For us it is not the being itself that constitutes itself in consciousness but rather its anticipation, its re-presentation [*Vor-Stellung;* Ed.], which is dependent on givenness precisely because its meaning lies in temporal transcendence. Presentation [*Vorstellung;* Ed.] does not mean simply standing before our gaze spatially, in the present, but also that which in some way indicates presentation before our gaze, and most important in this context is the type of indication which *anticipates.* For that reason the real world is not a presentation for us while temporality with its horizons and intentionality with its poles fall under the impression of a presentation. The real world however, is tied to anticipations and presentations generally by a lawlike bond of correlative relations between the structure of presentations of beings which include the mode of their verifiability, and the factual being itself. Thus the regularity of its manifestation, the only way it can show itself, that, what, and how it is, *belongs to the being itself, not only to its presentation.* Presentation, however, is necessary for the manifestation of being itself—a being cannot manifest itself, is not intrinsically manifest—a conception of being evident in itself is what idealism seeks to elaborate, but it is ultimately always forced to presuppose some *modus* or moment which is devoid of evidence.

Thus, from the point of view indicated, the importance of Husserl's analyses of time consciousness is not diminished but perhaps even expands into an understanding of transcendence itself. *Transcendence is at its core a temporal transcendence,* it is contact with being, retention, and anticipation simultaneously; that is, contact itself is meaningful only when anticipation and retention weave it into the unitary scheme of a presentation which transcends the present and projects an encounter with being itself *in persona,* though perhaps with corrections in a gradual and unending verification.

Thus on the one hand our presentations—everything that transcends, even if on the basis of experience, the givenness to the schemata of being into which being itself can enter by real verification—things, landscapes, nature, people—depend on a world which we anticipate as ordered and in that sense meaningful. On the other hand, however, if being in itself is not evident, if its evidence depends on the presentation in which the understanding of being, that is, the being of whatever is, is "constituted," lawfully established, then there is no reason to suppose that this presentation might be something other than the very manifestation of things and that the manifestation of things is anything other than this presentation in its factual unfolding.

Thus the world and the understanding of the world within a being who, as essentially temporal—that means, "internal time consciousness"—by its very nature relates to the world, to the totality of all that is, essentially belong together and constitute a unity. It is not possible to separate understanding and presentation of the world one-sidedly to the point of total autonomy. On the other hand, it is not possible to separate the world from the clarity and understanding to which the objectivities within the world on the one hand, the global schema of the world on the other, are bound by a more profound and intelligible bond than a factual connection, namely, by eidetic necessity.

This eidetic necessity, however, means nothing more than the possibility that clarity will erupt in the world, it contains no *total* clarity about it nor the possibility of a contemporaneous and uniform penetrability of its totality. Precisely the dependence of clarity on the constitution of a presentation of beings in the world is not only a proof that such total clarity is not a reality but is also a presumption that it is hardly possible. For the constitution of this presentation is nothing given once and for all, but is rather itself a temporal process, be it a historical process in real time or the genesis of the stream of consciousness itself in internal time consciousness. However, genesis in both senses presents difficult, unmanageable problems which cannot be resolved once and for all by reflecting on the givenness of purified consciousness as the ultimate foundation of all evidence, capable of providing us with a definitive scientific justification, binding for everyone and for all times, of all evidence and of all consciousness based thereon.

It is precisely the reflection on the eidetic nature of internal time consciousness and of the ultimate and all-constituting I, indissolubly bound up with it, that has shown that in the ultimate foundation itself we are not moving towards an ever greater and more evident clarity, but that our greatest insight is at the same time a *vision of what is escaping us*. Precisely the attempt at a radical clarity inevitably bears with it its dark places, dark not only for us but, rather, belonging to the very nature of clarity—that it is not a clarity of things themselves but rather a *clarity dependent on presentation,* and specifically on the presentation of a temporal being (which, as temporal, is in turn in principle possible only as finite). We have seen precisely in the case of the *nunc stans,* which Husserl presented as the ultimate core of the subjectivity of the subject, that a phenomenological, that is, a positive and direct self-givenness of this ultimately functioning foundation is neither possible nor thinkable, precisely because the functioning I is a process and because self-grasping is always a reification of something transposed thereby from a live process into a product, from creative to created, from subjectival to objectival, if it is to stand in the light of reflection.

Thus Husserl's philosophical conception transcends itself also at this point, where the reduction to immanence was to reach its culmination, producing a conception which may not conform to his initial intent but which shows, nevertheless, the possibility of a profound insight lying, to be sure, beyond the limits of a subjectivistic system.

The reference to the dialectical structure of reflection is eminently such an insight. As both Gerd Brand and Klaus Held pointed out, reflection presupposes a self-alienation which is at the same time bridged over, a surpassing of limits which are simultaneously confirmed and annulled; the reflecting being is simultaneously what it sees and more than what it sees. At the very edge of *phenomenological visibility* there appears yet another visibility which phenomenology did not explicitly thematize, even though it is not in conflict with its possibility—the visibility of relations even beyond the region of positive and objectival content—a dialectical visibility.

On the other hand, however, this instance also shows us that dialectical relations cannot be understood simply as the almighty power of an absolute concept which penetrates even where finite mind cannot tread, to the synthesis of all that seems opposed. In the given instance, dialectics does not demonstrate the power of the mind to force a thing to manifest itself where it closes up before finite reflection—for it demonstrates the powerlessness of reflection before its own reality, the impossibility of objectifying a being which is always already *ahead of itself* and which thus eludes all efforts of the concept at embracing it. Dialectics is not only an overcoming of finite intuition but also a recognition of the dark moment in the structure of objectivity.

The dark place in reflection itself is thus the presupposition of all conscious clarity, of all self-understanding, of all self-certitude. The transcendence which the *epoché* had driven out of the world has reappeared at the very root of immanence. This paradox, however, would be catastrophic for the phenomenological approach only if phenomenology were to become fixated on its Cartesian starting point, on the idea of basing philosophy as a science on the exclusive self-certainty of (purified) consciousness.

Phenomenology, with every justification, placed at the center of its studies the fact that things present themselves in consciousness *in persona,* in perception, in in-tuition (though clearly not "intuition" in the sense of an inspired guess!). However, it was less justified in supposing that it could in turn succeed in demonstrating in consciousness this process itself, with the same positive intuitive clarity, as one of the things that present themselves. Here phenomenology runs up against a limit contained in the very conditions of all clarity. Apparently, philosophy can no more be transformed into a theory of a pure inquiry into immanent perception than the classical rationalism of the seventeenth and eighteenth centuries could make it into a doctrine of a priori cognition and concepts. The world cannot be brought without remnant into the light of intuitive clarity; on the one hand, we are dependent on its facticity, on the other, there is the inevitable darkness which belongs to the temporal character of reflection. This temporal character probably also bears with it dark places other than those indicated in the instance of the *nunc stans;* there is the question of the overall meaning of the historicity of our knowing, whether the world might not be *in principle* susceptible to being uncovered only gradually and not as a whole, even though we intend it as a whole and so schematize it.

Still, this dependence and incompleteness of that uncovering of the world, unfolding in time in us as in a historical social aggregate, need not be understood as something purely negative. That neither the world nor our I can be rendered perfectly transparent has also the positive side that both the world and humans belong to each other so inseparably that a separation of these beings or even of some of their aspects—for instance, of the subjectivity of the human subject—is unthinkable. If the subjectivity of the subject is expressed as a *nunc stans,* as I in a constant, stable moment, then that means the subject must constantly objectify itself, transforming itself into an object, if it is to exist as a subject, and that ultimately means, if we look at all the implications of internal time consciousness, that it must become incarnate, that it must be the subjectivity of a *corporeal* subject.

This necessity, however, is twofold. It means on the one hand that only that being can be a subject which in a precisely definite, phenomenologically describable mode functions in a corporeity which it governs and animates. On the other hand, however, this fact of functioning in a body and in a world, without which subjectivity itself is impossible, means something more—it means that subjectivity is *called* to the world. Subjectivity depends on the world, it itself demands the world. We know, however, that subjectivity is in its eidetic nature the clarity, the uncoveredness of the world. The calling of subjectivity to the world may imply the incompleteness of that clarity, but also the "call of the world" to subjectivity, call to clarity. The order of the world is not a mere objectival order, it is not in things and in the way they present themselves to us, as simply given, rather, this order reveals itself, appears and is extended and deepened in its uncovering. The order of the world is not just a unidirectional mirroring but rather a dependence on a mutual encounter, on a deeper appropriation in the context of what was originally uncovered inauthentically, as well as an *authentic encounter* with what there is.

Thus human incarnation and worldliness are accompanied by a call to what is not *given* but must be uncovered, discovered, revealed in a deeper mode. The uncovering and the revealing of the world and of things in the world remains irreducible to the objective aspect of the world. This means that incarnate being is free with respect to the world, that it is not forced to accept it as finished, as it presents itself, but can also become aware how immensely it transcends everything given in that extreme distance which Husserl elaborated in his *epoché*. For the *epoché* is nothing other than the discovery of the freedom of the subject which is manifested in all transcendence, most of all in temporal, presentational transcendence—in our living in principle in horizons which first bestow full meaning on the present and that, in the words of the thinker, we are beings of the far reaches.

Chapter 8

Incarnate Being

Phenomenological clarification of the problem of constitution is not designed simply for describing what we know already. At first glance it may seem that we can learn nothing new by painstaking description and analysis of the meaning structure of the way we perceive and generally the way we live the daily experiences of our life at its most ordinary. The profound significance of such description lies in revealing the *genuine meaning* of these experiences, obscured by the transcendence of our practical life (including our theoretical practice, that is, the merely technical aspect of science).

Take as an example the things of our ordinary surroundings. These are realities we encounter *in persona*. The table, the typewriter, the landscape, the brook, the forest are there before me as themselves, not as represented by our subjective impressions, whenever I perceive them as present. However, for the physicist, who works with purely conceptual schemata, the real world is the world of physics, and that world seems to him related to our "subjective image" of this physical world by the causal bond of neurophysiology. Phenomenology reveals something important, that the thing, the real thing itself, *in persona,* is the thing of our perception and of our immediate practice—as opposed to its mere presentation, memory, verbal allusion when we merely speak of it, without its living presence; the thing with its practical qualities— the road as fit for walking or driving, the landscape that beckons us, the night forest with its terrifying and mysterious solitude, the joyful or the merciless blue of the sky above, these are *the things themselves,* not only their traits or qualities but their "expressive cast" as well, their mutual references, their contiguity of form that makes for the close solidarity of the "appearance" and the presence of each of them—all those are originary characteristics, not "inserted" secondarily into impressions. For things as they appear to us are aspects of the world in its relation to us, in dialogue with us, they are what we meet of the world and in the world, what suits us or repels us, simply what of it we understand and what "addresses us" directly as meaningful, and this grasping of a given meaning, continuing *in indefinitum,* this anticipation which is constantly being confirmed or denied, continuing through corrections, in surprising or tedious but ever ready twists, is the perceiving of things—the most important task in which the world manifests itself to us and coexists with us, continuously, ever anew, ever making a claim on us. The constitution of the thing is this *achievement,* continuous, spreading out endlessly. To say it is an achievement does not imply subjectification because meaning is not captured simply by opening our eyes but rather with "all of our soul"—we know already (from the example first presented in *Philosophy of Arithmetic* with respect to number) that activity is the presupposition for this capturing of meaning, that objectivity cannot become meaningful *for us* in any other way, and yet it does not cease to be objectivity: quite the contrary, it only becomes such on this basis.

Actually, the thing of physics is nothing other than the very thing of which we speak and with which we deal in our daily contact in the prescientific region, after it had been subjected to certain methodological, idealizing, and formalizing operations. The constitution of the physical thing shows us how it comes about— that the point is a higher, stricter objectification, a precision of data and of their identity at which we arrive with the help of geometrization of shapes and progressive application of the same method to qualitative moments as well.[1] It is really not a penetration to another reality but rather merely a systematic modification of the reality present to us. Modern natural science, ignoring the origin of the signification (essentially, the phenomenological constitution) of its object, substituted for it a metaphysical construct of a causal relation between a purely quantitative "true" transcendent physical reality and its subjective image in our consciousness. The body then is a mere part of the external world, an apparatus

---

1. See Edmund Husserl, *Crisis of European Sciences and Transcendental Phenomenology,* §9, pp. 21–60. [Ed.]

in which, for reasons unknown, certain physical processes are translated into a parallel "code" and that translation is then referred to, from the physicalist viewpoint, as "the process of consciousness."

If this perspective, for which meaning itself loses its meaning by becoming a part of a purely objective, meaningless process, is not in truth legitimate, if it cannot avoid psychologistic and naturalistic consequences, then we need a new understanding not only of the thing and of our relation to the thing in perception, but also of the role of our body. It is not simply that the relation to the thing in perception cannot be merely a causal one, taking place among "third person processes"—perception is a process of contact with things in the course of which objectivity acquires meaning for us, and not simply meaning which we would in some sense project onto it, but *its own* meaning, and yet *in relation to us;* taking place not in us but rather *in the world,* that is, in the universal whole of real, that is, temporally localized, being. It is no more than a prejudice to think that the world is full of nothing but physical and chemical processes and that it can be understood only in terms of them. Precisely if physics is merely an idealizing abstraction from the primordial rich perceptual contact with reality, we can understand quite well why in practice we cannot penetrate even psychological relations without taking physical processes and relations into account, and, for all that, that way the inmost nature of transcending grasping of being outside of us will elude us. To physics, the fact that we have a body inevitably appears as the starting point for explaining psychophysical relations, just as that the body is a body-in-space with which we deal by physical methods. Such an approach must in principle miss the point that, even though the body is an object, it is one that has and even is a meaning, can bestow meaning, moves within the field of meaning, and exists only within it.

And so precisely a phenomenology of corporeity, which Husserl barely sketched, though in a way that can provide a basis for further work, proves crucially important.[2] For Husserl the body is what finitizes the transcendental subject, the purified consciousness we achieve after the reduction. "Only by virtue of its experienced relation to the organism does consciousness

2. See Husserl, *Cartesian Meditations,* Fifth Cartesian Meditation; *Ideas II,* §§ 18, 35–42; *Crisis,* §47; and *Zur Phänomenologie der Intersubjektivität,* Hua XIII, which contains a number of the German revisions of the *Cartesianische Meditationen.* [Ed.]

become a real human or animate consciousness, and only thereby does it acquire a place in the space belonging to Nature and Nature's time."[3] Through this relation consciousness becomes the *mind of a psychophysical subject.* Now Husserl considers the body in two basic attitudes: the "naturalistic" attitude which starts with the *body as an object,* and the "personalistic" attitude which starts with the *context* as the correlate of personal acts and motivations.[4]

The naturalistic attitude sees humans as animated bodies, that is, bodies-in-space with characteristics which other bodies-in-space lack but which basically remain of the same type as "thing and its properties." Husserl does phenomenology in both attitudes but his more important, proper starting point is the personalistic attitude: here the actual circumstances on which I depend do not figure as physical conditions but as the whole of my experienceable context, and the relation to it is not merely a causal one but one of *motivation.*[5] Husserl then seeks to show that between physical reality and the world of mental motivation there can be no relation other than reciprocal coordination, conditioning without causality in the narrow, strict sense of the term; that physical causality might itself be merely an abstraction from an originally global and meaningful causation is an idea which does not yet appear in *Ideas II* (which is where Husserl deals with these problems), but which is, I believe, a consistent conception of the relation between the "natural" world and the world of natural science (in the modern sense).

The important distinction, though, is one which Husserl draws between the sensing and willing body on the one hand and the body-object on the other.[6]

Both bodies, the body as a complex of sensing and will and body as an object, are givens of the personalistic attitude, though of course this givenness of the body-object is not yet the physical body but only the basis for its possible thematization.

Husserl now analyzes the experience of the body within the "egological abstraction,"[7] that is, without taking into account the

3. Husserl, *Ideas I,* p. 125.
4. See Husserl, *Ideas II,* §§34, 49, 62. [Ed.]
5. Ibid., §56. [Ed.]
6. Ibid., §§18, 38. [Ed.]
7. For the concept of *inspectio sui,* see ibid., §§18e–f, 54, Beilage VI; in *Cartesian Meditations,* this "solipsistic" starting point is methodologically developed as a "reduction" to the "sphere of ownness." See *Cartesian Meditations,* §44. [Ed.]

things and the experiences of others or others themselves. (Some thinkers today reject that abstraction: for instance, Sartre believes that the experience of the body depends on the experience of the other because it is originally given when the other, who is my object, in turn makes me the other's object.[8] That, though, stresses one-sidedly the role of the body-object and ignores the fact that even in our relation to ourselves we are for ourselves for the most part "the other"). This abstraction is simply a methodological modification designed to simplify the situation and to bring out the primordial components of the experience of the other. Let us now briefly sum up Husserl's analyses first of the sensing, then of the willing body.

The body is the bearer of localized sensation,[9] we experience it as a thing but it is a thing which senses. Sensation here refers to a certain "tactile" sense datum. In the sensation of touching we have ourselves in a twofold fashion: when we rub our hands, we sense ourselves simultaneously as actively feeling and as the object felt.[10] In the left hand, when I feel it with my right, I experience localized sensations. These are certainly different from those in which the left hand is given as an object for the right hand. Thus my body is on the one hand a thing like all others, on the other hand it is felt inwardly and in a localized fashion, in sensations not belonging among the properties of the body as a mere physical thing.

Here the difference between visual and tactile data is remarkable.[11] The doubling we have pointed out in the tactile region, where the given includes not only an object but simultaneously both a sensing and a sensitive body, does not hold in the visual realm. In the visual realm we do not see ourselves, not even with the help of a mirror, because even here we have only an object which is not connected to us but is rather always at a distance. A visual appearance of the one who sees is absent in the seeing. The eye as a seeing organ is given internally in a *kinesthetic-tactile* fashion. This duality of kinesthetic-tactile is at the same time an indissoluble, unitary bond that is the basis for the aesthesiological appearance of the body. The kinesthetic-tactile sphere plays the

---

8. See Jean-Paul Sarte, "The Third Ontological Dimension of the Body," in *Being and Nothingness,* pp. 351–59. [Ed.]

9. See Husserl, *Ideas II,* §§36, 40. [Ed.]

10. Ibid. [Ed.]

11. Ibid., §37. [Ed.]

role of the self-sensing foundation even for the "higher," distantiating senses of seeing and hearing.[12]

The localization of sensation is substantially different from the
extension of the material determinations of a thing. Material
things are in space as unities in the play of spatial perspectives
which present them as the same from different viewpoints, in different aspects. The localization of sensation lacks this perspectival
character; there are no perspectives here, nor is there an overall
coextension amid the diversities of the given. Thus, in sensing, the
body as our own is sharply distinct from the modes of givenness of
other objects. (We could say that sensing our own body is similar
to grasping our own experiences, even though the two are not the
same: the body is something that persists, something that does not
flow with time as a lived experience, but, on the other hand, it
never stands at a distance, a perspectival synthesis has no meaning
for it—it is a *fundamentally present quasi-object*.[13] This problem of
the body also suggests that Husserl's distinction between the
being of an experience and the being of the thing might not prove
tenable.)

Thus sensation as a kinesthetic-tactile region is the basis for the
experience of the body as a body. To be purely visual or auditory,
a subject could not have a body, could not exist in a body as a corporeal being, a thing among things.

Now, though, let us note further that the sensitive body is
at the same time the *center of orientation*.[14] It is the point zero
from which all perspective on things is projected. The body and
things thus constitute a system, a firm structure from which no
component can be taken out. Thus things point to the body as the
center without which perspectives and their synthesis would be
impossible.

Within this structure, the kinesthetic-tactile moment constitutes the central layer without which nothing else could exist: the
layer of direct contact with things, our affecting things is possible
in it alone (though not the things affecting us). The differentiation within the sensory field between the kinesthesiological field of
proximity and the more removed, mediated fields further shows
that the qualities of individual fields are no mere a-rational givens

---

12. Ibid.; also *Ideas III*, p. 5. [Ed.]

13. See Husserl, *Ideas II*, p. 167: "The same Body which serves me as means for all
my perception obstructs me in the perception of it itself and is a remarkably imperfectly
constituted thing." [Ed.]

14. Ibid., §41a. [Ed.]

but are, rather, continuous with the constitution of the sensory field internally, in a way we can grasp. The entire sphere of tactile qualities (temperature, pain, movement, contact) is a region of proximity and of a physical self-sensing in direct contact with that amid which we are set. Similarly, visual qualities, colors, visual shapes, are fundamentally qualities of distance, they are always at a remove; a globally enclosing ever-present distantial datum is evidently not possible except as a visual datum.[15] Here we see before us a field of inquiry into something which, in a modified sense, could be called a "transcendental aesthetics," having to do precisely with that content of impressions which Kant considered essentially a posteriori, devoid of all intelligible, meaningful access.

The fundamental role of kinesthesis shows, furthermore, that the localizing function of the body is inseparable from the *willing body,* the body as the "organ of volition." This does not mean that I can treat the body as a mere instrument I control precisely already *with the help of* the body.[16] The body-as-own is the only object that can be spontaneously mobile, immediately available to the will of the pure I and is the "means for producing a mediate spontaneous movement in other things. . . . The subject, constituted as a counter-member of material nature, is (as far as we have seen up to now) an I, to which a body belongs as field of localization of its sensations. The I has the ability ('I can') to bring the body or its organs freely into motion and to perceive a world by means of such motions."[17] The awareness that "I can" is essentially a bodily awareness. The body-subject is basically what it "can," *is able to,* and, of course, the body-subject might also be *incapable.* However, this inability is something different from the absence of all *dynamis* of *poiein* and *paskhein,*[18] it is a privative mode based on a present potency. Should all ability to act disappear from the body, the body would cease to be a body: it would cease to be.

If, however, the body is not constituted in perspectival views, what does constitute its unity? Nothing other than this unitary, typical effect of the body in its sensory fields on things and the

---

15. Further, in *Ding und Raum,* the constitution of (visual) space is understood as that of the consciousness of *distance [Entfernung, Wendung]* via kinesthetic systems. See §§70–73; see also Ulrich Claesges, *Husserls Theorie der Raumkonstitution* for a detailed exposition of Husserl's texts on space. [Ed.]

16. See Husserl, *Ideas III,* p. 6. [Ed.]

17. Husserl, *Ideas II,* pp. 159–60.

18. "All potentiality/power of doing and bearing." [Ed.]

effect of things on the body. "In each bodily sensation, this sensation is not only grasped but also understood as belonging to
systems of possible functional consequences which correspond
exactly to the way a material reality must experience it consistently
with possible material effects."[19] In this dualistic manner Husserl
expresses the experience of an undifferentiated effectivity conce-
trated in the corporeal "I can" which has a rich structure of habitualities in mastering objects that might enter the sensory fields. The
constitution of the body is a constitution of these constantly available habitualities.[20] The body can thus integrate its activity into
the coherence of the material world without the subject penetrating this coherence in its understanding or, at least, without penetrating to the bottom, to the purely objective component.

In contrast with other material objects and processes, the body
is a center of orientation, the point zero of an ordered sequence
which we bear with us or, better, which we are. All things are oriented to the body which bears with it the primordial spatial orientation of near-far, above-below, front-behind, right-left. All these
topics represent themes for further investigation.—The circumstance that the body is defined in its primary function by its "I
can" and only secondarily by its objectivity also entails that certain
parts of the body are invisible and others only partially visible, as
well as that we do not see ourselves or hear ourselves as we do
other objects, that we do not recognize ourselves in profile, that
our own voice sounds distorted on tape. Furthermore, the bodily
"I can" is a correlate of the bodily "I must," and "I cannot," of
passive yielding and of being integrated into a perceptual field of
action; no "I can" is possible except on the ground of a passivity
into which the possibility of action is already placed and integrated.[21]

The bodily "I can" is the consciousness of freedom. Only
an incarnate being integrated into the rest of reality in a bodilyaes-
thesiological, meaning-bestowing, meaningful field can be free. It
is, however, a *freedom in dependence*. In order to bring anything
whatever about, we depend on this bodily field and on all that
opens before us within it. (This dependence also is what distinguishes waking experience from a dream—including a continuous,

19. Husserl, *Ideas II*, p. 162.
20. See ibid., §29; also Husserl, *Cartesian Meditations*, §32. [Ed.]
21. Thus passive constitution is essential to corporeity—a point which Landgrebe
details in his "The Problem of Passive Constitution." [Ed.]

systematic dream—directly and independently of any putative anticipated order of reality at large.) Here it might then be possible to go somewhat beyond Husserl's own analyses.

The dependence of freedom seems to us basic to a crucially important phenomenon that stands at the center of the fundamental layer of our activity. Our bodily existence is dependent on the objectively significant field also because the body here is not identical with itself as a passive datum. The body is not only the act center which initiates action but is also that at which its dynamics aim: it is hungry or thirsty, it desires air, light, movement . . . It is thus the starting point of an action which returns to it in satisfaction, and the polarity of dissatisfaction-satisfaction lies at the root of *need.* The body is in need *in principle,* not accidentally; it wants to be constantly cared for, and in this caring-for it is always *dependent* on its field.

Thus physical need paces our activity wholly naturally, automatically. Freedom in its everyday form is freedom within the matrix of a periodic demand and satisfaction of a need. Behind this periodic satisfaction, however, lies the fundamental need of a bodily being: the constant, unfading dependence of a bodily being is not something we know objectively but is, rather, a primordial impulse, the primordial "cannot be without . . ." Behind such need stands the finitude of bodily existence; freedom is essentially bodily, and as bodily it is essentially need-ful and as need-full it is finite and mortal. Thus every movement, be it ever so innocent and apparently insignificant, implies the finitude of a bodily being.[22]

The preceding raises a question: when we speak constantly of the body-subject, does that mean that the body—in the sense of a bodily subject—*is* identical with the subject? What is the relation of the subject, in its innermost sense, of the subject as the center of experience, of the living present source of the stream of time, to corporeity?

---

22. Needs have an "instinctual" basis throughout. The dependence of the body in its functioning in its context thus also reveals the realm of instinct. Instinct, though, is a sphere which we need to analyze separately—a phenomenology of instincts is still in its early stages. Instinct, as distinct from an autonomous, active will dependent on its own *fiat,* is that which in activity is not our *doing* as such but rather is that which we encounter in activity as a preceding determination of such doing and acting; while not wholly unrelated to the I, because its satisfaction/gratification turns out to be linked to a massive pleasure or elimination of suffering and unrest, thus constitutes a positive feel of life and of oneself—though in such a way that I uncover in them that into which the I in its deciding and determining is already integrated as a pre-ordained matrix. [See *Ideas II,* §3 of Beilage XII, pp. 349–51.—Ed.]

Modern philosophy has two extreme answers to this question, answers which, though not explicitly formulated in phenomenological terms, can yet bring about an ideal-typical clarification even when applied to a phenomenologically developed analysis of being-in-body.

The first answer is that of Descartes or of Cartesianism generally: the I is a pure spirit which, even though linked in a unitary substance with its corporeity, represents its form, its active component which is externally related to its material counterpart—it is not this substrate, it does not stand on the same level with it; therefore in its normal strong posture towards it can govern it; otherwise it is subjected to it, enslaved by it, becoming unfree.[23] The normal relation of mastery can also be expressed in saying that the spirit, the I, *has* a body, has it as an instrument of its essential noncorporeity and freedom.

The second solution is Nietzsche's: I do not have a body but rather I *am* a body. I am not body and soul but rather body throughout.[24] By body Nietzsche does not understand simply an objectively-physiological object but rather the body-subject. The view that the human being is cleft into the soul and the body is a product of a pathological cleavage in the subject itself, the subject losing the power of its vital unity. The will to master the bodily component in oneself assumes the form of self-hate and so of contempt for oneself. This pathological process and others similar to it must be evident even to the observer and the analyst of putatively "purely spiritual" historical processes.

The question now is what phenomenological analysis has to say to this opposition or what inspiration phenomenological analysis will draw from it.

Already in the first phase, phenomenological analysis discovered the duality of body-as-mine: the body-subject, sensing, actively capable and realizing its possibilities, always preceded by needs and integrated within a matrix of antecedent instincts; and body-object, body sensed and given in distantiating sensibility; body—the original proximate object which is a wholly exceptional, extraordinary "object," and body which is of the same

23. See René Descartes, *The Passions of the Soul*, part 1, pp. 328–48 (in vol. 1 of *The Philosophical Writings of Descartes*). [Ed.]

24. See Friedrich Nietzsche, *Thus Spoke Zarathustra*, part 1, "Of the Despisers of the Body"; also §14 of *The Antichrist*. Of course, Nietzsche's work is full of body metaphors and reflections on corporeity. [Ed.]

order as all other objectivities, body in the first person and body in the third person.

Already this recognition shows how complex and multilayered the problem of the body-as-my-own is. What does "being in body," being corporeal, mean in the region of the subjective or presubjective body? In no case does it mean being an object extended in space or an aggregate of objective processes therein. For the objectival realm includes no *relation of a subject to objectivity,* no possible access to it. In this sense, then, we are not our body. With respect to the body-object we are always at a distance. *Who* is at a distance?—Undoubtedly the one who asks and so already indicates that the connection between the self as the center of vital activity and the self as object is a mediated and nontransparent one: the personal I, the ultimate I of living presence, the free bearer and executor of all life. The I is not possible except as self-distantiating, as free; even when an instinctive action is wholly bound by instinct and passion so that it does nothing but what they demand, it must yet pass through our I, appeal to its consent—and that is an expression of freedom. For the I is not possible except as transcendence or, more precisely, as a dominance in time, as something that is neither at the mercy of the passivity of an inner stream nor scattered through the objective moments of time.[25] On the other hand, however, we have also seen that I-freedom, I-dominance, is a constant transition into an object, that it is constantly escaping from freedom to the other shore of objectivity without thereby losing its inner identity and so responsibility for what it does as active and creative.

To be at a distance, to be sure, need not necessarily mean being differentiated, divided, and separated in its essence with respect to that from which I am at a distance. I can be at a distance from that which I am as well as from what I am not. But only that which cannot be a pure object can be at a distance.

Being at a distance need not necessarily mean being by my very nature diverse, divided, and separated from that with respect to which I am at a distance. I can be at a distance with respect to what I am as well as with respect to what I am not. But only that can be at a distance what in principle cannot be pure object.

---

25. See Husserl, *Ideas II*, §§ 22–29. [Ed.]

However, in the case of a temporal subject such as we are, a subject of a living present which is in principle ever new as on the first day of creation and at the same time constantly passing, even ever already passed into objectivity of some order, subjective being is possible only as corporeal. Its subjectivity is freedom and freedom is always acting; acting, however, is possible only when I have the power, when I can, and I can only when I have a body at my disposal, a body that obeys me; when, that is, my I is the subject of corporeal habitualities. That in turn means that I cannot be only an absolute presence but must also be a substrate of what I have accumulated already; and since I can accumulate only on the basis of an already present definite ability to use a body, we can say that even innate dispositions are *already here* and in that sense past—I can be a free being only on the basis of a past, on the ground of a relation to it. Thus a free being, a free I, is corporeal in its entire substance; however, the primordial corporeity of a free being, capable of speaking of itself as "I," calling itself a subject, is a *subjectival corporeity* on whose basis and on the ground of an absolutely near objectivity perennially constituted in it, there first arises a relation to our own corporeity as fully equivalent with other objects in the world.

This relation to the body, graduated and mediated in many ways, at the same time gives birth to multiform relations to itself and to other things and beings. The primordial I, the primordial freedom is something I *am* in the purest sense of the word, never something I *have*. A free being, however, not only is but also *has* a body *at its disposal,* is in charge of its body, that is, of a corporeal subject and presubject with which *not only* is it never fully coextensive but which in some aspects ever elude it, containing presuppositions, instinctual matrices, situational moments which are never fully *before* us, finally even a purely objectively material substrate which as a dark, naturally causal bearer of its *own* vitality is also in some sense coextensive with me. In all these respects I may also *be my body,* though not in such a way that we could conversely say that my body is my I. My body is I in the sense of belonging with me, insofar as I cannot be without it; I presuppose it, but it is not the same as I—for simply for itself it is only a lifeless abstraction which only *I* make what it is. In that sense I can say that I am my body and at the same time that I have it, but I cannot say in the same way that my body has me and in that sense is my I. To be sure, it is not impossible, actually it is quite normal, for my body to *have me,* to determine me, to be superordinated to me. The reason, though, is not that it would itself in its freedom command me, imposing itself on me—it is possible only because I have submitted my I to it, have lent it to it, have alienated it into it.

The worth of the being of what we have is never on an equal level with what we are—Gabriel Marcel's thesis[26] is borne out by the relation of the free I, the subject body, to the object-body. I am not my body in the same sense that I am a free being; between the two there are a number of steps in which a free being *has within its power* its corporeal aspect in such a way that its inmost being stands above the rest. A self-alienation, a distantiation from ourselves, begins already in our internal time consciousness; it is wholly bridged over in passive, automatic self-awareness; it is no longer bridged over in the subjectival body which, as such, is no longer a lived experience alone but is at the same time a field of potentialities and habitualities which are ever present; and it is the perennially accompanying fact of our life as objectively corporeal formations.

Thus to the question, am I my body or do I have it? a phenomenologist opposes the question: what does it mean "to be," to say "I am" and "I have"? We need to distinguish the sense of our own being, in which I can only be myself, my I, from that in which I might not be fully identical with myself and in which I am also that which I *have* and without which I can have no access to that which I undoubtedly am not and what I might possibly *merely have.* I am then also that through which I pass over into what is alien to me; because this transition is a necessary part of me, I also necessarily am this transition. However, what makes this distinctive construction of my being possible is that I am temporally, that I am a free being, not only extended in time but temporal in my very nature. In this temporality, then, there is also present, as a possibility, a *perversion* of the primordial and normal relation between the core of a free being and that on which it depends. Only a free being can alienate itself from itself, and the context and means of this self-alienation are precisely the intermediate

---

26. See Gabriel Marcel, "Outlines of a Phenomenology of Having," in *Being and Having,* pp. 154–75. [Ed.]

zone between pure freedom and sheer objectivity which is our living
in a body, our corporeal subjectivity.[27]
The phenomenology of corporeity was made possible first by a
radicalization of the reduction (1) to a purely personal sphere,
purged of any relations to others as such—this reduction makes it
possible to understand the building up, the constitution, of body-
as-own as distinct from the constitution of the "objective" object
and simultaneously in an inseparable continuity with it (the
"objective" object is constituted in an unending synthesis of perspectives which is ever subjected to possible corrections and
presupposes a center of perspectives from which individual objectivities and their overall coherence are seen, so that the aesthesiological body and the bodily world mutually refer to each other,
though the experience of each is of a principally different nature—
perspectival mode of experiencing on the one hand and a perspectival architecture of habitualities on the other); (2) secondly, it
was made possible by a radicalization of the reduction to the
sphere of the "living presence" of the original *ego* which, in a
purely personal sphere, marks out for us a region of the pure self-
presence of the I and of its freedom. Only this dual reduction
makes it possible to explore the complex structure of our own
being and of the relation of freedom and corporeity within it.
Only that makes possible the distinction we attempted to carry
out, between the flowing purity of free subjectivity, the body-subject as the center of the habitualities of the sensory field (necessarily linked to a schematic corporeity which draws an ever present
boundary of corporeity, of its orientation, where is my head, my
hands, my feet, my back . . .) and the object-body which is initially present in the third person, given in impersonal sensory
fields just like any other object.
However, the reduction to the sphere of what belongs to me
personally, to purely private experience, reveals not only the difference between experiencing objects and experiencing the body-
subject—it reveals also one other distinction, one so important

---

27. The consciousness of the present I is thus always a consciousness of the I in a
body. That, however, does not yet necessarily mean a consciousness of the body's acts. Self-
experiencing is not always an experiencing of the body: for instance, imagination and
thought are not phenomenally acts of the body, not even of the subject body, though they
might be accompanied by certain corporeal experiences. Especially thought perception, in
spite of the corporeal metaphor, is not a corporeal act. When Aristotle spoke of the noncor-
poreality of thought he meant it phenomenologically. [See *De Anima* III.4—Ed.] A closer
characterization of these realms of "noncorporeity" would reveal in them that the I transcends its integration into a present actuality, thus escaping the field of bodily presence.

that it contains the source of the entire extensive significative dimension which ultimately deeply modifies our experience of ourselves as corporeal beings. That is the dimension of the experience of the other as such, as the other I. In its significative implication, this experience is so deeply interwoven with and built into our individual experience that we cannot reach its primordial nature without radical abstractive operations. For we see even ourselves, in our most ordinary experiences, "through the eyes of others," that is, we are for ourselves roughly what others see of us and in us, what they do or can encounter in lived experience: we are, even for ourselves, a bodily object visible like other things, accessible in perspectives, placed, in principle, on the same level with other things. At the same time, all objects of my experience are given objects, accessible to *all;* neither my perspective nor anyone else's is in any way privileged, objects are something absolute within the relativity of *all* private perspectives. If we now want to reach the originary experience of the other, we must reduce our own experience not only to the sphere of private experience but, within this private region, to the "primordial" sphere, that is, the region of what belongs *to me,* a region within the privacy of the originally given. Only then can we observe the specific experiences by which the experience of the other is built up in significative implications within this primordiality.[28]

In what way is the experience of the other adumbrated within this sphere of primordiality, that is, the sphere of that which is given to me as my own lived experiences and their aspects (my actual lived experience, sensory objects in their modes of self-presence)? It is, to be sure, certain that the other can never be originally given to me "from within" as I am given to myself in actual self-presence. But I am well aware that even my own I, as past, is never accessible to me in the original in such a way that I could relive it but, rather, can in principle be accessible to me only in the mode of a "quasi"-living. Are we not dealing with something similar in the case of the experience of the other?[29]

We shall present Husserl's theses about the experience of the other with a certain nuance suggested by the distinction between incarnate freedom, the body-subject and the body-object, at

---

28. Thus the necessity of the reduction to the sphere of "ownness" in *Cartesian Meditations,* §44, where Husserl explicitly recognizes the radical character of the exclusion of any sense in which the world is "other" or not (only) "for me." [Ed.]

29. See Husserl, *Crisis,* §54b. [Ed.]

which Husserl only hints and which we elaborated above. Consistently with that, precisely the experience of the *body-object* plays a primary role in the experience of the other. Only on the basis of the experience of the body-object do I become a thing among things, a thing on the same level as the objects of my perspectives. The experience of the object-body, the experience of *oneself in the third person,* which is already represented in the primordial sphere, though only as something essentially incomplete and marginal, becomes central in the context of the experience of the other and of his own experiences (including his experience of me, naturally mediated by the experience of me as an object, "in the third person").[30]

In order to understand the way the other being is constituted, the other I in my own experience, we must stress the following:

Life as my own, my own lived experience, is necessarily either graspable by present reflection or given in presentification, in recollection as belonging to the same stream; in that case, though, it is a nonpresent phase. *In the same I, actual presence and presentification exclude each other.* Still, there is something like a *present presentification of the I.* Whenever I see, hear, sense, touch, affectively sense and react to an alien bodily presence, whenever I have before me another organism, another living body in live experience, I have before me—mediated by its image—a *bodily comportment,* that is, an existence in a subject body, and in its case this existence naturally emanates from a realm no less purely subjective than my own. I have in this object an immediate and self-evident awareness of a subject, no less than in my own personal memory. However, unlike with the remembered object in which I conceptualize *myself,* I have here a subjective object which, for reasons cited (that it is no less present than I myself, presently perceiving), I cannot myself be—thus it is another subject, an *alter ego.*

This awareness of the other I is not given in experience as a judgment.[31] In reality it also does not rest on such a judgment, but rather only explicates a judgment, making it evident why the experience of the other as such is nothing absurd, which a living continuation of its syntheses could deny, but rather contains the matrix and the rule of its own possible verification and falsification. Where the ongoing experience of the live personal comport-

---

30. See Husserl, *Ideas II,* §§42–47. [Ed.]
31. See Husserl, *Cartesian Meditations,* p. 111: "Apperception [i.e., of another ego] is not inference, not a thinking act." [Ed.]

ment of the other, manifested in bodily appearance, is confirmed, we have before us a real organism as distinct from a mere appearance of an organism which "only looks" like one (a mannequin, an image, an illusion).

Husserl's conception of the experience of the other is thus in no sense a variant of the empirical conception which considers "empathy" a *judgment on analogy with our own lived experience*. In the first place, the *other* I is, for Husserl, an entirely original subjective structure which belongs among the fundamental modalities of subjectivity as such, just like the *I of lived presence and its objectification* in immediate and mediate memory. We could say that Husserl's entire analysis is an elaboration of this *idea of "thou-ness"* and of the way it is realized in our experience.

Another moment requiring some clarification has to do with the way this modality of subject being is realized. The experience of the other person, the realization of "thou-ness," presupposes the experience of oneself both *in the first and in the third person*. For the entire "projection" of subjectivity or, better, the verification of the idea of "thou-ness" in experience, presupposes the presence of something *in which* thou-ness, the second subjectivity, is presented and which itself is not subjective; for *subjectivity given in living presence* is mine, whereas *presentified* subjectivity is alien: the presence of the other as such in me must thus be nonsubjective; and if it comes about by my understanding it as an inverted, mirror image of my own external appearance, then this external appearance must be given even to me as something a-subjective—that is, it must take place in the manifestation of my *object-body*.

Husserl considers what he calls "appresentation" to be the primary, indispensable level of the manifestation of the other.[32] Appresentation is a type of association, initially wholly passive, with which the objective appearance of my subjective body, body as acting and comporting itself in given situations, automatically naturally associates itself with an analogous appearance of the second person: the hand with which I act and the hand with which I do not, the feet on which I walk and those on which I do not, the voice I emit and voice I do not. To be sure, the perspective of these objects is also different: appresentation associates them in this diversity and in spite of it. *This, however, would be impossible were I myself not given to myself as an object, as a body that exists in*

---

32. See Husserl, *Ideas II*, §44; *Cartesian Meditations*, §52. [Ed.]

alienation. Here then is the deepest, "transcendental" significance of objective corporeity—it is the locus on which the realization of thou-ness can build. The first and the third person are the inner presuppositions of the realization of the second person. The second person in its significance as person is derived from the first person, in its verification from the third person. Conversely, it will also turn out that if we are in the world also as a thing among others, on entirely the same level with what is verified in continuing syntheses, then it is thanks to the second person who perceives us in such an objective way and whose standpoint we accept by bringing the experience of the other in a synthesis of coextension with our own; the other being—other beings—objectify us ourselves together with all else—the world thus becomes a world for all, a world with a common validity, and within that matrix our subjective lived experience together with our bodily subject becomes mere "internal perspective" on the objective organism.[33]

At this point, however, Husserl carries out an important operation which is a special, transcendental parallel of this radically objectifying role of the second person, making everything subjective worldly and placing it in the power of the world. This radical objectification is accompanied by a self-forgetting, a forgetting that the other I is a constituted formation, a construct which presupposes a deeper, radically subjective layer. This self-forgetting has to do with my own I of the first person in which we already uncovered the transcendental subject by the reductive procedure. The uncovering of the transcendental subject in oneself leads to the recognition of the primacy of the first person. However, this recognition of its primacy, if it is consistent, must be not only a

---

33. This comment concerning the necessity of the objective body for the experience of the other as such, together with the explanation of self-objectification in the experience of my own body as an object in the experience of the other, shows that it is not really possible to present all of the experience of the other on the level of the I as reduced to subjective immanence. Such a reduced I is pure subjectivity; as such, it can have no common ground with another trait of subjective life. Constitution of the other I, however, presupposes that I and the other I are not wholly isolated streams but share a common terrain. This common terrain cannot be the mere phenomenon of my body—that is still strictly private—but only the object-body. Thus we need to admit that, if the experience of the other is really to be analyzed in its intentional components, it cannot take place entirely in the sphere of subjective immanence. Thus the structure of intersubjectivity is another reason for rejecting the reduction towards purely subjective immanence. In our interpretation, however, it is not the ultimate role of the *epoché* and reduction to create a sphere of a self-sufficient pure immanence, but is rather a new way of posing the question of the meaning of the world, the question of the meaningful role played by the world—a role the world can play only if it is essentially drawn into intentional structures quite apart from their being contingent or necessary in terms of the evident givenness of their being.

recognition of the primacy of *my own* first person but rather of any first person whatever, of all: it must lead to the recognition that the other I is not possible as only the idea of a certain object verified in successive experiences but, rather, exclusively *as I,* that is, as a functioning subjectivity in the first person, that is, ultimately, also as a *transcendentality.* If the way from the I as source and as free to the *monad* (that is, to the concrete unfolding of the I in the field of its experience of the world) is a necessary, internally logical progression, then we need go further still and recognize that I cannot posit only my own monad but a *transcendental universum of monads,* each of which is its own originary, free source. And that means that I may not reduce only my own private perceptions and intentions, my own faith in the world, but must, together with it and in it, reduce also the world experience of others, accepted into my own belief in the world and contained within it: I must carry out an *intersubjective reduction* and thereby extend subjectivity, this originary first person, into an entire plurality of first persons who, in mutual interplay and contact, carry out their constitutive syntheses.[34] All objectivity whatever and with it all constitution of meaning and meaning structures must then be related to this transcendentally monadic universum. Only here do we encounter the ultimate surd to which the question of foundation, of the demonstrative meaning of all experience, has led.

At this point we need to recall certain reflections about the nature of the reductive process in its relation to reflection which Husserl elaborated in the critical effort at a phenomenology of the reduction, especially of the reductive *epoché.*[35] Husserl did not rest content with the "Cartesian" way to a purified transcendental consciousness with which we are familiar from our earlier exposition.[36] The Cartesian way through a critique of knowledge of the world and of its evident givenness, as he presented it in *Ideen I,* has a number of shortcomings.[37] This approach to the transcendental region gives the impression of a loss (of the world and knowledge of it), furthermore, this approach does not achieve full subjectivity (in particular, it does not attain those modifications that now

---

34. See Edmund Husserl, *Erste Philosophie II: Theorie der phänomenologischen Reduktion,* Hua VIII, pp. 169–92. [Ed.]
35. Ibid., p. 40. [See also Ludwig Landgrebe, "Husserl's Departure from Cartesianism."—Ed.]
36. See chapter 6 of this text.
37. Iso Kern, *Husserl und Kant: Eine Untersuchung über Husserls Verhältnis zu Kant und zum Neukantianismus,* pp. 189ff, especially pp. 202–13.

interest us, modifications in contemporaneous presence), stopping
short with a "solipsistic" self-consciousness and not achieving even
this own-subjectivity in a full apodictic sense which would meet
the demand for an apodictic critique of knowledge, because the
temporality of consciousness stands in the way; we have seen
already, in the analysis of internal time consciousness, the difficulties of the last radicalized reduction which, after all, was the most
likely candidate to satisfy the requirement of apodicity, yet its
result is only a substantive latency of the ultimate originary I.

However, we can find and trace yet another path to the
absolute lived realm of subjectivity, one independent of objectivity.
Husserl seeks to point out the distinctiveness of this way by analyzing the idea of *interest,* in turn placing the analysis of interest
which he in turn places in the context of the recognition of the
constant self-conflict that is a part of the nature of the life of our
I.[38] The "I" is always in some sense also someone other. The I
acts; that means that all taking of position, all knowing, valuing,
practically deciding standpoints belong to it; however, already this
range of attitudes it can assume as the same I shows that it cannot
live simultaneously in all of them and that assuming different attitudes represents its partitioning. This partitioning can be such that
while the acting (and nonobjective, functioning) I might not be
assuming a certain stance at this moment, neither does it distanti-
ate itself from it already by not living in it; nonthematically, I can
continue to agree with that I which I do not happen to be at the
moment, whose role I am not exercising when I pass over from
the attitude of cognition into one of valuation and vice versa.
However, it is also possible that the I might assume two conflict-
ing postures: in simple perception a skeptic assumes or practices a
naive belief in the world which he does not share but rather rejects
in a philosophically reflective attitude. Thus the I can even reject
itself in various attitudes and live in opposition to itself and especially reflection, the great domain of self-division, is fecund in such
situations. So, for instance, every memory is a self-objectification
and a self-pluralization, for to remember something means to
remember oneself (nonthematically) together with the thing, the
self that lived that past event (for memory is a quasi-presence), if I
thus hold in memory my past I, I can assume a critical view of

---

38. See Husserl, *Erste Philosophie II,* Hua VIII, pp. 92–111. See also Landgrebe,
"Husserl's Departure from Cartesianism," in *The Phenomenology of Edmund Husserl,* pp.
103–17. [Ed.]

myself as past, as the I of my past memory.—Therefore, however
the subject is partitioned by standpoints and presentifications
(here we see that our life becomes partitioned and pluralized the
moment it steps over the bounds of living presence), it yet remains
one with itself, it is ever the same I-as-own reflecting on itself,
moving from latent to overt, criticizing or agreeing with itself.
The normal case, to be sure, is that the reflecting I is not only subjectively the same as the reflected I, but also that the reflecting I is
even *drawn* by the reflected I into its own attitudes, taking them
over. But even when it does not accept but criticizes them, there
remains through all the differences of attitude the identity of
interest. Thus for instance the skeptics do not agree with the naive
perceptual I in its belief in the world but rather deny it—yet that
means that they are still interested in the *positing of the world,* that
their criticism is guided by this interest. Interest means a unity of
ends; intentional activity which has the same goal manifests a unitary interest, for instance an interest in knowing the world, in
knowing things as they are in themselves, as distinct from a valuing or a practical, active interest.

Thus, in sum: every act is rooted in a certain *posture* guided by
a defining interest, that is, by a *goal* which marks out the relevant
background to the act; though the goal need not itself be the
"theme" of each individual act, the object intended in it—as, for
example, if a particular act is only a subservient, instrumental act
towards achieving the main goal—yet the theme of the primary
act still helps define the mediate, instrumental act.

Now we can say that the inevitable internal division of the I in
its various attitudes presents a certain philosophical possibility
which we can use in service of the *epoché* and of its clarification
from a new perspective. If we define the attitude in which naive
consciousness lives in the world in terms of the interest in what
there is, the world in which a worldly thinker and even a skeptic
both live, then we can also define an attitude from which all interest in and focus on the knowing of such existing beings have been
removed. It does not cease to be real for reflected consciousness,
but for reflecting consciousness it has not the least significance,
reflecting consciousness does not identify with it in the least but
rather maintains an absolute abstaining distance with respect to its
attitudes. By contrast, this reflecting consciousness in no sense
loses *all* cognitive interest, though its interest does not concern
knowing the objects in the world with which reflected consciousness

is preoccupied: it has to do exclusively with the reflected consciousness which as such becomes its thema. The interest of a reflecting thinker concerns exclusively thematized consciousness so that, with respect to the interests of reflected consciousness, the thinker becomes a pure disinterested observer. With that we have reached a definition of the *epoché* in purely psychic, internal terms without involving the problems of evidence and transcendence. Now the intent is to elaborate an entirely new mode and region of a consciousness for which, in contrast with the worldly I, the world and all the theses connected with the thesis of the world have no validity; clearly, a realm of consciousness so understood is truly virgin ground on which no one has yet trod because the thinkers who devoted themselves to an empirical inquiry into consciousness did not know the *epoché* while philosophers like Fichte, Schelling, and Hegel, who do suspend the thesis of the validity of the world (which they take not as something given and preexisting but as something constituted in absolute consciousness), do not engage in a reflective analysis and observation of the conscious process in a purified empirical experience.

Husserl originally thought that the *epoché* thus defined can best be demonstrated first on individual acts, though he soon realized that the *epoché* is indivisible, having to suspend not just interest in individual acts of the observed but the entire natural attitude with all its habitualities and horizons; nor that only: it must be applied consistently down to all subjective attitudes with their modalities which occur in experience. There is no modification of the subject, arising from the division of the I living in the diversity of its temporal possibilities and attitudes, that would not or need not be in principle affected by the modification of the *epoché*—only thus can we reach the universum of purified consciousness and not consciousness in a state of mere objectification. Even the I of memory and of fantasy can be subjected to such reduction. The fantasy consciousness, focusing its interest on its own fantasizing activity, can refrain from taking interest in its doxic acts—or, more accurately, in its quasi-doxic activity which it lives, in its fantasy-generated context, as if it believed it. Unbiased by such interest, it can then grasp such activity in full concreteness. The same is true of the presentified acts of another I which can be treated as not interesting in terms of their own content and so can become interesting solely with respect to their own inner processes.

The intersubjective reduction seems paradoxical and was also the most attacked among all of Husserl's constitutional analyses.[39] If the intersubjective reduction is to contribute to the constitution of a pure universum of subjectivity which *"nulla re indiget ad existendum,"* which needs no thing to be in the sense that even its intercommunication is possible without any objective bridge whatever, then we need to observe, with Alfred Schutz, that Husserl has demonstrated nothing of the sort anywhere in his known writings and that it has a strong tinge of the unthinkable. It is something else, however, if this reduction represents, as we have sought to show above, a reduction to a sphere of indubitably evident being. That turned out to be *being in presence* which was, on the one hand, the subjective givenness of external facts in the perceptual field and, on the other hand, the givenness of the subject with its noematic structures, adumbrating the frameworks of possible experience; ongoing through corrections. On our interpretation, the common unifying structural bond of the two is the temporality of the originally corporeal subject. Though this subject depends on objectivity, it is, for all that, a free subject: its freedom is manifested precisely in that, within its dependence and no less for it, it is *capable of truth,* that is, that nothing external stands between it and its object, between it and the world; for all its *factical* dependence and finitude, it has a direct relation to the object, to meaning, to truth, not a causally dependent one; thus a relation to meaning, to truth; truth is, for that subject, a matter of seeing, an object, and not a mere fact, swaying and manipulating the subject. This freedom manifests itself precisely in the *epoché* and in the reduction to the indubitable, that is, to what is seen as present. From this viewpoint, the intersubjective reduction, that is, the reduction of those modalities of I-ness which are capable of expanding the sphere of present experience indefinitely beyond my privacy, has the significance of a reassurance by that freedom even beyond the sphere of my personally present I to wherever there exists any being whatever that is capable of calling itself an "I." For what else is the reduction than the experience of self-assurance by the recognition that the I cannot lose its object *dum quassus illabatur orgis?*—that its relation to the object, essential for the understanding of things, is not a relation dependent on the facticity

39. Alfred Schütz, "The Problem of Transcendental Subjectivity in Husserl."

of the world? And what else is the intersubjective reduction than the reassurance that anything that calls itself "I" cannot be wholly alien, that, for all that separates it, it is not hopeless to attempt to approach another, to address one another, to understand another even if it were the understanding of the most extreme opposition and of the deepest enmity? In principle, no I stands outside the possibility of communication; no I is isolated, each is in its way only an inflection of all others as all others are inflections of its own.

In this sense we can consider the intersubjective reduction, as a part of the problem of thou-ness and of other subjective structures, a most important topic after all.

Now, though, we must take another look at that part of the intersubjective experience which Husserl finds so uncomfortable and which causes him difficulties; namely, the objective component—the body-object in its relation both to the I and to the other I.

For, undoubtedly, intersubjective communication takes place *solely by means of the body-object;* therein may lie the most essential role of corporeity, namely, that it is the medium of sociality. We surely need not emphasize how immensely indispensable sociality is to the life of humanity.

In appresentation, in the grasping of the other I as presently acting in an other organism, analogous to my own, the duality of *place* plays an important role. "I" is indissoluably linked to a "here," "thou" is equally linked to a "there" as the place of a central, thematic object. The place of the "thou" is an objective nearness in the original sense of the word; as soon as the "thou" no longer occupies it, as soon as it is also no longer in the "quasi-nearness" of a conceptual modification, it passes into a "her," a "him," or an "it," into the third part of the spatial structure of present-absent, passing gradually, unnoticeably into the unfilled spatial horizon.

The place of the "thou" is, as we have said, the optimal spatial nearness. That in itself means that the "thou" is originally perceptively present. However, the meaning of the second person pronoun is not merely *presence,* for even in the optimum of presence the second person can also be a "s/he." The nearness of the other in the situation of "thou" is transformed into *communication,* that is, into the community of activity in various modalities, in the modes of "together," "mutually," "against each other." Evidently the place of the other is the optimal nearness, because therein each thing is for perception fully what it is, in that place it does not fuse with anything else and has the least in common with the undifferentiated background to which the "it" leads.

Proximity-remoteness is a spatial structure which is essentially transferable: as soon as I pass over to where "thou" are, my present "here" will be for me "there" and vice versa. Proximity-remoteness as such, however, remain; the objectivity of the shared place extends through this polarity, independent of proximity-remoteness and manifesting itself in them. Proximity-remoteness is a structure through which alone the distance in the third person can become manifest, a distance independent of the subject. However, there is definitely a remarkable agreement between those spatial characteristics linked to objective corporeity and the primordial structure designated by the personal pronoun: "there" in the sense of proximity is definitely never as fully proximate as it is in communication. Thus "there," in the sense of that indispensable "ground zero" which represents a fixation of my standpoint, is indissoluably bound up with the *I*.

We can say that the condition of communication as well as of apperception of the other as such is the structure of place marked out by the duality here-there-over yonder, paralleling the I-Thou-he/she/it. Only in and through them can objective extension be given as something neutral with respect to them, untouched by them but capable of presenting itself (perspectivally) only through them. All objectivity with which we can have perceptual contact must enter into this spatial structure. It is an objectival structure, even though not an objective one. However, objective spatial structure, again, is in a different way something without which communication would be impossible: it is what is common in the reciprocity of two objectival situations, taken for granted as the common denominator of their co-presence and their mutual correspondence.

Under these circumstances—as a factor making communication possible—objectivity, that is, not mere objectness but common objectivity independent of situation, objectivity "in itself," begins to make sense. Objectivity is the context of communication and, as context, it is integral to that bestowal of meaning which takes place in the subject sphere. Could we not approach the problem of the meaning of this objectivity, the meaning of objective syntheses? Are not objective unities falling under the regional *eidos* "objective concretum" unities precisely with respect to communication? Is not the guideline according to which our universum is constituted—its categories, after all, make up the structure of the world—precisely the community in which we exist, and are not anticipatory steps of communication reflected in all the object-syntheses?

Husserl posed the problem of access to the world anew by showing how every object which becomes a pole of our intentional activities has its horizons into which experience enters, how these horizons, no less than explicit concrete objects and their aspects, have their significative references, implications, coherence, and how the world is adumbrated in these horizons as the ultimate collective horizon containing all others within itself. The world as horizon, however, is a world defined from a viewpoint which may be objectival, dealing with objects, but which is not itself objective; it is a world-perspective, world as it proves to be an indispensable margin persisting in all givenness and its transformations, just as horizon as such persists in all the stream of experience, in the changes of local horizons. Perhaps, though, that is true even of a world in the strong sense of the word: of the world as the aggregate of all realities, the sum of all that can be included in the unity of objective temporal sequence (however we define this flow in its concretely objective form in the objective sciences), can be equally thematized in the context of that fundamental question of meaning, of significance which is elaborated by phenomenology.

Only, this question must not be posed on the wrong grounds and in the wrong way. If it is to be elaborated without producing nonsense, we need to trace out the internal structure (we might also say the "logic") of those meanings through which our experience *is,* and, correlatively, the objectivities which in principle belong to it. That means that we must start working on it from the beginning, from the first elements of meaning, and not from the completed schemata of a world picture as it is presented to us in the complex, polished, and extensive secondary conceptions of the objective sciences.

Precisely the question of the foundation of such objective sciences can and must first be developed through this "logic of experience." That will show that here a mere formal analysis of first concepts and principles, of their possible unclarities, antinomies, and inconsistencies, is not enough. However, this grounding, which is all of which "natural" reflection is capable, demands a further, more radical reflection which will demonstrate initial concepts and axioms of the appropriate discipline in their correlation to the subjective lived experience in which they are accessible and can be demonstrated. Here the way leads to the actual genesis of their meaning by pointing to the prescientific sphere of experience which scientific concepts always in some way presuppose, which they make precise and which they objectify. That is how we can and must proceed in grounding the most basic, most general disciplines, in the logic of general meaning and formal ontology, that is how we need to proceed in other ontologies as well. For only by clarifying the transition from the prescientific sphere to science can we eliminate those opaque aspects, those metaphysical and generally prejudicial presuppositions which these disciplines tend to have in common awareness and which share the blame for their often critical situation.

All positive and objective disciplines thus presuppose a world which is in a certain sense already complete, functioning, ever valid for us, a world which is not the product of theoretical activity but precedes it; a world which not even scientific thinkers ultimately leave wholly behind, even though with the help of their abstractions, idealizations, and other operations yielding precise and effective concepts they move on a theoretical level, for they move also in that preexisting world as human beings and as the verificators of their conceptions. A description and an analysis of this original "natural world" or the world of our life are thus the common desiderata for the philosophical grounding of all science, both natural and social. Until this need has been met, we shall not be able to carry out either a genuine clarification of the foundations of the sciences or present the history of their meanings and ideas.

However, even though phenomenological descriptions and analyses have contributed to this task in numerous ways, as a whole it not only has not been mastered—it has not even been started. Husserl defined it in this basic role in his last, unfinished work.[40] This task itself is in turn only a prolegomenon to the subjective analysis itself, to the radical reflection which will investigate all the subjective structures, references, and connections in which

40. Husserl, *The Crisis of the European Sciences and Transcendental Phenomenology*. [A number of new texts have recently been published in a volume of *Husserliana* under the title *Die Krisis der europäischen Wissenschaften und die transzendentale Phänomenologie: Ergänzungsband: Texte aus dem Nachlaß*—Ed.]

the corresponding objectivity is given. Here our gaze need follow
not objectively positive structures, but rather the achievements of
subjective life. Thus this approach to the foundation actually
becomes another, third grand way of the phenomenological
reduction. For those who investigate the origin of objective structures, their necessary interrelation with subjective processes, must
not use those objectival theses under investigation as premises,
and consequently must carry out their entire reflection on the terrain of the *epoché*.

The task of ascertaining the place and constitution of all meanings thus leads to a preobjective "life"-world as to the native
ground of "pure" objectivity. This "natural world" or "world of
human life" is what should be described and analyzed;[41] it would
not be right to consider all the perspectival and other analyses
which Husserl presented in *Ideen I* and *Ideen II* as already a
description of this world, even though they are undoubtedly a
contribution to it. For even though they move within its matrix,
they do not thematize it directly *as a matrix*. This preobjective
world has precisely its own structure as world and matrix, its typical horizonality, its essential "situatedness," and that means basically that, as essentially situational, this world is basically a world
of acting, doing, deciding, working, and whatever else we can call
such modalities. Husserl managed only to adumbrate such problems, there are even numerous analyses, but they are certainly not
exhaustive and perhaps not even always central.[42]

What we could call the historical destinies of humans unfold
within the matrix of this situational practical framework. For
Husserl, this historical dimension of being human is linked with
the idea of a gradual objectification of the world in which the
world of individuals and of narrowly defined communities
becomes a common world for all. It cannot become this world for
all automatically—passively. Even though the passivity of the natural world always remains the basis of all the conceptual arsenal,
the fact is that in history there emerged, under certain circumstances, a new goal, a new idea, and with it a new possibility—the
possibility of humans actually taking over their conceptual universe and accepting responsibility for it, that is, to subject all its

---

41. See Husserl, *The Crisis of the European Sciences and Transcendental Phenomenology*,
§51. [Ed.]

42. See especially Ludwig Landgrebe, *Der Weg der Phänomenologie: Das Problem einer
ursprünglichen Erfahrung*, pp. 41ff.

meaningful relations to radical testing.[43] That is a new level of clarity and rationality, which does presuppose clarity, transparence already in the preceding world, though one that is not sufficient unto itself and calls for a further, deeper, specifically a universal clarity.

However, as we have had the opportunity to note frequently, this "call for" a further and deeper clarity is grounded in all experience. *An experience is a reference to a further experience.* It is a constant return to the same in ever new ways. The significance of time as a primordial horizon might be precisely that it makes something like this possible. Within the framework of the fundamental structure of temporality we return, through a constant renewal of being, to where we had been, building upon it. Thus in the given we find what we need for further progression. That means that, even in the most unusual undertakings, the ground is already prepared for us. Prepared ground represents a means to an end. Experience is thus teleological throughout. We have seen how experiences of perspectives, of proximity-distance, and of the "other" presuppose one another so that it is difficult to separate distance from personal pronouns which stem from the region of intersubjectivity: all of that reveals the teleological references in our lived experience, the fact that certain achievements are "pre-constituted" in it before they are explicitly grasped, and that in that way life does not create only itself, in the sense of its present phases, but also the means for future purposes and the purposes for past means.

This kind of life's working on itself, bestowing meaning on itself through a continuity, of which explicit reflection and critique and distantiation with it are also a part, is something eminently *historical.* Life in its very nature is a history, it is a process, not simply an event. Not only does it take place in a temporal framework as objective processes, not only is it a constitution of a temporal stream as subjectivity in pure streaming, but rather it is *a raising by time in time above time,* it is a way forward which is at the same time a way back to inmost beginnings for only in bestowing meaning on itself does it grasp itself and only thereby can it give itself that further and deeper meaning it needs. For that reason, however, the basic drive to ever greater clarity belongs to

---

43. See Husserl's Vienna Lecture, "Philosophy and the Crisis of European Humanity," in *The Crisis of the European Sciences,* pp. 269–99, wherein he presents this thesis of the history of Greek and Western thought. [Ed.]

historicity essentially, not accidentally, and if clarity (about myself as well as about what is in principle correlated with me) is by its nature *ratio,* then history is in principle a history of *ratio.*

To be sure, we must not give that word a narrow meaning, identifying *ratio* with one of its historical manifestations. *Ratio* is not the same as ancient or modern rationalism. It is neither mere practice nor theory. Most emphatically it is in no sense mere skill and technology. *Ratio* is clarity about oneself in the correlation "I—world" which is essentially a process, an awakening, and a growth.

All that means further that truth, absolute truth, is not a finished thesis but rather a process placed under the perspective of *idea.* Husserl distinguishes several substantive phases in this process.[44] The first has to do with human life as "generatively historical" [*"ursprüngliche generative Historizität";* Ed.], that it is a life of generations which take their successive turn, linked by the bond of biological origin and by shared activity in which all take part. This activity gives rise to the shared environment or surrounding world of a certain community—the world of cultural things which are passed on as the fruit of earlier achievements and of traditional forms as substantive cultural processes; together with this, however, persons, too, belong to the world with the entire personal horizon, the horizon of personal spirituality, the possibility of cultural activity constantly shaped by contact with the objective and personal world of others. All this is a meaningful unity, with meaning present as a preformed configuration, not as an end projected earlier by humans; humans neither are nor sense themselves to be executors in the service of a definite idea, but rather enter into a meaningful coherence as naturally as they breathe, taking part in the work at hand and carrying it on.

The second stage is one which we noted earlier (and of which our first chapter spoke as well): a new sense of purpose [*"Zweckleben"* in Husserl; Ed.] can arise in individuals and, starting with them, in the community as a whole, such that the new purpose bestows something of itself on all those meaning configurations [*"Zweckgebilde"* in Husserl; Ed.] and achievements already present as automatic, as obvious—the new purpose becomes a purpose of self-responsibility and, correlatively, becomes a will to transform humans, to integrate humankind into the global matrix of a

---

44. Husserl's *Krisis,* pp. 339ff and Beilage XXVI: "Stufen der Geschichtlichkeit: Erste Geschichtlichkeit" [appears in Hua edition of the *Krisis* only—Ed.], pp. 502–3.

wholly new framework. That is the moment of human awakening
to autonomy—to the will not to accept meaning passively as a fact
but rather to be responsible for it. That is the moment when
humans become aware of their freedom which thereafter becomes
their ultimate meaning and purpose. The agent of this new meaning is none other than philosophy, that radical self-reflection of
humanity.

> The universally, apodictically grounded and grounding science arises now as
> the necessarily highest function of humankind . . . namely, as making possible
> humankind's development into personal autonomy and into an all-encom-
> passing autonomy for humankind—the idea which represents the driving
> force of life for the highest stage of humanity.[45]

The third stage of rationality then is one which takes place
within the framework of this idea itself—in the context of the
struggle between modern fundamental ideas of science, between
physicalist objectivism and transcendental subjectivism. This is
where the clear idea of philosophy as the scientific foundation of
all science originates, as the foundation which itself is not objective but which justifies all objectivity; Husserl claims not to have
discovered this foundation himself but to have given it a form
capable of general communication and verification, a form in
which it will be scientific, not, to be sure, in a purely technical and
objective sense but in the sense of that optimum of clarity and
autonomous responsibility at which the idea of philosophy aims
from the very beginning. The discoverers of the idea of apodicity
and of its relation to subjectivity are Descartes and modern transcendental philosophy.[46]

And so we have now returned to the beginning, having
attempted to answer, in the spirit of Husserl, the question of the
meaning of Husserl's effort to make philosophy scientific. It is
nothing less than a striving for freedom and complete autonomy
of humankind; a freedom and autonomy to which there belongs
indissoluably an absolute responsibility for all meaning and significance which human thought and action can have.

After this brief overview we cannot remain unaware that
Husserl's idea of human autonomy as the guiding idea of the scientific transformation of philosophy builds on the tradition of classical

45. Ibid., p. 338.
46. Ibid., p. 274. [Ed.]

German philosophy, the philosophy of Fichte and Hegel. It is a part of this tradition not only in its humanism, but also in that, as a result of Husserl's conception of the *epoché* as the reduction to pure immanence, the representation of the meaning of the world which his philosophy seeks to uncover on all its levels in a radical reflection never goes beyond the subjectivity which constitutes this meaning, which brings it about *("zustandebringt")*. Husserl's philosophy not only emphasizes human autonomy, but does so together with the nonautonomy of the world, a grand subjectivism: perhaps, after our critical observations, we can say, an exaggerated one.

This subjectivism must inevitably lead to the question of whether the theme of meaning, of significance, which is the guiding theme of this philosophy, is not at the same time undercut by this subjectivism. For meaning constituted by subjectivity as a universum, as a world, is a *rediscovered* meaning; rediscovery presupposes a loss; why did the primordial absolute subjectivity lose or lack its own self? How can we explain this fact with which phenomenology begins and which we can only accept? For Hegel and his theological philosophy, the answer is given in the idea of the creation of the world out of the absolute freedom of the divine Being which is also an absolute necessity. For Husserl, who seeks to philosophize nontheologically, only a question mark remains.

Something else goes with this. Husserl is a modern philosopher who from the very start takes the mathematical-objective ideal of science very seriously, returning to the beginnings in the rationalistic tradition in Descartes, Galileo, and Leibniz in order to transcend it in an original way to show that in the objectivism of this ideal there is no room for a radical self-justification. His way from this abstract realm to the concrete ultimately leads him, as we have seen, into the realm of historicity, to the foundations of history. Here, though, Husserl goes no further. Husserl never did more than simply proclaim the task of analyzing the natural world and its historicity or the rise of the great objective spiritual configurations (which in classical German philosophy was the topic of such great works as Fichte's *System of Morality* and Hegel's *Phenomenology of Mind*). Quite the contrary, the historicity he describes was so reduced and rendered abstract by his proclamation of philosophy as the highest spiritual activity, of objectification as its primordial form, and of phenomenology as its highest aim that we can hardly see in it anything more than a partial contribution to the questions of a historical—and that means of genuinely con-crete—perception of the relation of humans and the world.

Husserl does see that the teleology of history is not a teleology of predetermined and predefined goals, that it is, rather, a *reinter-pretation of the preconstituted,* but he seeks to proclaim such an absolute goal nonetheless; he transcends a short-range finite tele-ology, but then tries to sneak it back in under a different guise. The problem of a positive bestowal of meaning upon the stream of history, *if it is not simply an elimination of what is meaningless and contradictory,* if it is not a mere manifestation of what is purely given and its overcoming in the project of pure rationality, that is, of clarity and justice, is not clearly posed in Husserl's thought because it is not clearly defined. Husserl restricts the pos-sible global conceptions of life basically to science-philosophy; is this viewpoint really critically justified? Does it rest on sufficiently profound illumination, on a philosophy of human possibilities? What if we encounter, at the base of human potentiality, an inevitable plurality, which might entail a plurality of goals as well? What does that mean for the historical self-formation of humanity? To these questions we no longer find answers in Husserl's work.

In the foregoing we have attempted a certain criticism of Husserl's basic speculatively analytic conception of the *reduction to pure subjective immanence.* According to our critical comments, this immanence, that is, the immanent going beyond what is directly given, itself presupposes a nonimmanent beyond, an awareness of the *fact* of a global and in that sense worldly given-ness. This givenness is inseparable from the meaning of our experi-ence, but we cannot say that it is throughout its achievement; it is nothing constituted but rather a presupposition of all constitution. Thus we cannot say that any meaning of the world is coextensive with meaning constituted by subjectivity. Meaning is the joint product of the world and the "subject." That the subject, the dependent, finite subject, can nonetheless carry out a transcen-dence, that is, constitute transcendence in immanence, appears to me as a justifiable claim, the positive aspect of Husserl's analyses of subjectivity. Do these analyses, however, go far enough, as far as we need to go to understand historical being? Is not their mean-ing too conditioned by the speculative thesis that we are dealing with the absolute creation of meaning and not with creation of meaning dependent on an exterior and on a community, on others as such, on continuity, cooperation, and conflict with them? Did not Husserl become too fixated at the place of his breakthrough from a mathematical to a mentally historical ideal of scientific understanding? And do not his philosophical analyses (his profound probings of time, of living presence, of corporeality, of the Other, of generative sequence) for that reason remain fragmentary where they are concrete and too abstract where they are global, where they reach for an overview of the history of humankind?

Once we formulate these questions, others easily arise: if Husserl's philosophy is, in its positive achievements, an incomplete philosophy, a philosophy in progress, what use can it be to us in our present-day tasks and difficulties? Is it not something dated, belonging basically to the past?

The answer lies in the question itself. Phenomenology helps not in spite of but precisely because of its not being a closed system. An incomplete philosophy means at the same time an *open* philosophy. It means a philosophy which in a sense begins anew at each step, at each problem. A philosophy which is far more a reflection about method, about the way of grasping a problem, than a finished product, and which therefore also teaches us to evaluate results according to what they are really worth: as only stages on the way. There is no absolute truth as a product.

At a time when all the traditional modes of conceiving of society and of history face a recognized need to renew their conceptual arsenal, a need to forget what they have learned and to begin anew without spiritual blinders, a philosophy of this kind, teaching us to look at things systematically with a fresh eye, is a fundamental desideratum.

Besides, Husserl's phenomenology is the only great modern philosophy that carried out, in an exemplary fashion, the breakthrough from the modern mathematico-physicalist objectivism, attacking its basic conceptions not from without but rather by striving from the start for its consistent, absolute elaboration and justification. That enables it not to become bogged down in a specialized scientific positivism while at the same time not losing contact with the problems and methods of the special sciences.

If in closing we were now to characterize the results of Husserl's life's work in philosophy, we would present the following summary.

Husserl contributed to the liberation from psychologism in the grounding of abstract science, especially logic; to its liberation from psychologism and so indirectly also to exorcising psychologism from other disciplines, especially the social scientific ones. He could resolve this problem thanks to his conception of the perception of universals, which at the same time opened up for him a new approach to the perennial problem of a priori knowledge: not an a priori which definitely closes up the subject to the world but rather one which builds a bridge between the two. The program of eidetic ontologies which he had projected became a signal for the rebirth of philosophy not merely as a formal methodological discipline but as one *dealing with a content*. An eidetic psychology, a conception he had adumbrated, rested on a new conception of *intentionality* (leaning towards but also in opposition to Brentano's conception of intentional inexistence). Tracing out the problems of intentionality, along with the effort at a pure description of what is given in inner perception with the guarantee of evident givenness, led to the "phenomenological reduction": first to an *"epoché"* of all transcendent knowing and then to the reduction of transcendence to "pure phenomenon." Husserl may not have carried to completion this profound and extensive thought construct which was to be the definitive foundation of philosophy as a science, but along the way he discovered many of the themes of contemporary philosophy and so enriched it with highly interesting topics: the problems of time, of the awareness of time, of temporality, of the relation between time and the world; a new conception of the world as not only the sum of existing things but as the locus of the encounter of subject and object; the problem of the subject as corporeal, that is, as living in a body, understood not as a thing but as a perspective on things and as the possibility of affecting them directly (the difference between body-subject and body-object whose consequences lead beyond the original abstraction of a purely spiritual subject); the problems of intersubjectivity as the proper realm of reason which discovers itself and unfolds in history; the problem of the historically teleological continuity of subjects called not only to uncover but rather freely and out of freedom to deepen the world order, going beyond all that is merely given to what is universal and therein truly rational. Thus Husserl started out with the problem of the foundations of science and was led to the problems of history, of historical social being whose crises and vicissitudes are for him at the same time crises and vicissitudes of the European sciences. Thus if not in his systematic writings, then at least in practice Husserl transcended the scientific ideal of a mathematizing scientism with its quest for absolute certainty and showed the way to a new, more active and free conception of science and of being human; though perhaps the most important of all the prospects this philosophy opened is the perspective of the unity, of the mutual interlocking and inter-dependence of humans and the world, an interdependence which will not let us consider the world without taking humans into account, or humans without taking into account the world.

Translator's Postscript to the English Edition of Jan Patočka's *Introduction to Husserl's Phenomenology*

My translations from Czech have been a labor of devotion and defiance—of devotion to Czechoslovakia, my sorely tired native land, and of defiance of its Soviet rulers. I was determined that Czechoslovakia shall not disappear behind an iron curtain of censorship and silence.

The translation of Jan Patočka's *Introduction to Husserl's Phenomenology* was a challenge as well. It is a highly professional text and the then ever-present censorship gave Patočka added reason for concealing the philosophical implications of his technical analyses behind a veil of professional terminology. In addition, at the time of its writing, neither Czech nor Slovak had as yet a stabilized phenomenological terminology. Thus Patočka often uses several terms from ordinary usage to point to a concept which, in later years, would come to be designated by a specific technical term. It is often not clear at first reading whether a common usage term like *po ruce* is intended in its ordinary sense of *available* or in the sense of the technical Heideggerean *zuhande*.

In establishing an English text, I have relied on three sources. The first is the original text written and prepared for print in the early 1960s. The relaxation of censorship was not yet sufficient to permit a publication in book form, but the work did appear in installments in the philosophical journal published by the Institute of Philosophy of the Czechoslovak Academy of Science, *Filosofický časopis* (13.5 [July 1965]: 693–701; 13.6 [September 1965]:

821–49; 14.1 [January 1966]: 1–21; 14.3 [May 1966]: 289–305; 14.5 [July 1966]: 269–89). This is the text I have treated as authoritative, both for the text and as an indication of Patočka's overall orientation, since this text underwent his own thorough editing in galley proofs.

The introductory first chapter makes it clear that Patočka here approaches Husserl from a Heideggerean standpoint. He is, in effect, convinced that reality is Heideggerean and himself opts for a Heideggerean approach (for instance, in the conclusion of chapter 5), though that makes his appreciation of Husserl no less genuine nor his interpretation of his work any less brilliant. Still, all other things being equal, I believe we are justified in reading ambiguous terms in a Heideggerean sense.

However, Patočka also demonstrates his deep respect and appreciation for Husserl, especially for Husserl's earlier work. While he was familiar with the first parts of Husserl's *Crisis of European Science* already in manuscript—it was, after all, Patočka who organized Husserl's Prague lectures in 1935 on which *Crisis* was based—and while the Husserliana edition of *Crisis* was available to him (so notes to chapter 8), it is clearly Husserl's more technical works, like *Logical Investigations* or *Experience and Judgment,* which Patočka considers definitive. For that reason, I believe we are justified in reading Husserl's terms in Patočka's works in the sense they have in the earlier works rather than that which they acquire in *Crisis* and in the posthumously published texts, with the possible exception of chapter 8, devoted to Husserl's late writings.

Here a second edition of the text, *Úvod do Husserlovy fenomenologie* (Praha: Státní pedagogické nakladatelství, 1969) can be of help. It is not, strictly speaking, a second edition, but rather a mimeographed verbatim copy of the first, serialized version, traditionally termed *scripta.* Normally, *scripta* are the written version of a professor's lectures prepared by the professor for duplication as a teaching aid for the students. However, when during the thaw of Czechoslovakia's "Dubček Spring," when Patočka was briefly permitted to return to teaching, he did not have time to prepare his new lectures on phenomenology in manuscript and so had his earlier text mimeographed as *scripta* instead.

By and large, the two texts are identical, though the latter is less carefully copyedited, except for some most helpful insertions.

For instance, while in the journal version Patočka uses simply the term *reálný*, in the *scripta* he adds to it Husserl's German *reell* in brackets, indicating that the term is to be read in the technical sense of *reell* (really immanent) rather than of *real* (occurring in spacetime). The Czech term used in the first edition could mean either.

Here a third, much more recent text proved rather helpful. It is Jiří Polívka's *reportata* of the lectures Patočka actually gave at the University in the academic year 1969–1970, *Úvod do fenomenologické filosofie* (Praha: Edice Oikoumene, 1993). The text is reconstructed from the notes a group of Patočka's devotées took at the lectures, though it represents a far more accurate record than medieval *reportata*—such as those of Duns Scotus' Paris lectures—based on shorthand notes alone. It was also most scrupulously edited by some of the very finest Patočka scholars in the former Czechoslovakia, doc. dr. Pavel Kouba, dr. Miroslav Petříček, dr. Ivan Chvatík, and doc. dr. Jiří Polívka.

While the text roughly follows the outline of Patočka's printed text, it is far more detailed and there are some interesting differences. Patočka here sets his task as one of showing "the extent to which Husserl's heritage remains alive in contemporary philosophy" and presents as Husserl's focus the return *zu den Sachen selbst*, to actual lived experiences. His approach in the lectures is systematic as well as historical, the technical terminology is stabilized (though it is not clear whether by Patočka or by the editors), and the entire tone is much more popular, aimed at a student audience rather than at professional colleagues. While the text represents a *reportata*, not even a *scripta*, and so needs be used with caution, as all apocrypha, I believe that on the whole it does confirm the reading I presented in *Jan Patočka: His Thought and Writings* (Chicago: University of Chicago Press, 1989)—that Patočka is not a minor Heideggerean but an original thinker who has undertaken the daunting task of fusing Husserl's rationalism with Heidegger's romanticism. Or, as he puts it in the present volume, the real needs to be thought, but thought as other, not reduced to mere object of thought (chapter 5).

None of the sources cited, however, can resolve the problem of translating Husserl's term *Wesen*. Etymologically, it means *being* in the sense of *typical mode of being* and is so defined by philosophical dictionaries of Husserl's time, such as Eisler's *Handwörterbuch*

der Philosophie (1903). Patočka translates it as *podstata,* the etymo-
logical equivalent of *sub–stance;* later Czech writers will use an
artificially coined equivalent of the German *Wesen, bytnost.* In English, the most common translation is *essence*—but that is most
unfortunate. The word *Essenz* does occur in German, but to the
best of my knowledge Husserl *never* uses it as a synonym of *Wesen.*
The word he does use as a synonym is the Greek *eidos* and, far
more suggestively, the German *ideale Möglichkeit,* the ideational
possibility.

That is what I find most helpful. The point, after all, most
emphatically is not that the object *chair* somehow contains within
itself a magic essence of *chairness* which we could isolate in a
process of abstraction. Patočka makes that amply clear (so chapter
5). It is, rather, that, apart from any factual existence of any
objects fulfilling it, the structure of our being in the world is such
that there is an a priori possibility of supporting our bodies from
below in a sitting position. That is an ideal possibility, present, in
principle, entirely a priori, not in an object, but in the structure of
experience itself. An object will only contingently instantiate it the
first time humans sit on a stump rather than on their haunches.
That is *Wesen,* the a priori possibility which makes an instantiating
actuality intelligible.

I have therefore avoided translating *Wesen,* Patočka's *podstata,*
by the English *essence.* At times simply the Greek *eidos* proved
appropriate, at first with explanatory parentheses (*Wesen* or
"essence"), later without them. However, there are times when
Husserl uses *Wesen* to indicate not simply the *ideale Möglichkeit,*
but that *ideale Möglichkeit* as constituting an instance, actual or
imaginary—say, not the pure possibility of an elevated surface but
that possibility as incarnate in an actual or imaginary table. In
those cases I have resorted to the translation *eidetic nature,* all the
while repeating to myself Martin Luther's dictum, "Sin bravely
but believe more bravely." (In the same spirit I discarded that
time-honored Teutonic monstrosity, "It belongs to the essence
of . . . ," in favor of the English "The eidetic nature of . . . is such
that. . . .") As a rule, then, in this text *eidos* refers to pure ideal
possibility, *eidetic nature* to Husserl's *Wesen,* usually but mislead-
ingly translated as "essence."

As for Patočka's *funkční,* a cognate of Husserl's *fungierend,* I
should have liked to have rendered it *acting* or *agent,* especially

when speaking of *fungierende Subjektivität,* subjectivity as an agent, in first person, rather than as object of contemplation. However, that daring I am not, and so I remained with the uninformative English cognate *functioning,* enshrined by no lesser translators than David Carr in *Crisis* and Dorion Cairns in his *Guide to Translating Husserl.*

No such relatively easy solution proved possible in the case of Patočka's quotations from Husserl. At the time of writing, there were no Czech translations of Husserl's work, and Patočka's translations often diverge widely from the translations of John Findlay, W. R. Boyce-Gibson, Fred Kersten—though, interestingly, seldom from those of David Carr. Since Patočka's interpretations are often based on his translations of Husserl's text, I could not simply use existing English translations. However, since these are quotations, I could not simply translate Patočka's text. In such cases, I prepared my own translations of Husserl's text which would be consistent both with Husserl and with Patočka's interpretation, even though they diverge from the existing English text, especially in the case of William P. Alston's and George Nakhnikian's English translation of *The Idea of Phenomenology.* Husserl's German terms, inserted by the editor, can be helpful but are not always a reliable guide to the Czech original. I have done my best, but I would urge any readers concerned with detailed exegesis to refer to the German text, prepare their own translation, and see if it bears out Patočka's interpretation. Such an exercise, incidentally, throws an interesting light on the question of how faithfully Husserl can be read through Heideggerean eyes.

*   *   *

My debt of gratitude to my colleagues in America and, after my return to Czechoslovakia in 1991, in Prague, especially to dr. Josef Moural and to dr. Ivan Chvatík, is too great to detail here. However, I owe special thanks to my former student, present colleague, and ever a friend, James Dodd, and to Open Court Publishing Company and its editor, Kerri Mommer, without whom this text would never have seen the light of print.

I completed a draft of this translation in 1987, but after the fall of the Communist regime set it aside: with freedom restored and my return to Prague, other tasks seemed more urgent. It was dr. Dodd's enthusiasm—and willingness to undertake the tedious labor of editing—and Open Court's enthusiasm for publishing the product that encouraged me to gather up my materials yet once more and to revise my rough original translation for dr. Dodd's editing and publication. So, thank you. I trust you will agree it was worth it.

Erazim Kohák
28.X.1996

Bibliography

All works cited, either by Patočka or in the editor's notes, are included in the bibliography.

Adorno, Theodor. *Against Epistemology: Studies in Husserl and the Phenomenological Antinomies*. Trans. Willis Domingo. Cambridge: MIT Press, 1983.

Aristotle. *De Anima*. Trans. R. D. Hicks. New York: Arno Press, 1976.

———. *Metaphysics*. Trans. Hippocrates G. Apostle. Grinnell: Peripatetic Press, 1979.

Arnauld, Antoine, and Claude Lancelot. *A General and Rational Grammar*. 1753. Translation, reprinted in series *English Linguistics 1500–1800*, ed. R. C. Alston. Menston: Scholar Press, 1968.

Arnauld, Antoine, and Pierre Nicole. *The Art of Thinking*. Trans. James Dickoff and Patricia James. Indianapolis: Bobbs-Merrill, 1964.

Becker, Oscar. "The Philosophy of Edmund Husserl." In *The Phenomenology of Husserl: Selected Critical Readings*, trans. and ed. R. O. Elveton, pp. 40–72. Chicago: Quadrangle, 1970.

Bergson, Henri. *Time and Free Will: An Essay on the Immediate Data of Consciousness*. Trans. P. L. Pogson. New York: Humanities Press, 1971.

Berkeley, Geroge. *A Treatise Concerning the Principles of Human Knowledge*. Indianapolis: Hackett, 1982.

Biemel, Walter. "The Decisive Phases in the Development of Husserl's Philosophy." In *The Phenomenology of Husserl: Selected Critical Readings*, ed. R. O. Elveton. Chicago: Quadrangle Books, 1970.

———. "Husserl's *Encyclopedia Britannica* Article and Heidegger's Remarks Thereon." In *Husserl: Expositions and Appraisals*, ed. Elliston and McCormick. Notre Dame: University of Notre Dame Press, 1977.

Bochenski, I. M. *A History of Formal Logic*. Trans. and ed. Ivo Thomas. New York: Chelsea Publishing, 1970.

Bolzano, Bernard. *Theory of Science*. Trans. and ed. Rolf George. Berkeley: University of California Press, 1972.

———. *Paradoxes of the Infinite*. Trans. D. A. Steele. New Haven: Yale University Press, 1950.

Boethius of Dacia. "Every Man is of Necessity an Animal." In *Cambridge Translations of Medieval Philosophical Texts*. Vol. 1, *Logic and the Philosophy of Language*. Ed. Norman Kretzmann and Eleonore Stump. Cambridge: Cambridge University Press, 1988.

————. "Modi significandi sive Quaestiones super Priscianum Maiorem." In *Copus Philosophorum Danicorum Medii Aevi*. Vol. IV, ed. Jan Pinborg and H. Ross. Copenhagen: 1969.

Brand, Gerd. *Welt, Ich, und Zeit: Nach unveröffentlichten Manuskripten Edmund Husserls*. Hague: Nijhoff, 1955.

Brentano, Franz. *Psychology from an Empirical Standpoint*. Ed. Oskar Kraus and Linda McAlister, trans. Antos C. Rancurello, D. B. Terrell, and Linda McAlister. New York: Humanities Press, 1973.

————. *Philosophische Untersuchungen zur Raum, Zeit, und Kontinuum*. Ed. Stephan Körner and Roderick Chisholm. Hamburg: Meiner, 1976.

Claesges, Ulrich. *Husserls Theorie der Raumkonstitution*. Hague: Nijhoff, 1964.

Descartes, René. *Meditations on First Philosophy*. In *Selected Writings of Descartes*, vol. II, trans. John Cottingham. Cambridge: Cambridge University Press, 1990.

————. *Passions of the Soul*. In *Selected Writings of Descartes*. Vol. I, trans. Robert Stoothoff. Cambridge: Cambridge University Press, 1990.

Ehrenfels, Christian von. "Über Gestaltqualitäten." In *Vierteljahrsschrift für wissenschaftliche Philosophie* 14 (1890): 249–92.

Eley, Lothar. *Die Krise des Apriori in der transzendentalen Phänomenologie Edmund Husserls*. Hague: Nijhoff, 1962.

Fichte, Johann Gottlieb. *The Science of Knowledge*. Trans. Peter Heath and John Lachs. Cambridge: Cambridge University Press, 1982.

————. *Systeme der Sittlichkeit*. In *Sämtliche Werke III*, ed. I. H. Fichte. Maner und Muller, 1845.

Fink, Eugen. "Die Spätphilosophie Husserls in der Freiburger Zeit." In *Edmund Husserl: 1859–1959: Recueil commemoratif publié a l'occasion du centenaire de la naissance du philosophe*, pp. 99–115. Hague: Nijhoff, 1959.

Frege, Gottlob. *The Foundations of Arithmetic*. Trans. J. L. Austin. Evanston: Northwestern University Press, 1980.

————. *Funktion, Begriff, Bedeutung*. Ed. Günther Patzig. Göttingen: Vandenhoeck and Ruprecht, 1986.

————. "On Sense and Reference." In *Translations from the Philosophical Writings of Gottlob Frege*, ed. and trans. Paul Geach and Max Black. Oxford: Blackwell, 1960.

————. "Review of Dr. E. Husserl's *Philosophy of Arithmetic*." In *Readings on Edmund Husserl's Logical Investigations*, ed. J. N. Mohanty, trans. E. W. Kluge, pp. 6–21. Hague: Nijhoff, 1977.

Gründer, Karlfried, and Joachim Ritter, eds. *Historisches Wörterbuch der Philosophie*. Darmstadt: Wissenschaft Buchgesellschaft.

Hamann, Johann Georg. *Vom Magus im Norden und der Verwegenheit des Geistes: Ausgewählte Schriften*. Ed. Stefan Majetschak. Bonn: Parerga, 1993.

Hamilton, William. *Lectures on Metaphysics and Logic*. Edinburgh and Boston: 1859–1860.

Hegel, Georg Wilhelm Friedrich. *Phenomenology of Spirit*. Trans. A. V. Miller. Oxford: Oxford University Press, 1977.

Held, Klaus. *Lebendige Gegenwart*. Hague: Nijhoff, 1966.

Helmholtz, Hermann von. "An Epistemological Analysis of Counting and Measurement." In *Selected Writings of Hermann von Helmholtz*, ed. Russell Kahl. Middletown: Wesleyan University Press, 1971.

Herbart, Johann Friedrich. *Sämtliche Werke.* Vol. 6, ed. G. Hartenstein. Leipzig: Voss, 1851.

Herder, Johann Gottfried. "Essay on the Origin of Language." In *On the Origin of Language,* trans. John Moran and Alexander Gode. Chicago: University of Chicago Press, 1966.

———. *Ideen zur Philosophie der Geschichte der Menschheit.* Riga: Hardknoch, 1884–92.

Héring, Jean. "Bemerkungen über das Wesen, die Wesenheit, und die Idee." In *Jahrbuch für Philosophie und phänomenologische Forschung* 4 (1921).

Hobbes, Thomas. *Computatio sive logica=Logic,* Part 1 of *De Corpore.* New York: Abaris Books, 1981.

Hume, David. *A Treatise of Human Nature.* Ed. L. A. Selby-Bigge, revised by P. H. Nidditch. Oxford: Clarendon Press, 1983.

Husserl, Edmund. *Analysen zur passiven Synthesis (1918–1926).* Husserliana XI, ed. Margot Fleischer. Hague: Nijhoff, 1966.

———. "Author's Preface to the English Edition of Ideas." Trans. W. R. Boyce Gibson for *Ideas: General Introduction to Pure Phenomenology.* New York: Humanties Press, 1931; reprinted in *Husserl: Shorter Works,* ed. Peter McCormick and Frederick Alliston, pp. 43–53. Notre Dame: University of Notre Dame Press, 1981.

———, *Cartesian Meditations.* Trans. Dorion Cairns. Hague: Nijhoff, 1969.

———. *Crisis of European Sciences and Transcendental Phenomenology.* Trans. David Carr. Evanston: Northwestern University Press, 1970.

———. *Ding und Raum Vorlesungen 1907.* Husserliana XVI, ed. Ulrich Claesges. Hague: Nijhoff, 1973.

———. *Erste Philosophie (1923/24). Zweiter Teil: Theorie der phänomenologischen Reduktion.* Husserliana VIII, ed. Rudolf Boem. Hague: Nijhoff, 1959.

———. *Experience and Judgment: Investigations in a Genealogy of Logic.* Trans. James S. Churchill. London: Routledge and Kegan Paul, 1973.

———. *The Idea of Phenomenology.* Trans. William P. Alston and George Nakhnikian. Hague: Nijhoff, 1964.

———. *Ideas Pertaining to a Pure Phenomenology and to a Phenomenological Philosophy. First Book: General Introduction to a Pure Phenomenology.* Trans. Fred Kersten Hague: Nijhoff, 1983. [Kersten's translation is based on the 1973 edition of Husserliana III—Ed.]

———. *Ideas Pertaining to a Pure Phenomenology and to a Phenomenological Philosophy. Second Book: Studies in the Phenomenology of Constitution.* Trans. Richard Rojcewicz and Andre Schuwer. Dolbrecht: Kluwer, 1989.

———. *Ideas Pertaining to a Pure Phenomenology and to a Phenomenological Philosophy. Third Book: Phenomenology and the Foundations of the Sciences.* Trans. Ted Klein and William Pohl. Hague: Nijhoff, 1971.

———. *Die Krisis der europäischen Wissenschaften und die transzendentale Phänomenologie. Ergänzungsband: Texte aus dem Nachlaß, 1934–1937.* Husserliana XXIX, ed. Reinhold Smid. Dordrecht: Kluwer, 1993.

———. *Logical Investigations.* 2 vols., trans. J. N. Findlay. New York: Humanities Press, 1970.

———. *On the Phenomenology of the Consciousness of Internal Time (1893–1917).* Trans. John Barnett Brough. Dolbrecht: Kluwer Academic Publishers, 1990.

———. *Die Philosophie der Arithmetik*. Husserliana XII, ed. Lothar Eley. Hague: Nijhoff, 1970.

———. *Zur Phänomenologie der Intersubjektivität: Texte aus dem Nachlaß*. Husserliana XIII, XIV, XV, ed. Iso Kern. Hague: Nijhoff, 1973.

Ingarden, Roman. "Discussion de la conférence Biemel." In *Husserl,* Cahiers de Royaumont-Philosophie no. 3. Paris: Minuit, 1959.

———. "Essentiale Fragen: Ein Beitrag zu den Wesensproblem." In *Jahrbuch für Philosophie und phänomenologische Forschung* 7 (1925).

James, William. *Principles of Psychology*. New York: Holt, 1927.

Kant, Immanuel. *Critique of Pure Reason*. Trans. Norman Kemp Smith. New York: St. Martin's Press, 1965.

———. *Lectures on Logic*. Ed. and trans. J. M. Young. Cambridge: Cambridge University Press, 1992.

Katzmann, Norman, A. J. P. Kenny, and Jan Pinborg, eds. *The Cambridge History of Later Medieval Philosophy*. Cambridge: Cambridge University Press, 1982.

Kern, Iso. *Husserl und Kant: Eine Untersuchung über Husserls Verhältnis zu Kant und zum Neukantianismus*. Hague: Nijhoff, 1964.

Kirk, G. S., J. E. Raven, and M. Schofield. *The Presocratic Philosophers*. Cambridge: Cambridge University Press, 1990.

Kronecker, Leopold. "Über den Zahlbegriff (1887)." In *Werke,* vol. III, ed. K. Hensel, pp. 249–74. New York: Chelsea Publishing, 1968; reprint of Leipzig: Teubner, 1895–1931.

Landgrebe, Ludwig. "Husserls Departure from Cartesianism." In *The Phenomenology of Husserl: Selected Critical Readings*. Ed. and trans. R. O. Elveton. Chicago: Quadrangle Books, 1970.

———. "The Problem of Passive Synthesis." In *The Phenomenology of Edmund Husserl: Six Essays*. Trans. Donn Welton. Ithaca: Cornell University Press, 1981.

———. *Der Weg der Phänomenologie: Das Problem einer ursprünglichen Erfahrung*. Gütersloh: Mohn, 1963.

Leibniz, Gottfried Wilhelm. *De Scientia Universali seu Calculo* Philosophico. In *Die Philosophische Schriften von Gottfried Wilhelm Leibniz*. Vol. 7, ed. C. J. Gerhardt. Hildesheim: Georg Olms, 1960.

———. *De Synthesi et Analysi Universali*. In *Die philosophische Schriften von Gottfried Wilhelm Leibniz*. Vol. 7, ed. C. J. Gerhardt. Hildesheim: Georg Olms, 1960.

———. "From *Of the Art of Combination* (De Arte Combinatoria)." In *Logical Papers*. Ed. and trans. G. H. R. Parkinson. Oxford: Clarendon Press, 1966.

———. *New Essays on Human Understanding*. Ed. and trans. Peter Remnant and Jonathan Bennett. Cambridge: Cambridge University Press, 1982.

Levinas, Immanuel. "Intentionalité et sensation." In *Revue Internationale de Philosophie* 19, nos. 71–72 (1965): 179–203.

———. *The Theory of Intuition in Husserl's Phenomenology*. Trans. André Orlanne. Evanston: Northwestern University Press, 1973.

Lipps, Theodor. *Grundzüge der Logik*. Leipzig: Voss, 1893.

Locke, John. *An Essay Concerning Human Understanding*. Ed. A. D. Woozley. New York: Meridian, 1974.

Lotze, Hermann. *Metaphysic in Three Books: Ontology, Cosmology, and Psychology.* Trans. Bernard Bosanquet. Oxford: Clarendon Press, 1884.

Lullus, Raymundus (Raymond Lull). *Ars Magna et Ultima.* In *Raymondi Lulli Opera ea quaed Adinventam ab ipso Artem Universalem . . . Pertinent.* Argentorati, 1617, pp. 218–663.

Mach, Ernst. *The Analysis of Sensations, and the Relation of the Physical to the Psychical.* Trans. Sydney Waterlow. New York: Dover Publications, 1959.

Marcel, Gabriel. *Being and Having.* Trans. Katherine Farrer. New York: Harper and Row, 1965.

Martin of Darcia. "Modis Significandi." In *Copus Philosophorum Damicorum Medii Aevi.* Vol. 2, ed. H. Ross. Copenhagen: 1961.

Marty, Anton. "Über das Verhältnis von Grammatik und Logik." In *Symbolae Pragenses. Festgabe der deutschen Gesellschaft für Alterhumskunde in Prag zur 42. Versammlung deutscher Philologen und Schulmänner in Wien 1893.* Prag, Wien, Leipzig: 1893.

——. *Untersuchungen zur Grundlegung der allgemeinen Sprachtheorie.* Halle: Niemeyer, 1908.

Merleau-Ponty, Maurice. *The Phenomenology of Perception.* Trans. Colin Smith. London: Routledge and Kegan Paul, 1962.

Mill, John Stuart. *A System of Logic Ratiocinative and Inductive, being a connected View of the Principles of Evidence and of the Methods of Scientific Investigation.* London: Longman, Ltd., 1970.

Mohanty, J. N. *Husserl's Theory of Meaning.* Hague: Nijhoff, 1964.

Nietzsche, Friedrich. *Twilight of the Idols/The Antichrist.* Trans. R. J. Hollingdale. New York: Viking, 1968.

——. *Thus Spoke Zarathustra.* Trans. Walter Kaufmann. New York: Viking, 1966.

Patočka, Jan. "Husserls Subjektivismus und die Möglichkeit einer a-subjectiven Phänomenologie." In *Die natürliche Welt als philosophisches Problem: Phänomenologische Schriften I,* ed. Klaus Nellen, Jiri Nemec, Ilja Srubar. Stuttgart: Klett-Kotta, 1989.

——. *Die Bewegung der menschlichen Existenz: Phänomenologische Schriften II.* Ed. Klaus Nellen, Jiri Nemec, Ilja Srubar. Stuttgart: Klett-Kotta, 1989.

——. *Jan Patočka: Philosophy and Selected Writings.* Trans. and ed. Erazim Kohák. Chicago: University of Chicago Press, 1989.

Plato. *Theaetetus.* Trans. M. J. Levett, revised with an introductory essay by Myles Burnyeat. Indianapolis: Hackett, 1990.

Russell, Bertrand. "On Denoting." In *Logic and Knowledge: Essays 1901–1950.* London: Routledge, 1992.

——. "The Philosophy of Logical Atomism." In *Logic and Knowledge: Essays 1901–1950.* London: Routledge, 1992.

Russell, Bertrand and Alfred North Whitehead. *Principia mathematica.* Cambridge: 1910, 1912, 1913.

Sartre, Jean-Paul. *Being and Nothingness.* Trans. Hazel Barnes. New York: Philosophical Library, 1956.

——. *The Transcendence of the Ego: An Existentialist Theory of Consciousness.* Trans. Forrest Williams and Robert Kirkpatrick. New York: Noonday Press, 1970.

Schütz, Alfred. "The Problem of Transcendental Subjectivity in Husserl." In *Collected Papers*. Vol. III, *Studies in Phenomenological Psychology* (Hague: Nijhoff, 1970), pp. 51–53.

Sokolowski, Robert. *The Formation of Husserl's Concept of Constitution*. Hague: Nijhoff, 1964.

Stern, William. "Psychische Präsenzzeit." In *Zeitschrift für Psychologie und Physiologie der Sinnesorgane* 13 (1897): 325–349.

Strawson, P. F. "On Referring." In *Logico-Linguistic Papers*. London: Methuen and Co., 1971.

Volkmann-Schluck, K. H. "Husserl's Lehre von der Idealität der Bedeutungen als metaphysiches Problem." In *Husserl et la Pensée Moderne/Husserl und das Denken der Neuzeit*. From colloquium in French and German: *Actes du deuxième Colloque international de Phenomenologie. Krefel, 1–3 Novembre 1956/Akte des zweiten internationalen phänomenologischen Kolloquiums. Krefel, 1–3 November 1956.* [Patočka cites German version, pp. 230–41; French is on pp. 241–50, translated by J. Ladriere as "La doctrine de Husserl au sujet de l'idealitie de la signification en tant que problème metaphysique."]

Wittgenstein, Ludwig. *Philosophical Investigations*. Trans. G. E. M. Anscombe. Oxford: Blackwell, 1958.

Name Index

Analytic Table of Contents

(In the original, the author prefaced each chapter with the brief out-line reproduced here in place of a topical index. Tr.)

Chapter 1: Phenomenology as a Philosophy and Its Relation to Traditional Metaphysical Approaches

Chapter 2: The Philosophy of Arithmetic

Precisely the clarification of the contradiction mentioned outlines the problem for Husserl's further philosophizing. 25 • (Other important motifs of the *Philosophy of Arithmetic.*) First we need to secure the objectivity of ideal contents. Not on the grounds of mathematics but more generally, on the ground of pure logic. 26 • No such logic exists so far. *Logical Investigations I* carries out such securing against "psychologism." 27 • The problem of whether logic is an art or a science. Theoretical foundation of a practical discipline—logic—is, according to the psychologizers, only psychology (thought). 28 • Psychologism confuses psychic experience and its objects, the different cast of empirically psychological and purely ideal, exact lawlike ordering. 29 • Psychologism as a skeptical relativism is in conflict with the conditions of possibility of all valid theory. 34 • Psychological prejudices and their dissolution. The idea of a pure logic, its components, its structure. 37 • Besides formal ontology there are indications also of material theories of substances and ultimately a theory of substantive relations among subjective substances and objective formations which are the objects of subjective processes. 39

Chapter 3: Pure Logic: The *Logical Investigations*

Is not built up without regard for the subjective aspect, thought as such. 41 • The basis of the proof of the objectivity of the ideal is a special act of universal intention 42 • as distinct from the act of individual intention. This act can be neither defined nor deduced, only induced like the definition of the primary concepts of multiplicity and quantity in the *Philosophy of Arithmetic*. The act of universal intending is built up on acts of individual intending. 43 • Intending and fulfillment. Static and dynamic fulfillment. 44 • The intending of universal intending fulfilled in a special manner, categorial or (in the special case when individual members of categorial relations do not enter into the fulfillment of a higher level) by a universal perception (intuition). 45 • That justifies the broadening of the concept of perception (intuition). A presentifying original perception (intuition), self-evidence = perception (intuition). Broadening of the concept of perception (intuition) to the regions of categories and of the universal. Categorial and universal perception (intuition) are not always one-stroke acts. 46 • Universal perception (intuition) and phantasy (productive imagination), variation of example in free fancy as a method of achieving the universal.

The theory of signification or pure logical grammar as the first chapter of pure logic. 47 • The problem of signification, theory of signification (Mohanty): theory of the sign, operational theory, Husserl's theory of signification—units whose singularization is the act of intending. Its relation to the operational theory. 49 • The theory of the formal object as such as the third chapter of an objective pure logic. 51 • The problems of the *Philosophy of Arithmetic* fall within its framework. Husserl's logicism is not that of Frege or Russell, does not reduce mathematics to logic. 54 • Pure logic as a sphere of "mental" ("spiritual") relations. 55

Chapter 4: The Concept of *Phenomenon*

The constitution of a pure logic requires a resolution of the question of a bridge between the subject and the object, of the transition from the subjectivity of lived experience to the objectivity of knowing. This transition must be carried out on the subjective side, that is, by a *new theory of subjective processes and sequences.* 58 • A psychology defined by empiricism is not adequate for this; might Brentano's "intentional" psychology do? Brentano's conception of psychology is built up on a differentiation between physical. and psychical phenomena. Physical phenomena lack the evident warrant of existence intrinsic to psychic ones. 59 • Difficulties with Brentano's starting point, its metaphysical component, overlooked by Brentano. Brentano's intentional psychology does not include the problem of *conception,* of the interpretation of the given. By contrast, Husserl sees the need of including within the intentional conception the problems of *the same* which appears in various representations and of various objectivities attached to the same representation. 60 • Husserl's critique of Brentano's characterization of physical and psychical phenomena. It does not lead to a complete abandoning of Cartesianism and of its conception of internal evidence but rather to the demand for purifying the phenomenon of all assumptions. Three

conceptions of phenomenon in Husserl. 62 • The act and the
sense content as real components of lived experience. Three
"components" of the intentional experience, the schema of its
functioning—intentional achievement = the object on the basis
of the *interpretation* of meaning intentions, one oriented by data,
by "representations." New conception not of the intentional
object, *completely given* in the intentional act, but rather *constituted* by the intentional act—the conception of constitution. 64 • The synthetic character of effective intentionality.
Generalization of the problems of the *Philosophy of Arithmetic.*—
Correlative problems: the mutual relation of the unitary object
and the manifold of lived experience, as a field of eidetic laws.
Concerning the "givenness" of intentionality. Intentionality functioning covertly. The latent nature of the intentional act in Heidegger's and Sartre's existential interpretation. 65 • Husserl
himself does not take this path but rather follows out a noetic
interpretation of the constitution of objective unity. 66 • Intentionality and the problem of the unconscious and the subcon-
scious.—Equivocation in Husserl's conception of *"reell* nonintentional component" of lived experience. 68 • The need for
further distinctions. 70

Chapter 5: Pure Logic and the Problem of the Grounding of Experience

Fact, *Wesen, eidos.* 72 • Eidetic generality and eidetic singularity.
Regional eidos. Formal region, generalization, and formalization.
The substrates: final material singularity and "this here" *(tode ti).*
75 • Independent and dependent, concrete and abstract *eidos.*—
Cognition of *eidos* makes cognition of fact possible; eidetic disciplines are *a priori* foundations of the empirical. Types of a priori
sciences: material and formal eidetic disciplines, exact and inexact
disciplines, disciplines of definitive and indefinitive diversities.
77 • The need for further regional ontologies.—*Eidos* and experience of *eidos.* Protointention to unity and adequation at the basis
of association. Empirical typicality and empirical generality: the
idea of an infinitely corrigible universal structure on the basis of a
sensual starting point. Abstract and regional pure *eide.* 80 • *Critical comments:* The founding of factual experience cannot be

transferred to relations in the eidetic region, as Husserl de facto does. On the one hand the idea of eidetic intuition is not carried out to dialectical structures, on the other hand it is overextended into an a priori project of all possible worlds. 82

Chapter 6: The First Explanation of the Phenomenological Reduction

Problem of pure phenomenon. 87 • The relation between intentional acts and their objects cannot be reduced to purely objective eidetic relations. The psychic in psychological sense is not purely immanent. 88 • Pure phenomenon reached by reduction to immanence. 89 • *The Idea of Phenomenology:* The reduction presented in three stages: (1) the problem of transcendence, (2) *epoché*, exclusion of all objective theses and transformation to real immanence, (3) finding transcendence in immanence. *The Idea of Phenomenology* does not elaborate the difference of two types of being (immanently subjective and absolute, transcendentally objective and relative): therefore also the derivation of transcendence fails here. 90 • A new attempt in *Ideas I.* 97 • Exposition of the problem of the world, of cognition within the world, general thesis of the natural standpoint. Reduction is not designed to reach an indubitable remnant of knowledge of the world but a wholly new region of being (or better, "before being"). 98 • The law of contrast of two modes of being: self-evidence in objective region does not, in the subjective region does, guarantee being. The presuppositions of this law. Husserl revives Fichte's attempt at winning absolute subjectivity and explaining the object from the subject. The difference in method. 103 • A critique of the idea of the reduction. The reduction cannot succeed in excluding sense certainty, if we mean by it awareness of the fact of transcendent contact. Husserl illegitimately identifies immediate givenness and subjective immanence. Further identification: the presentival and the subjectival immanence and transcendence. Presentival and subjectival transcendence differ. Destruction of the orderly world does not mean destruction of the world as such. 104 • If reduction cannot be carried out as Husserl expected that does not mean rejection of the *epoché* and of its achievement. However, the significance of the *epoché* changes:

it makes possible a study of transcendence as a self-opening of the subject for being. Husserl and intuitive realism; the primacy of the one and of the other. 105

Chapter 7: Analysis of Internal Time Consciousness

Analysis of internal time consciousness.—Analysis of time precedes systematic presentation of the reduction and applies its principles. 107 • Explanation of the consciousness of time: (1) building on Brentano, (2) description and analysis of time consciousness, (3) constitution of internal time, of temporal objects and of transcendent objects in objective time. 109 • Problem of the self-constitution of the temporal stream. Radicalization of the reduction to "living present," bracketing of the lived stream. 112 • Reduction to the "nunc stans." Problems of "nunc stans": How is reflection possible? What is the final ground of self-constitution of the inner temporal stream. The elusiveness of the agent I. 124 • Its "preexistence," nonindividuality. *Nunc stans* as a limit concept, a constantly intended idea.

In analysis of internal time consciousness Husserl's phenomenology progresses from innerworldly objects to the problem of relation to the world as a whole. 128 • The world and the temporal horizon. The world, the idea of the world, the uncovering of the world. The significance of temporality for this uncovering. 130 • Transcending Cartesian reflectively intuitive certainty, of the idea of clear, positive intuition of a content ("back to the things themselves"): *nunc stans* and the dark area within it. 133 • Dialectical structure of reflection does not represent an absolute method but rather signals the finitude of reflection; the positive aspect of the finitude of reflection: incarnation of the subject, the call of the subject to the world, the call of the world in humans. 135

Chapter 8: Incarnate Being

The thing we see and the thing of physics. 137 • There is no causal connection between them. Living and psychophysical things. Consciousness in the form of transcendental subject and as a psychophysical reality. How does consciousness become an